Friends In Deed

FIRST EDITION

**Library of Congress Cataloging in
Publication Data**

Rampton, Sheldon, 1957-
    Friends in deed: the story of
U.S.-Nicaragua sister cities: a how-to manual
and directory for sister city organizers/Sheldon
Rampton; photographs by Liz Chilsen;
introduction by Vincent Kavaloski.
        p.   cm.
Bibliography: p.
Includes index.
1. United States–
Relations–Nicaragua.
2. Nicaragua–Relations–
United States.
  I.   Chilsen, Liz, 1957-   . II.   Title.
III.   Title: Sister cities.

E183.8.N5R36 1988   88-17161
303.4'8273'07285--dc19   CIP

ISBN0-9620731-0-5 (lib.bdg.)

**Alternative Cataloging
in Publication Data**
Rampton, Sheldon, 1957-
    Friends in deed: the story of U.S.
Nicaragua sister cities; a how-to manual and
directory for sister city organizers. Sheldon
Rampton, author; Liz Chilsen, photographer.
Madison, WI: Wisconsin Coordinating
Council on Nicaragua (WCCN), copyright
1988.

PARTIAL CONTENTS: Citizen-based
foreign policy. -How to start a sister city.
-Person to person exchanges. -Directory of
U.S.-Nicaragua sister cities.

APPENDICES: Suggested reading.
-Directories of organizations.

1. Sister cities movement (United
States-Nicaragua).
2. Citizen diplomacy. I. Wisconsin
Coordinating Council on Nicaragua.
II. Chilsen, Liz, illus.   III. Title.   IV. Title:
The story of U.S.-Nicaragua sister cities.
V. Title: U.S.-Nicaragua sister cities.

327.73072

The Wisconsin Coordinating Council on Nicaragua (WCCN) was formed to promote the
official sister-state relationship that has existed between Wisconsin and Nicaragua since
1964. Since hosting the U.S.-Nicaragua Friendship Conference in 1986, WCCN has
played a leading role in the sister cities movement nationwide, providing advice and assistance to new sister cities, and promoting cooperation and information-sharing among existing projects.

Friends In Deed:
The Story of US-Nicaragua
Sister Cities

Liz Chilsen & Sheldon Rampton
Foreword by Vincent Kavaloski, PhD

**In Association with
The Wisconsin Coordinating
Council on Nicaragua**

Acknowledgments

The Wisconsin Coordinating Council on Nicaragua thanks the following foundations that have supported WCCN's work, directly or indirectly making this book possible: The CarEth Foundation, The Field Foundation, National Community Funds, Norman Foundation, Peace Development Fund, Samuel Rubin Foundation, Threshold Foundation, The Tides Foundation, and The Youth Project. Thanks also to Becky Glass, Pratt Remmel, Jr., and to donors who asked to remain anonymous.

The authors wish to thank the WCCN board of directors and former board members for their endorsement and support of this project. Special thanks to all the members of the WCCN advisory board, who have given not only their names but their money, time, wisdom and hearts to our work. Numerous individuals have contributed in many different ways, including hundreds of dues-paying members and volunteers.

The Nicaraguan Department of Municipal and Regional Affairs (DAMUR) contributed phenomenally, providing us with transportation throughout the country despite considerable difficulties due to the war. We especially want to thank Carlos Tunnermann and Rosa Carlota Tunnermann, Francisco Campbell, Mónica Baltodano, Zelmira Garcia, and the members of the DAMUR staff with whom we have been privileged to work.

Thanks to Michael Shuman of the Center for Innovative Diplomacy and to Gale Warner, co-authors of *Citizen Diplomats*, whose writings and research on the subject of municipal foreign policies were a frequent resource. Thanks also to the *Bainbridge Review* for permission to use parts of a January 21, 1987 article by Theresa Morrow titled "Esterberg's Quest Turns Up Nicaraguan Sister Island" as the opening to chapter 5. The *Twin Cities Reader* of Minneapolis, Minnesota gave permission to use excerpts from the November 19, 1986 story, "Nicaragua to Minnesota: A Cultural Exchange," by Jon Kerr. Thanks to Marja Eloheimo for permission to use her lovely poem. Sue Lyons of the Brooklyn/San Juan del Rio Coco Sister City Project wrote a substantial portion of the section dealing with news media in chapter four, and gave permission for its incorporation into this book. Steve Watrous of Milwaukee, Wisconsin allowed us to use his "Steve's Travel Tips to Nicaragua" as a resource in writing chapter five. A-R Editions, Inc., of Madison, Wisconsin, provided excellent guidance in the book's design and production.

Personal appreciation to: the Rev. Art and Sue Lloyd, Donna Vukelich, John Stauber, Gini Waddick, Diana-Eréndira Castillo Reina (Yendi), David Merritt and Jean Hopfensperger; to George Talbot, Christine Schelshorn, Myrna Williamson and Steve Cagan for their flexibility and encouragement of the photographer; to Jim Danky for help with cataloging and promotion; to Nora Cusack and Donna Kruse at K-C Graphics, and to Walda Wood for showing patience with a frequently tired and distracted writer. Thanks to the organizers of sister-city projects around the country, who not only created the subject matter of this book but also provided us with information, support and insight. A prophetic thank-you to the organizers of sister-city projects which have yet to form. Thanks also to colleagues and friends not mentioned here, who nevertheless are an important part of this book.

Finally, we wish to express our deep gratitude to Mirette Seireg, WCCN's first executive director and a co-founder of the organization. WCCN's survival in its formative years is due largely to her dedicated work, which frequently involved almost supernatural commitments of time and energy. We also owe thanks as individuals to Mirette for encouraging us to use our interests in writing and photography to promote friendship between the United States and Nicaragua.

Whatever virtues this book has are due in large measure to the groups and individuals mentioned above. The authors alone claim responsibility for its failings.

Contents

**Children in Ciudad Darío ▲
during the annual poetry
festival honoring Ruben
Darío, Nicaragua's national
poet. Known internationally
as the founder of the modernist movement in Spanish
poetry in the nineteenth
century, Darío is a major
reason that Nicaragua is often
described as a "Nation of
Poets."**

Foreword:
The Alchemy of Love

This is a book that will not only change lives, but save lives. It chronicles one of the most positive movements in the long and troubled history of U.S.-Central American relations. It is a book that gives hope. But even more importantly, it gives a reason for hope, and a way to translate that hope into constructive social action.

Friends In Deed tells the story of the burgeoning U.S.-Nicaragua sister-city movement, and how you can become part of it. It shows the lives and faces of the U.S. and Nicaraguan citizens who have made themselves citizen-diplomats, and reached out across the sea of official hostility with the warm hand of friendship. It tells the dramatic stories of forward-looking cities in the U.S. and Nicaragua which have joined themselves together across the boundaries of space, culture and politics, to affirm their larger common humanity and to work together toward a better world.

But *Friends In Deed* has an even broader significance. It gives us an in-depth description and analysis of the new "people-to-people movement toward peace" — a movement that is broader, more creative, and more inspiring than traditional peace movements have been. It signals a new era in thinking about peacemaking and international relations.

"With every true friend-ship, we build more firmly the foundation on which the peace of the whole world rests."
M.K. Gandhi

Moving Toward Peace

Historically, peace movements tend to arise as a reaction to war or the impending threat of war. Because of their roots in the "politics of protest," traditional peace movements have the following characteristics:

- They are *primarily reactive* against the belligerence of their own governments. Therefore, they not only get typed as "Dr. No's," but they tend to lack an affirmative vision of peace and a long-term strategy for peace.

- Traditional peace movements *seek peace indirectly* by pressuring or petitioning their governments to make peace for them. In other words, their peacemaking with the "other side" is mediated through official diplomatic and political channels.

- Traditional peace movements *arise spontaneously* out of a felt sense of crisis, and usually outside the conventional institutions of the society. Hence, they tend to subside quickly once the crisis dies down. They *lack continuity* for the long haul.

- Traditional peace movements tend to attract a *left-liberal constituency* of people opposed to the current government. Hence they are often "marginalized" and fail to become a mainstream force.

The emerging "people-to-people" peacemaking movements, which bring together ordinary citizens and cities of the U.S. with those from officially "hostile" countries such as Nicaragua and the Soviet Union, go beyond traditional peace movements in each of these four respects:

- They are *"pro-active" and positive,* in that they initiate constructive programs of transnational cooperation. Their "no" to violence and hate is founded on a resounding "yes" to grassroots friendship and cooperation. This not only inspires and energizes the participants but it gives their work a positive public image.

- They *build peace directly,* not just through the mediation of their governments. By way of grassroots international contact, the new people-to-people movement goes beyond demanding peace to actually *manifesting* peace.

- They *institutionalize* spontaneous peacemaking action through formal sister-city (or sister-church, sister-school) relations, or through international organizations such as the International Physicians for the Prevention of Nuclear War, Co-Madres, or the Alliance of Nurses for International Health and Peace. Thus they build a sustained, ongoing peace and development process for the long haul, instead of fading away when the crisis abates.

- They attract a *diverse constituency* of people, left, right and center on the political spectrum — and even many who define themselves as "nonpolitical." People-to-people cooperation has been endorsed by Republican leaders such as Eisenhower and Reagan, as well as Democrats like Carter and Johnson. But in a deeper sense, people-to-people peacemaking transcends conventional political categories. It is, at bottom, a politics without politicians, a form of international populism that has a place in it for every citizen who cares not only about his or her country, but about the future of our war-imperiled planet.

The Ancient Tradition of Guest-Friendship

In the middle of one of the bloody battles of Homer's *Iliad,* a totally unexpected event occurs. The Greek hero "Diomedes of the Great War-Cry" is about to attack a Trojan soldier and shouts out for him to identify himself. In the typical fashion of the day, the Trojan, Glaukos, gives not only his name but his ancestry. Suddenly Diomedes throws down his spear and cries out "in moving words of friendliness" that they must not fight one another because Glaukos' grandfather, Bellerphontes, once visited Diomedes' grandfather as a guest. The tradition of guest-friendship possessed such cultural power that it forbade fighting even between distant descendants. So, in the fury of the battle raging all about them, Diomedes and Glaukos exchange the "promise of friendship" and also their armor, so "that others may know how we claim to be guests and friends from the days of our fathers."

Of course the guest-friendship of Glaukos and Diomedes did not end the Trojan War, but it did exemplify an ancient and profound truth of human culture: despite our tragic history of warmaking, we also possess the ability to form positive human bonds across the chasms of race, nationality and animosity. These bonds are capable of binding up the wounds of hate and ending violence.

This healing power was recognized by the Greek poet Aristophanes in his play, *Lysistrata*, in which the solidarity of Spartan and Athenian women ends the bitter war between their cities. The philosopher Aristotle devoted two chapters of his *Ethics* to arguing that *philia* or friendship was the essential foundation of a healthy social-political life.

The actual use of international friendship through the linking of cities from hostile countries is, however, a recent phenomenon. After World War II, people on both sides of the French-German border wondered how to end the deep bitterness caused by war. Two Swiss writers brought Kolbe, mayor of Frankfurt, together with Godaalt of Normandy. In a dramatic gesture, the two embraced and joined their cities in a friendship pairing. Thus began Europe's "Jumelage" (twinning) movement. Across the bridge of these "twinned" cities journeyed vast convoys of grassroots citizen encounters, which did something no diplomats or government treaties could ever do: they transformed the centuries-old hostility between France and Germany into an emerging culture of cooperation. Like Glaukos and Bellerphontes before them, the people of the sister cities vowed on the basis of their guest-friendship never to fight again.

Today this same process is beginning to transform the relationship of the U.S. to Nicaragua and to the Soviet Union. Organizations such as Witness for Peace, Peace Brigades International, Co-Madres, CISPES, the Accompaniment Project, and Quest for Peace are joining with the people of Central America in their struggles for peace and social justice. Groups like the National Council of Churches, the Friendship Force ("A World of Friends is a World of Peace"), the National Resources Defense Council, the International Physicians for the Prevention of Nuclear War, and more than 250 other grassroots groups are building cooperative projects with the Soviet people.

What is the source of this power? How is it that ordinary citizens are able to bridge the gulf of political animosity with the healing bond of friendship? Philosophically, I think the answer to this question has to do with the unique ability of friendship to "re-humanize the de-humanized."

Manufacturing the Enemy Image

Before ordinary human beings can begin the organized killing known as "war," they must first "kill" their opponents psychologically. This is the ritual — as old as civilization itself — known as "becoming enemies." The "enemy" is described by our leaders as "not like us," almost inhuman. They are evil. They are cruel. They are intent on destroying us and all that we love. There is only one thing the "enemy" understands — violence.

This "logic of the enemy image" leads to one inescapable conclusion: the enemy must be killed. Indeed, destroying the enemy is an heroic act, an act of salvation and purification.

The great demagogues of history, from Attila the Hun to Hitler, have been masters of this crude but venomous psychology. But in more recent years, this hate-filled stereotyping has been augmented by a more ideological and sophisticated version of the enemy-image. If depersonalizing a whole people by painting them as subhuman monsters is no longer effective, they can be equally depersonalized by abstracting their humanity away. They can be turned into political abstractions.

On March 29, 1971, after Lieutenant Calley was found guilty of personally murdering 22 Vietnamese civilians at My Lai — all children, women, or old men — he made the following statement: "Nobody in the military system ever described them as anything other than Communism [sic]. They didn't give it a race, they didn't give it a sex, they didn't give it an age. . . . That was my *enemy* out there."

A New Beginning

Friends In Deed cuts through this insidious veil of distorted perception, in order to retrieve the precious humanity of the "Other." It gives back to the struggling Nicaraguan people "a race . . . a sex . . . an age." Here we see their faces, hear their names and learn about their lives and hopes.

People-to-people contact re-humanizes the de-humanized images manufactured by the political factories of hate, the images which prepare us to do violence to one another. As a form of cultural understanding, of course, it can be augmented by literary and academic study of one another's societies. But people-to-people contact does something nothing else can do. By touching our hearts, it returns us to the primordial truth of our species, a truth that lies deeper than politics, deeper than hate: that beneath the rich diversity of cultures and societies, we are one humanity, sharing one fragile common planet. As the great Russian seer Leo Tolstoy put it: "My essential unity with all people cannot be destroyed by national boundaries and governments."

The Wisconsin Coordinating Council on Nicaragua (WCCN) has been a leader in building what Liz Chilsen and Sheldon Rampton call the "tradition of friendship" that is slowly transforming the cultural basis of U.S. foreign policy. Through the sister-cities connection, a vast web of cooperative projects and communications is being created. Every strand in this web, every true friendship, brings us closer to a new beginning, a world of peace with justice, a world of one human family.

Long ago, the ancient Greek poet, Aristophanes, experienced another war between neighbors. As he walked among the ruins of his once beautiful city, he offered an anguished prayer for peace:

> *From the murmur and subtlety of suspicion*
> *With which we vex one another,*
> *Give us rest.*
> *Make a new beginning*
> *And mingle again the kindred of nations*
> *In the alchemy of love.*

May this book continue and strengthen the "new beginning" — the U.S.-Nicaragua sister-city movement — which mingles the people of our two nations in the timeless and healing "alchemy of love."

Vincent Kavaloski
Ecumenical Partnership for Peace and Justice,
Wisconsin Conference of Churches

Authors' Preface

The idea for this book originated during the 1986 U.S.-Nicaragua Friendship Conference, where participants expressed a need for greater information-sharing between projects. At the invitation of the Nicaraguan Department of Municipal and Regional Affairs (DAMUR), we spent two months in Nicaragua in 1987, documenting existing sister cities and exploring potential new projects. Since then, the number of sister cities has more than doubled, and regional coordinators have begun to emerge in several parts of the United States. We see this book as part of an ongoing process of documentation, and expect further growth of the sister-cities movement to require updates in its directories. We hope that organizers will notify us of address changes and other information pertaining to their projects or new projects in their area. Write to: Wisconsin Coordinating Council on Nicaragua (WCCN)/Friendship Project, P.O. Box 1534, Madison, WI 53701; phone (608) 257-7230.

A number of excellent books have already been written, from various viewpoints, describing political and social conditions in Nicaragua. We have not attempted to duplicate those efforts. Political and social questions are important, but the beauty of the sister-cities movement is the way it answers those questions, through personal friendships as much as through ideology or analysis.

The sheer number of projects underway across the United States has made it impossible to include a complete listing in the directories at the back, but the Central America Resource Center in Austin, Texas has compiled a directory of over 1,100 Central America organizations throughout the United States. That directory is available by contacting them.

While researching this book, we have been privileged to meet some of the U.S. and Nicaraguan citizens whose lives have become intertwined through the sister-city movement. What we have seen convinces us that the democratic principles which inspired our own revolution are alive today in the United States. These principles are more than mere rhetoric; they are concretely demonstrated in the ability of our people to challenge the "established authorities" in Washington and to invent literally thousands of creative alternatives to war. We hope that the methods outlined here can serve as a blueprint for building friendship and peace, not just between the United States and Nicaragua, but throughout the world.

Baseball, Nicaragua's national sport, in the autonomous region on Nicaragua's Atlantic Coast.

New Pilgrims in the Americas 1

"It was the best of times, it was the worst of times . . ."

Charles Dickens
A Tale of Two Cities

"When Eugene Hasenfus was captured," said Pedro Zúñiga, smiling rather apologetically, "most of us wanted to see him dead."

At first we hadn't noticed him, a slim, athletically built young Nicaraguan dressed in a tank-top T-shirt, army camouflage pants and a visor cap that bore the slogan, "Coppertone." His appearance, combining the styles of guerrilla militance and American advertising, typified the contrasts and incongruities that we had seen throughout the country, then in its seventh year of revolution and its fifth year of war against the U.S.-backed "contra" army. Soldiers armed with machine guns guarded the streets of Nicaraguan cities, yet seemed surprisingly casual as they chatted with civilian passers-by. In streetlots beneath graffiti denouncing Yankee imperialism, we had watched Nicaraguan children played baseball, the national sport which was popularized in the 1920s by invading U.S. Marines. We had heard Nicaraguan President Daniel Ortega speak angrily against the aggressions of the United States, and we had strolled past movie theatres advertising American war films with heroes like Charles Bronson, Clint Eastwood and Arnold Schwarzenegger. Nicaragua, it seemed, was a country full of contradictions, not least of which was its love-hate relationship with the United States.

As citizens from the state of Wisconsin, we embodied our half of this contradiction. It was a Wisconsin man, Eugene Hasenfus, who became the first modern U.S. prisoner of war in Nicaragua after his airplane was shot down while delivering weapons and supplies to the contras. Yet Wisconsin has also had a decades-long "sister state" relationship with Nicaragua, a friendship that precedes the years of war, revolution and political controversy. Over the years, this relationship has led to hundreds of exchanges between Wisconsin and Nicaraguan teachers, politicians, social workers, and religious leaders. After an earthquake devastated Nicaragua's capital city of Managua in 1972, Wisconsin sent planeloads of food, clothing and medicine to help the victims. Throughout the 1979 Sandinista insurrection and afterwards, Wisconsin volunteers provided assistance to children orphaned by war. During 1986, the year that Eugene Hasenfus was shipping weapons to the contras, Wisconsinites sent the people of Nicaragua over $1 million worth of agricultural supplies, firefighting equipment, and every other imaginable type of aid.

1

The Luciano Vilchez Agricultural Cooperative, where Pedro Zúñiga lived, was one beneficiary of this relationship. People fleeing the war zones of El Salvador and Nicaragua had resettled there, with assistance from the United Nations High Commission on Refugees and Nicaragua's Institute of Social Services and Welfare. People from the Wisconsin city of La Crosse had pitched in with donations of tools, supplies, and five high-producing dairy cows. As members of the Wisconsin Coordinating Council on Nicaragua (WCCN), an organization promoting sister-state exchanges, we were visiting to announce that the La Crosse People's Food Coop had raised additional money for a refrigerator so the farm could store veterinary medicines. The refugees listened solemnly to our news and then led us on a brief tour of the farm, proudly showing off several young calves produced by their Wisconsin cows.

Pedro Zúñiga joined the other members of the cooperative, following our tour at a shy distance, listening. Finally, as we were getting ready to leave, he introduced himself.

A member of the Sandinista Youth, he was living on the farm temporarily to carry out a literacy education project, identifying peasants who already knew how to read so he could train them to teach others. He was a student at the Nicaraguan National University in Managua, majoring in English, but his studies had fallen behind recently while he served a tour of duty in the Sandinista Army.

"A lot of us tend to forget the friendship between Wisconsin and Nicaragua," he said. "I was in the army when they captured Hasenfus, and when we saw in the news that our vice president was going to Wisconsin, and that Wisconsin was a sister state with Nicaragua, I didn't believe it. I thought the government was just throwing stories at us so we wouldn't be so upset when they pardoned Hasenfus.

"Then I came to this farm, where I had milk to drink every day. I thought, 'This is strange. Usually farms don't have this much milk. They aren't this well off.' I saw these cows that they had, and they were dairy cows. And when I asked where they came from, the people here said Wisconsin."

His face broke into an enthusiastic grin. "That's when I realized they weren't lying to us," he said. "I had wondered, you know, because sometimes you think these are just stories people tell. But now to see you here, face to face, makes it a reality for me."

Breaking the Barrier

Pedro Zúñiga's experience upon meeting us was remarkably similar to the feelings that North Americans often express after their first encounter with Nicaraguans. Hostilities between the U.S. and Nicaraguan governments have been intense and prolonged, and for many North Americans, regardless of their political philosophy, it is impossible to think of Nicaragua without harboring some sort of caution, suspicion or fear. For some, this feeling reflects their belief that Nicaragua is a totalitarian, communist country hostile to the United States. Others, who oppose U.S. military actions against Nicaragua, anticipate resentment or hostility from the Nicaraguan people. Many simply fear the idea of visiting a Third World country, particularly a country at war. "Nicaragua? Why the hell are you going *there*?" asked one person as we made preparations for our trip. "From what I hear, you can get shot there just for looking at people the wrong way."

In fact, one of the biggest shocks that North Americans experience upon visiting Nicaragua is the discovery that these fears are groundless. Many Americans express joy and astonishment at the warm greetings they receive from the Nicaraguan people. "The first surprise came at the Managua airport," said Dawn Jax Belleau, a reporter for Wisconsin's *Sheboygan Press* who toured Nicaragua in 1987. "A Nicaraguan woman approached a member of our group and, in English, said, 'Thank you for coming to visit my country.' This welcome was repeated numerous times during our stay."[1] Judith Anne Singer of Milwaukee, who fell from a horse and suffered several broken bones during a 1983 visit, recalled her experience in a Nicaraguan hospital with "smiling food workers, doctors who checked on me more than once a day, floor sweepers, and others who wanted to look at this injured North American. People who were visiting sick or injured relatives would help me eat, wash me, brush my hair, help me out of bed, push me in a wheelchair, take me outside, and bring me Pepsi. I speak very little Spanish, but it didn't present a problem. I spent a week in that hospital and was never afraid or lonely."[2]

One irony of the current crisis in U.S.-Nicaraguan government relations is that it has contributed to an unprecedented growth of friendship between the people of the two countries. Concerned at the growing war in Central America, tens of thousands of United States citizens, representing a broad range of talents, backgrounds and political viewpoints, have visited Nicaragua hoping that face to face contacts will transform hostilities into mutual understanding. Often, these efforts have gone beyond individual expressions of goodwill and led to formal partnerships between U.S. and Nicaraguan institutions. Wisconsin's once-unique sister relationship with Nicaragua is rapidly becoming commonplace throughout the United States, as part of a "citizens diplomacy" approach to improving U.S. relations in Central America.

Perhaps the most striking indicator of this movement's growth is the number of U.S. cities that have adopted Nicaraguan counterparts. In 1985, there were only 10 such sister cities, whose representatives met for the first time at a small gathering in Boulder, Colorado. By June of 1986, when Wisconsin hosted a "U.S.-Nicaragua Friendship Conference," the number had risen to 20. A year later, when another conference was held in Seattle, the number had risen to 77 and appeared to be growing exponentially, in places like Topeka, Kansas; Gainesville, Florida; and Washington, D.C. And in addition to cities, countless U.S. groups including university departments, churches, schools, cooperatives, nurses, computer buffs, students, daycare workers and journalists have established links with parallel groups in Nicaragua.

Many of these relationships began spontaneously. Someone from the U.S. would visit Nicaragua, see a particular need, and organize a project back in his or her home community to meet that need. Often these projects started on a small scale and grew more rapidly than their organizers anticipated. Some now provide hundreds of thousands of dollars worth of assistance each year. But the most important achievement of the sister-city movement has been the formation of ongoing, long-term ties between the people of our two countries, ties which break down stereotypes and suspicions.

Although often they began out of fear that Nicaragua would become "another Vietnam," these sister pairings are more than a response to fear. They are laying the basis for a thoroughly new, positive relationship between the people of the United States and the people of Central America. The sister cities

"The whole sister-city movement is expanding so rapidly that in comparison to the new groups, a 4-year-old group like Boulder has more experience. That may seem strange, because we have our own problems to work with, and we think, 'How can we be a role model for other groups?' "

Sara Lee, Boulder/Jalapa
Friendship City Projects

that have been established can be expected to survive longer than the current crisis. Hopefully, they will last for generations. Sister cities are building a *tradition* of friendship between our cultures. They are transforming the cultural basis of our foreign policy, and eventually may create a political climate in which a U.S. war in Central America becomes not only undesirable but unimaginable.

The Hasenfus Case

Historically, the events that have led to hostilities between the United States and Nicaragua are easy to identify, however unpleasant they may be to acknowledge. Since the 1800s, Nicaraguans have resented U.S. power and military dominance in their country, dominance that culminated with 45 years of U.S. government support for the Somoza dictatorship, one of the most cruel and greedy regimes in Latin America. Instead of helping the people of Nicaragua, U.S. economic aid was diverted into Somoza's personal fortune, while military aid and "police assistance" went to Somoza's National Guard, which machine-gunned villages, dropped peasants out of helicopters, and decimated Nicaraguan cities with aerial bombings during its final campaign of terror. These abuses led almost inevitably to revolution, and when the Sandinistas overthrew Somoza, their new national anthem pledged to "fight against the Yankees, enemies of humanity." In turn, this rhetoric has been quoted by the Reagan administration to justify its fight against the Sandinistas, and the resulting contra war continues to create new grounds for escalating hostility. But if the 1986 capture of Eugene Hasenfus inside Nicaragua shows the extent of those hostilities and the threat of a direct U.S. war, it also illustrates the ways sister cities can help to reduce hostility and promote peace.

By the time that Hasenfus was captured, over 20,000 Nicaraguans had died in the contra war, the country's economy had been devastated, and public emotions had reached a boiling point. The *Mexico Daily News* quoted street interviews with Nicaraguans whose suggestions included shooting Hasenfus, locking him up without food until he starved to death, and taking him to a public place "so everyone can hit him."[3] His capture was depicted on Nicaraguan posters and billboards, accompanied by a message to the United States. Before the U.S. could conquer Nicaragua, it warned, "More than a battalion of your blond invaders will bite the dust in our rugged mountains."

In the United States, on the other hand, passions about Nicaragua remained comparatively mild, despite the warfare in which we had become engaged. Until the Hasenfus capture, many North Americans remained unaware or unconcerned about events in Central America. Even in Hasenfus' home town of Marinette, a "Free Hasenfus" fund failed to attract significant contributions. "The comment that you hear frequently is, 'He got himself into it, it's his own problem,' or, 'The government got him into it, the government will get him out of it,' " said Ernest Pleger, a Marinette lawyer helping the Hasenfus family.[4] But the United States, anxious to minimize its embarrassment, denied any connection to his activities and publicly offered him no assistance. "As far as my government saying anything, it's forgotten," Hasenfus said. "Whoever I was working for out there, they just say, 'Sorry about that, Gene.' "

Ironically, the sister-state relationship became a channel of communication for members of the Hasenfus family, who contacted the Wisconsin Coordinating Council on Nicaragua for help in arranging delivery to Eugene's jail cell of a "care package" containing soap, deodorant, candy bars, and other comforts unavailable in Nicaragua. More importantly, the sister-state connection helped answer public concerns that had been raised by Hasenfus's capture when Wisconsin received a visit from Dr. Sergio Ramírez, Nicaragua's vice president. After receiving a welcome at the airport from Wisconsin Governor Anthony Earl, Ramírez toured the state capitol, spoke to large gatherings at a local church, and, through WCCN's mediation, met privately with members of the Hasenfus family.

"They are human beings," Ramírez said afterwards. "We know the problems they have because we know of suffering from war. We are concerned with the worries of the Hasenfus family, but we are concerned too with with the worries of thousands of families in Nicaragua. Our main interest is that in the future, a new Hasenfus case will not occur." This sentiment, and the fact that Governor Earl and other U.S. friends of Nicaragua had requested leniency in the Hasenfus case, were the reasons given by Nicaraguan President Daniel Ortega when he chose the birthday of Adam Hasenfus, Eugene's son, to announce that he would be released from prison and could return to the United States.

As the Nicaraguan government itself has stated, the release of Hasenfus was not a "humanitarian act." The Sandinistas obviously had political motives for their treatment of him, as did the United States government. The question, however, is not *whether* politics prevailed but *what kind* of politics prevailed — the politics of hatred and escalating hostility, or the politics of reconciliation and understanding? Whatever their differences of ideology, the Nicaraguan and U.S. governments both operate within an environment of public opinion and shape their policies in hopes of attracting public support, both domestically and internationally. In the case of Eugene Hasenfus, domestic political considerations could have motivated the Sandinistas to take a harsh, unforgiving position, appealing to nationalist sentiments and popular resentment of the United States. Instead they chose a conciliatory approach. Our encounter with Pedro Zúñiga illustrates some of the factors underlying that decision and the value of people-to-people friendship campaigns.

A Psychological Answer to the Problem of War

Significant differences exist between Nicaragua and the United States in terms of politics, culture, and ideology, but these differences are not the sole reason for the tensions between our countries. There is also a psychological aspect to the war in Central America, and the power to resolve this psychological aspect rests with our people, not our governments.

According to foreign affairs experts Joseph V. Montville and William D. Davidson, official relations between governments operate according to different psychological rules than informal, people-to-people relations. In government-to-government encounters, national leaders "are like tribal chiefs because they must assure their followers they will defend them against enemies — other tribes or nations — who want to conquer or destroy them." Unfortunately, this role can lead to posturing and misunderstandings based on hostile assumptions about other countries. Private, unofficial encounters, however, are "always open-minded, often altruistic," and proceed from the assumption that "actual or potential conflict can be resolved or eased by appealing to common human capabilities to respond to good will and reasonableness."[5]

People-to-people diplomacy is not a substitute for defense against a hostile enemy, but it can reduce and sometimes eliminate the sources of hostility. The

"There is a new stage arriving in the history of the U.S.-Nicaraguan confrontation. We believe, both as Christians and as revolutionaries, that everyone can repent sometime."

Alejandro Bendaña
Nicaraguan Foreign Ministry

rapid growth of U.S.-Nicaraguan sister cities reflects heightened concern among the United States people at the official level of hostilities and the escalation of U.S. military involvement in Central America. But it also reflects a desire to find a constructive, positive way of acting on that concern, an approach that represents and includes the participation not only of anti-war protesters but also of mainstream U.S. citizens who ordinarily would not become involved in political demonstrations.

The sister-city approach — locally-based programs of humanitarian assistance coupled with the opportunity for direct human contact and exchange — offers a means for U.S. citizens to learn more about Nicaragua without adopting a political commitment that they may not feel comfortable making. "I support this because I believe in clean water, but I'm not going to support the Sandinistas," says an Arkansas conservative who joined a project to develop drinkable water systems in Nicaragua's war zones. Most sister-city projects do not attempt to assemble "politically correct" people for the purpose of expressing their already-formed consensus. Rather, they establish a common ground within which people of divergent viewpoints can work together, developing and learning from one another in the process. Successful sister cities are often built around the moderates of a community as much as the political activists — not the "wheelers and dealers" but the "doers and joiners" who lead their civic groups and PTAs, whose lives are wrapped up in their churches and their jobs and with their children. For them, the sister city is a tool that enables them to contribute their talents towards peace and a better world.

Sister cities also offer a particularly effective way of teaching and learning about Nicaragua because they approach people through their own community involvements and interests — doctors on the issue of health care, baseball players through their interest in sports, teachers through their concern with education. Sister cities therefore attract the participation of people for whom Central America is not necessarily a primary concern. For this reason, the forms of sister-city work are nearly as diverse as the forms of human activity itself. In California, a group of disabled people is sending orthopedic equipment to disabled Nicaraguans. The city of Ann Arbor, Michigan provided a garbage truck for its sister city of Juigalpa. In locations throughout the United States, environmentalists, engineers, musicians and farmers have become involved in Nicaragua through their particular interests.

Finally, by building on the strengths and abilities of their communities, and by emphasizing humanitarian, friendly gestures, sister cities offer a positive approach that enables people to feel good about their relationship with Nicaragua, rather than negative and cynical. This sets sister cities apart from conventional approaches which think of Nicaragua primarily in terms of emotions such as fear — fear of war on the one hand, or fear of communism on the other. Both of these concerns are important in the minds of the U.S. people and must be addressed, but dwelling on fear alone can lead to feelings of powerlessness, apathy, and despair, or, in the worst case, to hatred and militarism.

Historically, it is not these negative emotions that have underlain the U.S. public's perceptions of foreign policy. In fact, one of the striking aspects of our society has been the almost supernatural optimism and self-confidence with which we have viewed our role in the world. Even before the United States existed as a nation, the early Puritan settlers were comparing the American continent to a "shining city on a hill," an example whose moral purity should

"Come hither, and I will show you, an admirable Spectacle! 'Tis an Heavenly CITY . . . A CITY to be inhabited by an Innumerable Company of Angels, and by the Spirits of Just Men . . . Put on thy beautiful garments, O America, the Holy City!"

Cotton Mather, Puritan preacher
Theopolis Americana: An Essay on the Golden Street of the Holy City (1710)

inspire the rest of the world. Later generations have spoken in similar terms of the United States responsibility to serve as "a beacon of democracy, freedom and prosperity" for the rest of the world. Politicians have used these phrases to cover up a multitude of sins, and reformers have used the same language to denounce those sins and demand change. Even when our nation's behavior has not lived up to its rhetoric, the words themselves have embodied hope. It is only in recent years, with the trauma of Vietnam, the disillusionments stemming from Watergate and similar scandals, and growing fears of unemployment, inflation and other symptoms of distress, that these higher aspirations have begun to sound hollow in our ears.

The sister-city approach, which is based on the positive emotions of personal friendship, has the potential to renew the idealism of the U.S. people and rekindle a positive sense of national self-respect. This aspect of sister cities — the emotional relief they offer to people whose pride in country has been repeatedly challenged over the last two decades — may be the most important psychological reason for their growth.

An artisan in Masaya, sister
city to Santa Cruz, California.

A woman expresses concern over housing problems to the Minister of Housing at a weekly "De Cara al Pueblo", or "Face the People" meeting in Managua. These weekly town meetings are televised nationally and offer an opportunity for citizens to discuss their concerns directly with national government leaders. ◄

Just 12 miles from the Honduran border, Ocotál is a sister city to Hartford, Connecticut. ▼

A volunteer from Managua assists the Nicaraguan coffee harvest, January, 1987. ◄

Madison resident Helen Aarli, a high school teacher, chats with a student at the Elvis Diaz Romero High School in Managua. ▼

Estelí, 1985. Buildings in ▲
Estelí were severely damaged
during the 1979 revolution,
and are slowly being repaired.
Estelí is a sister city to
Highland Park, New Jersey.

A Sunday afternoon chess
game in Managua.   ▶

Over 1,000 people filled Saint
Paul's Catholic Church in
Madison, Wisconsin to meet
with Dr. Sergio Ramírez,
Nicaragua's Vice President,
when he visited Wisconsin in
November, 1986.   ▲

During his visit to Wisconsin,
Dr. Ramírez met with
Governor Tony Earl.   ▶

12

Wisconsinite Rosie Rice
working in the Luz Dilian
Arévalo day care center for
Salvadoran refugees in
Managua.

Sylvia Fox, coordinator of the Sandinista Children's Association, shown here with her son Martin Luther. Her city of Bluefields is paired with Brooklyn, New York. She expressed interest in forming a sister relationship with children in kindergartens and day care centers in the United States.

"Do-It-Yourself Foreign Policy" 2

According to international-relations scholar Hans Morgenthau, diplomats play a role in promoting peace by negotiating agreements between nations; they serve as symbolic representatives of goodwill; and they serve as a channel for communicating information between their own nation and others. Gale Warner and Michael Shuman, authors of the book *Citizen Diplomats*, point out that while private citizens cannot represent the United States government in performing these functions, "they often can claim to represent smaller chunks of America — churches, businesses, civic groups, local governments, or other Americans of like mind. On behalf of their constituencies, the citizen diplomats often negotiate and enter into agreements. . . . They demonstrate their respect and goodwill . . . through singing, dancing, feasting and toasting. And they maintain their own two-way traffic of information and impressions." On some occasions, they may provide an alternative channel for carrying out diplomatic functions that traditional diplomats are unable to fulfill. "More often, however, they affect the political context in which leaders operate by spreading information and forming people-to-people relationships."[1]

American citizen diplomacy has been recorded as early as 1675, when a Quaker delegation from Rhode Island attempted unsuccessfully to mediate between warring Indians and settlers in New England's Plymouth Colony. According to Warner and Shuman, however, a similar effort by Philadelphia Quaker George Logan in 1798 managed to prevent the United States and France from going to war: "France, which was then battling Britain, had begun attacking American ships and taking prisoners because of growing U.S. political cooperation with Britain. To the amazement of everyone, Logan returned to the United States with a decree from France indicating its willingness to end its trade embargo and free all captured U.S. seamen."[2] In subsequent years, the Quaker Society of Friends has repeatedly offered its services as an informal channel for communication between hostile groups, during the Crimean War in 1854, the First and Second World Wars, in Northern Ireland, and elsewhere.

Even the protracted conflict between the United States and the Soviet Union has been repeatedly bridged by U.S. citizens acting in private capacities. Shortly after the Russian revolution, U.S. capitalist Armand Hammer carried out several profitable negotiations with the Bolshevik government, winning the

15

respect even of Lenin himself. In the 1950s Roswell Garst, a farmer and businessman, toured the Soviet Union, selling hybrid seed corn and touting the accomplishments of U.S. agriculture. In 1960, *Saturday Review* editor Norman Cousins founded the Dartmouth conference, an annual get-together for private, off-the-record talks between prominent Soviet and U.S. citizens, including influential leaders and writers such as James Michener, David Rockefeller, John Kenneth Galbraith, Margaret Mead, and Paul Warnke. Cousins also acted as an unofficial diplomat in the aftermath of the Cuban missile crisis, personally delivering messages between President John F. Kennedy, Pope John XXIII, and Soviet Party Chairman Nikita Khruschev. Thanks largely to this private "shuttle diplomacy," the Soviet Union agreed to release two imprisoned Catholic archbishops, and the U.S. and Soviets successfully negotiated an end to above-ground testing of nuclear weapons.

Local governments also have a long history of participating in foreign affairs, many of which are documented in a handbook by Shuman entitled *Building Municipal Foreign Policies.* "Benjamin Franklin, for example," Shuman writes, "shuttled repeatedly to Paris and London, representing mercantile interests of Pennsylvania and three other colonies. . . . During the early years of the Republic, the states continued promoting trade and often engaged in diplomatic negotiations. In the 1820s, several southern states imprisoned black British seamen, prompting Great Britain to set up consulates in the southern states to negotiate for their release and to lobby for new laws dealing with black foreigners. . . . For decades, American border states and communities adjacent to Canada or Mexico have entered into agreements" on issues ranging from road maintenance, water management and fire prevention to illegal immigration, acid rain, and drug trafficking.[3]

"If involvement in foreign affairs by those outside national government was infrequent in the late 1700s and early 1800s," Warner and Shuman observe, "it was probably because very few individuals or private organizations could afford to participate. Indeed, for most of U.S. history, the costs of ongoing international communications and travel — the basic tools of diplomacy — were simply prohibitive for almost anyone outside the national government. Today, however, the real costs facing citizens who wish to practice diplomacy are plummeting." Modern technological advance has brought global communication and transportation within the affordable reach of millions of North Americans. "With inflation factored out, the cost of an overseas cable today is now a thousandth of what it was in 1866 and a sixth of what it was in 1970. The cost of an overseas flight is now a sixth of what it was in 1940, and an overseas telephone call costs a sixtieth of what it did in 1935." Channels for dissemination of public information have multiplied and decentralized, thanks to "the increasing availability of compact, easily transported shortwave radios, tape recorders, videocassette recorders, personal computers, and satellite transmitters. . . . If technical developments like computer networks and broadcast satellites continue lowering the costs of global communication, and if more discount airlines continue lowering the costs of overseas transportation, we may soon be entering an era in which millions of Americans could practice . . . some types of diplomacy on a significant scale."[4]

Futurologists such as John Naisbitt and Alvin Toffler have written best-sellers arguing that these innovations are revolutionizing the way citizens relate to government. "Spectacular advances in communications technology open, for the first time, a mind-boggling array of possibilities for direct citizen participation in political decision-making," argues Toffler, the author of *Future Shock* and *The Third Wave*. "The old objections to direct democracy are growing weaker at precisely the time that the objections to representative democracy are growing stronger. . . . [A] building block of tomorrow's political systems must be the principle of 'semi-direct democracy' — a shift from depending on representatives to representing ourselves."[5]

Traditionally, direct democracy has seemed impractical, first because it was logistically impossible, and second because it was believed that everyday citizens lacked the information and expertise necessary to make wise decisions. But as Naisbitt argues in his book, *Megatrends*, "along came the communication revolution and with it an extremely well-educated electorate. Today, with instantaneously shared information, we know as much about what's going on as our representatives and we know it just about as quickly."[6]

Opinion pollster George Gallup, Sr. reaches similar conclusions. "In fact, the public generally is decades ahead of Congress. . . . We've found that there is a cultural lag, if you want to call it that, between the time people accept an idea and the time Congress is willing to act on it." George Gallup, Jr. observes that on the one hand, barely one-fourth of U.S. citizens bother to vote, reflecting "frustration and disillusionment with our governmental leaders and institutions" that has "placed us among the most apathetic people in the world in terms of our participation in the governmental process." On the other hand, "More than one out of two Americans are willing to work free of charge for a cause they believe in. . . . The low voter turnout isn't due to the fact that Americans don't care about their government. Rather, the problem seems to be that they think the government doesn't care about them. . . . When we asked people in our polls if they would be more inclined to vote on national *issues* as well as candidates, a significant number responded yes. In fact, we've estimated that voting turnout would skyrocket up to about 80 percent of eligible voters, in contrast to the present 27 percent for national elections. In other words, people don't want to shirk their responsibilities as citizens. They just want a more direct voice in government — a purer form of democracy than they have now."[7]

People from diverse political viewpoints now agree on the need to decentralize government authority and strengthen citizen influence at the local level. Conservatives have been among the most vocal critics of "big government," advocating what they refer to as "new federalism" or "states' rights." From a leftist perspective, Janice E. Perlman has praised the "plethora of grassroots organizations involving local people mobilized on their own behalf,"[8] and Princeton University Professor Sheldon Wolin argues that "Our whole mode of thinking must be turned upside down. . . . A political being is not to be defined as the citizen has been, as an abstract, disconnected bearer of rights, privileges, and immunities, but as a person whose existence is located in a particular place and draws its sustenance from circumscribed relationships: family, friends, church, neighborhood, workplace, community, town, city."[9]

Birth of the Sister-Cities Idea

In foreign affairs, the federal government's dominance has made local citizen initiatives less visible, but in fact the movement toward decentralized, local foreign policies has been growing steadily since the 1950s, and in the 1980s has begun to mushroom rapidly. In 1956, President Dwight D. Eisenhower initiated a broad-scale People-to-People program, as "an effort to stimulate private citizens in many fields — the arts, education, athletics, law, medicine, business — to organize themselves to reach across the seas and national boundaries to their counterparts in other lands. If we are going to take advantage of the assumption that all people want peace," he said, "then the problem is for people to get together and to lead governments — if necessary to evade governments — to work out not one method but thousands of methods by which people can gradually learn a bit more of each other." A forerunner of President Kennedy's Peace Corps, the People-to-People program also launched the sister-cities concept, which Eisenhower described as an expression of two deeply held convictions: "First is our belief in effective, responsive local government as a principal bulwark of freedom. Second is our faith in the great promise of people-to-people and sister city affiliations in helping build the solid structure of world peace."

For Nicaragua and the rest of Latin America, these initiatives acquired special significance in the aftermath of the Cuban revolution, as the United States became increasingly concerned with the growth of anti-U.S. sentiment south of its border. The depth of this hostility became painfully evident in 1958, during an intended "goodwill tour" of Latin America by then-Vice President Richard Nixon, which was shaken by a series of violent incidents. "In Lima, Peru, an attempted debate with the students at San Marcos University turned into a riot between police and demonstrators, one of whom spat in Nixon's face as he turned back to his hotel," write Jerome Levinson and Juan Onís in their book, *The Alliance That Lost Its Way*. In Caracas, Venezuela, "a howling mob tried to overturn the official car in which Nixon was riding. Nixon had a moment of real danger as local security police struggled to control the rock-throwing mob. While U.S. Secret Service men were beating off the attackers, the driver of the car saw an opening in the crowd, gunned the motor, and sped Nixon away to the safety of the U.S. embassy residence. . . . The violence of this incident, in which the life of a vice-president of the United States had been endangered, told the world that something was seriously wrong" in the relationship between the United States and its neighbors in Latin America.[10]

During his 1960 presidential campaign against Nixon, John F. Kennedy accused the Eisenhower administration of alienating the people of Latin America by supporting dictatorships while ignoring the poverty-stricken masses in those countries and their demands for reform. "Latin America is seething with discontent and unrest," he said. "If the only alternatives for the people of Latin America are the status quo and communism, then they will inevitably choose communism." He proposed a new approach — an "Alliance for Progress" linking "nations with a common interest in freedom and economic advance in a great common effort to develop the resources of the entire hemisphere, strengthen the forces of democracy, and widen the vocational and educational opportunities of every person in all the Americas." The purpose of the Alliance, Kennedy said, would be not merely to combat communism, but to help "our sister republics for their own sake."[11]

As Kennedy saw it, the need of Latin America for homes, work, land, health, and schools was so "staggering in its dimensions" that only a bold program — "a vast effort unparalleled in magnitude and nobility of purpose" — could hope to meet it. He called for a decade of "maximum effort," towards which the U.S. would contribute as much as $20 billion to support economic development, food aid, and social reform including land redistribution and other efforts at reducing the large and serious gap between rich and poor people in Latin America.[12] In addition, the Alliance for Progress established a variety of exchange programs to promote sharing of advances in science and research through cooperation among universities and research institutions; expanded programs of technical training; and an educational and exchange program to increase appreciation in the United States of Latin American culture and accomplishments in thought and the creative arts. Through these efforts, Kennedy promised to "transform the American continent into a vast crucible of revolutionary ideas and effort" and "demonstrate to the entire world that man's unsatisfied aspiration for economic progress and social justice can best be achieved within a framework of democratic institutions."[13]

In retrospect, as Kennedy aide Arthur Schlesinger, Jr. admitted years later, this language was extravagant and unrealistic. "In our public utterance we were an over-rhetorical administration," Schlesinger said. "We underestimated the strength of inertia and rigidity. . . . The Latin American oligarchs simply denied Kennedy's thesis that the choice was between peaceful and violent revolution; they were well accustomed to calling out the armed forces in order to prevent both." Moreover, there was "an intrinsic contradiction between the Alliance and the rest of the United States government. When the Pentagon, the CIA, and, to a degree, the State Department thought about Latin America, the first problem they saw was 'hemisphere security.' In the atmosphere of the late cold war, this preoccupation seemed more virile and patriotic than the Alliance's interest in development, democracy, and reform."[14] These pressures led to the abandonment of the Alliance's original emphasis on social and political reform, and in fact the Alliance began to sponsor "police training" programs that provided support to Latin American dictatorships. By the late 1960s, the Alliance for Progress had become simply another U.S. aid program, and in 1969 it was discontinued altogether.

Ultimately, Eisenhower's original ideas — people-to-people programs and sister cities — have proven more effective than massive U.S. government aid as a means of strengthening friendships between the United States and other countries. By June of 1987, Sister Cities International, a private foundation formed in 1967, had recognized 1,282 sister city arrangements between 786 American and 1,153 foreign cities, ranging across all 50 states and 86 foreign countries.[15] The sister-city concept had won praise from a wide spectrum of U.S. leaders. President Lyndon B. Johnson noted that city-to-city programs "work outside government in a field vital to the promotion of friendship among citizens of every land so they will understand each other and peace." Highlighting the benefits of community interaction across national boundaries, President Ronald Reagan said, "Out of this effort comes a spirit of friendship, which, multiplied by thousands of sister cities, results in improved economic, cultural and social relationships between people everywhere."

Kennedy's Alliance for Progress deserves credit, however, for helping to spread the sister-city concept. Through the Alliance-sponsored Partners of the Americas program, many countries in Latin America acquired U.S. "sister states." In Central America, the state of Oregon adopted Costa Rica; Alabama paired with Guatemala; Louisiana with El Salvador; Vermont with Honduras; and it was through the Partners of the Americas program that Wisconsin first became a sister state to Nicaragua.[16] These pairings were set up, Kennedy said, so that "through personal relations our curiosity can be fulfilled by a sense of knowledge, cynicism can give way to trust, and the warmth of human friendship can be kindled."

Words Become Deeds

During the Eisenhower-Kennedy era, sister cities functioned as obedient servants of U.S. foreign policy, and although the idea of cities as a force for peace received verbal homage, in practice only a few pairings were formed with cities in countries that did not already enjoy friendly relationships with the United States. In launching the sister-state relationship with Nicaragua in 1964, Wisconsin Governor John W. Reynolds described the program's objectives in military terms, praising the Somoza dictatorship as a "bastion of Western democracy and freedom, facing Castro and Communism. I know of no better way to directly demonstrate our support, and at the same time counter-attack hostile infiltrations, than by this type of people-to-people exchange."[17]

Mirette Seireg was a high school student in Madison, Wisconsin in 1972 when Nicaragua suffered a devastating earthquake, and then-Governor Patrick Lucey issued an appeal for donations to help the victims. As president of her school's Spanish club, she helped organize collections of canned food and clothing, which were gathered in huge bins in the school cafeteria and flown to Nicaragua. "We didn't have a clue as to what type of government existed down there or how the donations were going to be distributed," she recalls. "All we knew was that there was a need, and we wanted to help." In fact, most of the donations sent to Nicaragua after the earthquake never got to people who needed them. Food supplies, for example, were taken by Somoza and sold for profit in his supermarkets.

Nearly a decade later, Seireg witnessed and actively participated in a transformation in the nature of the Wisconsin-Nicaragua relationship following Somoza's overthrow. In 1981, after receiving a master's degree in nutrition from the University of Wisconsin, she was hired by Harvard University as a visiting professor at the University of Central American in Managua. "I was still politically illiterate," she says. "It didn't occur to me that there would be personal danger, because the insurrection was already over, and at that time the contras were not a significant force. My reasons for going were purely career-related. But it was through this professional exchange that I came to know Nicaragua."

At that time there were only 12 nutritionists in all of Nicaragua, and 60 percent of the children under age five suffered from some degree of malnutrition. "I spent the first year I was there basically just teaching and absorbing a great deal of information," she says. "I gained an appreciation for all that's needed to accomplish things that in the States I took for granted. I was impressed by the friendliness of the people, by how young everyone was, and their courage in pursuing areas of study that perhaps they knew nothing about but were very interested in learning. I was impressed by what it meant for some students just to get to the university. Some would travel from Masaya or Masatepe, a distance of 30 to 50 miles by bus, just to attend classes. I was impressed by the fact that there were no textbooks, and so I began to type up all of my class notes, including tables and charts, and mimeograph them so students would have something to refer back to after the class was over."

While in Nicaragua, she attempted to work with the Wisconsin-Nicaragua Partners, but discovered that the organization's past involvement with the Somoza regime had aroused suspicions on the part of the new government and

"There was a tremendous need for the people of Wisconsin to have a better grasp of the situation. The Nicaragua they were reading about in newspapers just didn't jive with what people experienced when they came down."

Mirette Seireg
Wisconsin Coordinating
Council on Nicaragua

the director of the school of nutrition where she worked. Moreover, after misleading articles about one of her projects appeared in a U.S.-backed anti-government newspaper, she became aware of the danger that, in the context of the growing hostility between the U.S. and Nicaraguan governments, her work could be used as a pretext for political manipulations. The biggest shock, however, came in 1983 when one of her students was killed in a contra attack. "It was earthshaking," she recalls. "Suddenly the war, which had seemed like something faraway and irrelevant, entered my classroom. I began to feel torn. There I was, on the one hand, working on a U.S.-sponsored project as a teacher to help people improve their lives. And on the other hand, I was a citizen of the same government that had created the contras who had killed one of my students."

That same year, she became acquainted with Wisconsin Secretary of State Douglas La Follette when he visited Nicaragua on a fact-finding tour. La Follette and a number of other influential Wisconsinites were interested in expanding the sister-state relationship. "We also were in agreement that there was a tremendous need for the people of Wisconsin to have a better grasp of the situation," Seireg says. "The Nicaragua they were reading about in newspapers just didn't jive with what people experienced when they came down."

In January of 1984, Seireg returned to Wisconsin and attended a gathering organized by Harvey Stower, a retired state assemblyman and Methodist minister. Other participants included the governor, the president of the University of Wisconsin system, several bishops and other Wisconsin leaders. "The situation in Nicaragua had become critical," Seireg recalls. "There was incredible antagonism between the two governments, and yet there were somewhere between 45 and 75 groups across Wisconsin providing material aid to Nicaragua. The people at the meeting felt there was a need to coordinate the efforts, to do what we could to promote the sister-state relationship and use it as a vehicle to promote peace, goodwill and understanding. Harvey asked me: 'Could you help us get this thing off the ground?' I said sure."

On behalf of the newly-formed Wisconsin Coordinating Council on Nicaragua (WCCN), Seireg and La Follette began traveling around the state, giving talks about their experiences in Nicaragua and reaching out to traditional, sometimes quite conservative groups. "I found that having his support was an enormous boost," she said. "When he visited a city in northern Wisconsin, it was news because he was a state official. People listened whom otherwise we might never have been able to reach."

In addition to these educational activities, WCCN became a clearinghouse for other organizations and individuals — churches, farmers, solidarity organizations. A poet in Milwaukee sought WCCN's assistance in putting together a collection of Nicaraguan poetry. Seireg organized a tour of health professionals and educators from the University of Wisconsin Medical School. She communicated with state and national politicians, lining up the support necessary to bring Nicaraguan visitors to Wisconsin.

At the same time, Nicaraguan sister-city projects began to spring up almost spontaneously in other parts of the country, such as New Haven, Connecticut and Seattle, Washington. "It was one of those ideas that seemed to come from a lot of places at once," recalls Nancy Cummins of Boulder, Colorado. "In November of 1983, Boulder had an election in which voters passed a ballot initiative calling for an end to military intervention in Central America. There was a group of us who had been active around the issue and wanted to do some-

"It was one of those ideas that seemed to come from a lot of places at once. Once it was proposed, I don't think we ever had any doubts that it would work."

Nancy Cummins
Boulder/Jalapa
Friendship City Project, Inc.

thing positive with the sentiments expressed by that vote. We got together and started talking, and the idea of a sister-city project emerged. Once it was proposed, I don't think we ever had any doubts that it would work. Virtually everyone we invited to take part in the discussions was open to the idea. We discussed it with people from the business community, the religious community, not necessarily people who were activists. And the city council was there, endorsing what we were doing — as long as we were the ones doing the work."

After forming ties with Jalapa, Nicaragua, one of Boulder's first projects was the construction of a pre-school, which attracted the attention of Sara Lee, a Boulder building contractor. "I had a growing interest in indigenous methods in building technology, and I was curious about Central America," Lee says. "I just got interested in the project because they were building something and it was taking place in Nicaragua. It seemed like a really positive, hands-on thing to do, regardless of whatever everybody's politics turned out to be. I met a lot of key people, got more interested, and started learning about Nicaragua."

The project was catching on in the community, but Cummins and others felt isolated. "We knew that other projects existed in other parts of the country, and we had the feeling that our work could be more effective if we had some communication with them. We decided to get together representatives from as many projects as we could and see if we could have a conference about forming a national network. We had already had contact with some groups such as Port Townsend, because it was also a sister city of Jalapa. We knew about New Haven. We asked the embassy for a list of projects, but at that time they had no list and no clear idea of what projects there were, where they were located, or anything like that. We made up a conference invitation and sent it to as many projects as we knew existed."

The conference, held on the last weekend of April 1985, attracted 15 people, including Luís Mendez who had been invited from the Nicaraguan embassy. "We did it with very little money," Cummins recalls. "We fed people with potluck dinners and housed them in people's homes."

Sara Lee, who was just beginning to get involved, remembers the Boulder get-together as "pretty informal; just everybody sitting around in a circle, talking about the concept of what we could do with sistering relationships. We talked about ways to facilitate logistics and material aid. There was a feeling that it was going to catch on, but I don't think anybody expected it to catch on as much as it did."

For Cummins, those feelings were stronger. "I felt mostly just happiness and energy to know that there were people all over the country working towards the same goal, and it seemed to me very interesting that people around the country at the same time felt the need to do sister cities work. I think there were a lot of high hopes that we could become a national movement, that there were principles that would keep us together. We felt our conference was just the tip of the iceberg. We knew there were more projects we hadn't been able to locate, and those that did come represented very diverse regions of the country."

Within a year, those hopes had been realized. On June 27, 1986, just two days after Congress voted to send $100 million in aid to the Nicaraguan contras, a much larger U.S.-Nicaragua Friendship Conference was hosted by the Wisconsin Coordinating Council on Nicaragua in Madison, Wisconsin. It drew 150 participants from 24 states. The number of material aid projects had grown phenomenally. "Churches, labor unions and school boards are exporting everything from baseball gloves to ambulances to water pumps," reported *Newsweek* magazine. "New Haven recently sent $10,000 worth of sewing equipment, children's clothes and agricultural tools to its sister city of León. Minnesota, which has also adopted León, sent a surgeon for a two-month tour of duty at a local hospital, and an electrical engineer to build incubators for newborn babies."[18]

Mirette Seireg, who organized the conference with WCCN Projects Director John Stauber and representatives of already-established sister-city projects, remembers that "we began to get flooded with letters from across the country, wanting to know how their city could become a sister city. As a result of the conference and working with the Nicaraguans, there was an actual procedure for doing that, and the number jumped incredibly rapidly."

Growing Local Independence

The sister cities movement is part of a larger nationwide trend towards local community independence from and even opposition to the foreign policy establishment in Washington. "The *Christian Science Monitor*, describing what it termed 'the invisible story of the 1970s,' found that one-third of all adults in large cities claimed to have been active in recent years in some form of community group," writes author Harry C. Boyte. "The Presidentially appointed National Commission on Neighborhoods listed more than 8,000 community organizations, almost all formed since 1970. . . . Perhaps most striking of all has been the growing protest against the nuclear arms race, reaching from the smallest villages in New England to the Catholic bishops."[19]

According to the Center for Innovative Diplomacy in Irvine, California, which researches and promotes municipal involvement in foreign affairs, over 900 local governments created pressure for arms reductions talks with the Soviet Union by passing nuclear freeze resolutions. Furthermore, says the center's *CID Report*, "By refusing to cooperate with the Federal Emergency Management Agency's 'crisis relocation planning,' more than 120 cities helped derail its nuclear war civil defense program. And by divesting billions of dollars from firms doing business in South Africa, more than 70 cities, 13 counties, and 19 states helped persuade the administration to replace 'constructive engagement' with limited economic sanctions."[20] Close to 150 communities have passed zoning ordinances banning nuclear weapons production within their city limits, "disengaging from the nuclear arms race by the operation of their own local laws," in the words of Irvine Mayor Larry Agran, who serves as one of the center's directors.[21]

During the December 1985 convention of the National League of Cities, Los Angeles Mayor Tom Bradley made municipal foreign policies the topic of his keynote address. "The right of cities to be heard on these crucial issues derives from two fundamental principles," he said. "First, local government is closest to the people." Second, "many of our national policies are felt first — and in the end most profoundly — in America's cities. . . . Cities can enfranchise many who might otherwise never be heard." As an example of the practical connection between local municipal decisions and U.S. foreign policy, he said, "Thousands of people from the war-torn countries of Central America have taken refuge in Los Angeles. Many of these refugees are living in violation of federal law. In too many cases, they are also living lives of poverty, fear and desperation. And the city has an obligation to provide all of its inhabitants with fire, police and other essential services. The city of Los Angeles is now on that

"Compared with the loony grandmothers in the U.S. who have discovered Central America 'down at our church,' the Sandinista supporters in Europe are a piece of cake."

from "Why Europeans Support the Sandinistas,"
by Mark Falcoff, U.S. Information Agency spokesman
Commentary, August 1987

course, along with a growing number of other cities. To encourage refugees to report crimes and health hazards to the city, Los Angeles city employees do not provide federal authorities with information regarding the immigration status of undocumented aliens who are otherwise law-abiding citizens."[22]

This growing independence of cities and states has of course raised concerns at the federal level. "We cannot have individual states and cities establishing their own foreign policies," said Senator Richard Lugar (R-Indiana), chairman of the Senate Foreign Relations Committee, in an August 1986 speech concerning local South Africa-related divestment. After several U.S. governors refused to send their state National Guard units to participate in military maneuvers and road-building exercises in Central America, Congress passed new legislation taking away the governors' veto powers. "The authority granted state governors made them susceptible to political pressure on controversial administration policies," said Assistant Secretary of Defense James Webb. "Moreover, such pressure could be exerted at the local level and, due to media interest in such controversy, given national exposure. Consequently, the governors' authority has become a vehicle to debate or influence foreign policy. This is no longer a case of a few isolated incidents; it is a demonstrated way for dissent groups, state legislators, and state governors to seize a forum."

Ultimately, however, the growing role of municipalities in foreign affairs may be unstoppable, Shuman argues. The growth of international markets and the increasing economic interdependence of nations has created a situation in which "international affairs, like many domestic issues, have become too complicated to run effectively as a monopoly. . . . The last thing an overworked, underfunded executive branch needs is direct micromanagement of thousands of local investment, cultural exchange, and border coordination activities." Also, attempting to limit the ability of cities to participate in international issues would entail severe restrictions of America's democratic principles. "Cutting off consciousness-raising measures ultimately means suppressing basic freedoms of speech, assembly, and travel. Restricting unilateral measures means trampling on traditional local autonomy in zoning, policing, contracting, and investing — an outcome that states-rights conservatives would oppose as vigorously as internationalist liberals. And restricting cities' ability to enter into foreign economic agreements means dismantling the principles of free trade. . . . Unless America becomes a police state, municipal foreign policies are here to stay."[23]

Trying a Different Door 3

"The moment that took the statistics and made them human for me was when a village woman asked if we could enlarge photographs for her," says New Haven, Connecticut resident Alan Wright. "They were pictures of her sons, who had been killed by the contras. The struggle in Nicaragua is not a joke, not a matter of politics. It's a matter of murdering people. I felt that unless I were to act on my disagreement with the federal government, I would in some sense be complicit in the murders committed by the contras."

Wright and his wife Paula Kline visited Nicaragua for the first time with a Witness for Peace delegation in February of 1984. They spent five days in the Nicaraguan war zone. They met with Salvadoran refugees, Sandinista government officials, church leaders and U.S. embassy personnel. They helped villagers dig a bomb shelter, and they stood in a peace vigil. They hand-carried medical supplies worth more than $3,000 to hospitals and relief groups, and they visited the office of Salvatore Meléndez, mayor of the city of León, to deliver an invitation from the New Haven City Council.

Upon learning of their plan to visit Nicaragua, New Haven Alderwoman Janet Stearns had introduced a city council resolution endorsing their trip, and a second resolution offering to begin a sister-city relationship with León, "a city which like New Haven is the site of a university and a medical school." Both resolutions received the council's unanimous support and were signed by Mayor Biaggio DiLieto.

"We were eager to do something positive with the people of Nicaragua. At the same time we aimed at avoiding many of the frustrations suffered by those who attempt to change Washington by opposing government policies through protest and letter writing," Kline said.

Upon returning to New Haven, Wright and Kline gave presentations at local churches and on the radio and formed a committee for ongoing projects. Through the Tools for Peace program of Oxfam America, they organized a material aid drive that collected over $10,000 worth of sewing equipment, children's clothes, medicine and other supplies. By September, they had contacted 47 community groups in the areas of art, health, education, youth, economic development, labor, social services, neighborhood organizations, Hispanic organizations, women's groups and churches. But only seven people

"*Current policies in Washington are not our main problem in Central America. The problem we've got to face is the powerlessness of the American people and the oppression that exists both here and in Nicaragua. Empowerment is our main issue. We don't simply complain about Washington's foreign policy. Our city has a foreign policy too, and that's empowering.*"

Alan Wright
New Haven/León Sister City Project

25

were active in the project, and although they had enjoyed some initial successes, they had no clear idea of how to proceed.

At that point, the sister-city project hosted a visit from Sixto Ulloa, the director of international relations for CEPAD, an organization of Nicaraguan Protestant churches. Ulloa invited them to send a delegation from New Haven to observe Nicaragua's national elections, which were scheduled to be held in November of 1984. With only a month's notice in which to make all the arrangements, the group came up with a list of names of 15 potential delegates, representing a political, ethnic, social and cultural cross-section of New Haven. Seven agreed to participate: a Yale University law professor, the executive director of a women's health clinic, a nurse, a representative of a local organization of Native Americans, an admissions officer at the University of New Haven, a labor leader, and Lee Cruz, the New Haven director of the League of United Latin American Citizens. "Although I was not particularly informed about Nicaragua, I was immediately interested, as was my wife," said Cruz, who later became New Haven/León's project coordinator in León.

The delegation's trip to León lasted five days, two of which were spent on travel. Their three days in Nicaragua were spent entirely in León, pursuing a busy schedule of interviews with election administrators and people from five of the seven political parties which participated in the election. "Because of the elections, there were people there from all over the world," Cruz said. "Ghana, Sweden, England — it was like the United Nations." In addition to observing the voting procedures, the New Haven delegates held quiet conversations with randomly chosen voters standing in line at polling places in poor, middle-class and wealthy neighborhoods. They also met with León educators, health workers and people representing a variety of other fields, obtaining names and addresses of contact people interested in supporting the sister-city project. They delivered $1,000 worth of medical supplies to a León health center. One Nicaraguan Indian chief was so touched by a gift from a Connecticut tribe that he gave the group a 500-year-old statue to carry home.

"We arrived back in New Haven, dead tired, and went straight from the airport to Channel 8 to be interviewed," Cruz recalled. "That evening, the 1984 elections were held in the United States, and for some reason in New Haven that year they were a complete fiasco. The computer got screwed up, and people's names got lost from the voting lists. This actually contrasted with the orderly and clearly very well-run elections that we had just witnessed in León." Not only were they impressed with the efficiency of the process, their experiences contradicted President Reagan's claim that the Nicaraguan elections had been "a sham." Yale Law School professor Harlon Dalton came back "absolutely convinced that the Nicaraguan election is as fair as humanly possible. We witnessed incredible enthusiasm, bordering on euphoria, about the process of having the first free election in the nation's history."

Later that month, the delegation delivered a formal report on their trip to a gathering attended by 200 New Haven residents, and invited interested people to attend a follow-up organizational meeting. At that meeting, which attracted 60 people, the New Haven/León Sister City Project established four initial committees, reflecting points of correspondence that had been identified between the two sister cities:

Education Task Force. Both New Haven and León are university centers. On the basis of this similarity, several sister-school relationships were estab-

"We witnessed incredible enthusiasm, bordering on euphoria, about the process of having the first free elections in the nation's history."

Harlon Dalton
Yale University Law Professor

lished between public and parochial schools in New Haven and León. Ongoing projects were organized to promote literacy, school art and poetry exchanges, educator and student delegations, and drives to collect school supplies and toys for local classrooms and day care centers in León.

Health Task Force. Both cities have major teaching hospitals. Since its founding, the task force has sponsored discussions about health care delivery in the two cities, sent supplies to answer León's shortages of equipment and medicine, helped build a health clinic in a León neighborhood, and sent New Haven health care workers to study Nicaragua's innovative methods of low-cost health care delivery.

Arts and Culture Task Force. Both cities have museums and are famous for their architecture. Both have important Hispanic populations with similar ethnic traditions. The task force attracted dozens of New Haven area painters, dancers, sculptors, singers, photographers, poets and dramatists. They have sponsored a national poetry competition, local poetry readings, musical exchanges and a major photo exhibit introducing the people of León to the people of New Haven. New Haven volunteers helped with building restoration at León's Museum of the Americas. A collection of works by New Haven artists will be permanently housed in the León museum, and León art is exhibited in local New Haven galleries. In addition, local artists have contributed their talents through music and dance concert fundraisers.

Religious Task Force. Religious buildings dominate the center of both cities; in fact, León's basilica is the oldest cathedral in Central America. The religious task force runs an "adoption service" which helps New Haven congregations find the right match in adopting a church in León. Churches have exchanged Bible readings and sermons as well as Sunday School art. One church has helped its sister church in León obtain a "boom box" tape recorder so their folklore dance group has music to dance by. Each church exchanges a photo panel and agrees to common days of prayer.

Although the New Haven/León organizers continue to hope for a change in Washington's policies towards Central America, it is not their main emphasis. "So long as the government remains our intermediary with Nicaragua," Wright says, "we will be perpetually tied to their will, voicing opposition to their policies but unable to develop a positive, constructive alternative. This is exactly what Washington hopes will happen: that all discussion and debate will focus on Washington's agenda. They want us to marshall all of our energies organizing expensive, large rallies to protest what they're doing and beg them to change. So long as that's all we do, the government can use our protests as evidence that the 'democratic system' is working, since people are freely exercising their right to demonstrate, while at the same time they ignore our requests, thereby making our energies worthless. When the rally is over, people in Nicaragua are no better off, while people here who are committed to social justice are poorer and exhausted, with no tangible evidence that policies in Washington have improved. The experience of seeing your time, money and energy have no effect ultimately frustrates and disempowers those who give of themselves."

Wright compares these efforts to pushing on a jammed door. "You can either stand there and keep pushing, hoping eventually to break it free, or you can try a different door. We're not trying to open doors in Washington. That's not our goal. Our goal is to empower people in our own community to build a better world. An empowered church or school is one which takes the initiative to develop a positive program and then acts to carry it out. Having accomplished a relatively minor project they will be emboldened to pursue more difficult and ambitious programs."

As the New Haven/León project has grown, new committees have been added in fields such as labor, science education, day care, and economic development. Project organizers have developed a three-step approach aimed at diversifying and incorporating new sectors of the community:

1) Approach a population which has clearly identifiable interests, interests which touch the people's own personal identities. Offer to make a presentation to their group about people who are similar to themselves in Nicaragua. "Examples of this might include health workers, educators, trade unionists, construction workers, artists, bicyclists, or even bird watchers," Wright says.

2) Teach them about the revolution by showing them how the sector with which they identify has taken a role and been affected.

3) Give them concrete and achievable tasks, the consequences of which will be an empowering belief in their ability to have an impact on the world around them.

"Let me give an example of how this has worked," Wright says. "Take a difficult population, those traditionally outside the 'political' arena, high school students at a private school. Imagine for a moment that you are a student at one of New Haven's very elite college prep schools. Were I to come in railing against Reagan and the contras, I would immediately divide the audience into those who were already with us and those who are 'with the president.' But since one major goal of our work is to engage and empower new people, it doesn't make sense to begin by setting out the traditional lines of division.

"Instead we talk about 'prep school' education in Nicaragua. We tell them that before the revolution 55 percent of the Nicaraguan population was illiterate, 80 percent had no access to formal schooling. For the most part, the only people who could get a quality education were the rich who sent their children to expensive prep schools. Since the revolution in 1979 the number of teachers in Nicaragua has tripled, the number of students has more than doubled, and in León, our sister city, the new government has built a new prep school. Like our New Haven prep school, it aims at giving the best possible, most intensive education to young people, to prepare them for college and for lives as professionals. But the prep school in León has one difference. It is reserved for the children of poor people, workers and farmers, whose kids have been disadvantaged by economics, who have had to work at an early age to help the family survive, but who would like to go to college. All the students are on scholarship and they are getting, for the first time in their lives, an opportunity to have quality education.

"Now you, as students, can have a sister prep school with these young people. You can exchange poems and letters, banners and souvenirs. Just think of the following: Baseball is the national sport of Nicaragua, just as it is here. Your sister school in León has several teams but they don't have balls, bats, gloves or uniforms. They have a beautiful science laboratory but without any lab equipment such as microscopes, bunsen burners and the like. You could play an important role in this noble project. Let's organize a commitee and begin to develop this sister-school project. Perhaps the first thing we should do is organize a delegation of student representatives to go down to León during your spring break. When you go, you could carry down baseball gloves, balls and bats, and perhaps even some lab equipment to contribute to their science department."

Using this method, the New Haven/León Sister City Project had organized 30 delegations as of June 1988, sent seven major material aid shipments, and given countless educational presentations. The sister-city project had a mailing list of 3,000 New Haven area residents, representing over two percent of the city's population of 120,000. "The enthusiasm is really incredible," said Cruz. "One minister heard I was traveling to Nicaragua, so he gave the sister-city project a check for $1,000. And this is a retired couple, for whom $1,000 has a tremendous economic impact."

In 1986, New Haven began to shift its fundraising emphasis away from large donors and towards sustainers who can contribute $50 or $100 per year. Instead of "blue chip" projects like museum restoration, organizers are focusing on efforts to provide water and housing for the poor. Its budget for 1987 — most of which had already been raised by the start of the year — was $51,150. The actual value of its projects amounted to several hundred thousand dollars. Through non-profit discount channels, for example, the health task force obtained $150,000 worth of medicine for León's hospital at a cost of only $5,500. Other efforts for 1987 provided: sewing machines for a sewing collective; an IBM clone computer for the university; a "foster parent" program to subsidize an orphanage for girls; health and safety equipment for León's sewer workers; and generators for yet another health clinic.

"We were very fortunate," Cruz said. "We had a lot of good things happen, and we had some very enthusiastic people who knew a lot about organizational development. I think we've gotten the participation of a whole bunch of people who wouldn't otherwise get involved in Central America, and it's because we approach people in terms of who they are and their interests — law, religion, or whatever — rather than try to bring them around to our point of view and emphasis on Central America, which is what a lot of other groups try to do. Our membership ranges from diehard Sandinista apologists on the one hand, to people on the other hand who simply feel that we should help the people of Nicaragua regardless of what type of government exists there. So we say we're not a political group, but there is no doubt that the people involved are acting politically. This is simply the most effective way we've found of empowering ourselves and saying to the people of Nicaragua that we stand in solidarity with them. We are organizing on the basis of our strengths, not our weaknesses. There's no way we can take on the State Department or the CIA when it comes to military or covert activities. That's their turf, and if we tried to compete with them on their terrain, they'd kick our butts, hands down. But if you force them to come into our arena — grassroots organizing, material aid — then *they're* the ones who can't compete."

The National Planning Committee for the 1986 U.S.-Nicaragua Friendship Conference, left to right. Back: Gary Handschumacher, Disabled Peace Project, Denver; Debra Ruben, Nicaragua Network, Washington DC; Roy Wilson, Seattle-Managua Sister City Association; Alan Wright, New Haven-León Sister City Project; Mary Foster, Project Minnesota-León. Front: Mirette Seireg, Wisconsin Coordinating Council on Nicaragua (WCCN); John Stauber, WCCN; Anne Hess, MADRE.

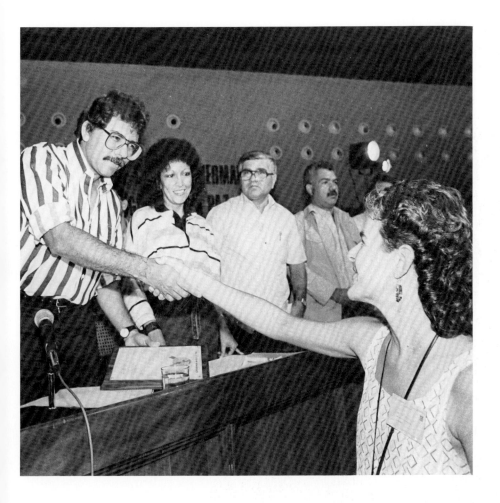

At the sister cities conference in Managua, WCCN Executive Director Liz Chilsen presented Nicaraguan President Daniel Ortega with a resolution from the Wisconsin State Legislature commending "the efforts of . . . conference participants to promote peace, understanding and goodwill between our two countries." Pictured to Ortega's right is Comandante Mónica Baltodano, leader in the revolutionary government who supervises the government's involvement in sister-city projects. ◄

"It's a very long list, very impressive. Brooklyn, New York; Arcata, California; Madison, Wisconsin; . . . What this proves is that the true values of the American people are manifesting themselves. The true values of the American people cannot be denied by unjust policies carried out by the government. Their values stand for peace and against war. By nature, man cannot see in another man an enemy. He has to see another man, a friend, a brother. Peoples, by nature, cannot be enemies, even though there be policies that try to have countries confronting one another . . .

Those values have left us here in Nicaragua full of hope for the future. To you, brothers and sisters in the United States, we thank you for your interior moral force which has enabled you to rise above the rhetoric of hatred launched by the U.S. administrations against Nicaragua. You are an expression of the American people, who are willing to tighten their links and extend their hands to the Nicaraguan people."

Nicaraguan President Daniel Ortega
addressing the 3rd U.S.-Nicaraguan Sister City Conference
Managua, Nicaragua, June 21, 1988

Adolfo Madrigal, a fisherman
from Solentiname. "So you're
from the United States," he
said. "What are you going to
tell people when you get
back? Are you going to tell
people that this is the greatest
country on earth? Are you
going to tell people how
beautiful Nicaragua is? Are
you going to tell them how
much better our lives are
now, how many more pos-
sibilities we have than we
ever had before?"
Solentiname has a sister
relationship with Mollis, Italy,
one of over 200 links between
European and Nicaraguan
cities.

The fishing island of Solentiname is famous for its paintings and poetry. In the 1970s, Solentiname was the home of a religious community founded by Ernesto Cardenal, a Catholic priest and world-renowned poet. After the revolution, Cardenal became Nicaragua's minister of culture and organized poetry workshops throughout the country, modeled after workshops he held with Solentiname peasants and fishermen. The resulting poetry often resembles Chinese or Japanese poetry, with its delicate and beautiful juxtapositions of natural scenes. "I don't think they are familiar with Chinese poetry," Cardenal says. "I think the similarity you find in their cases arises out of a natural affinity toward nature that they have as peasants."

The village of Comalapa, in ▲
Nicaragua's Chontales re-
gion, has a sister-city relationship with Worcester, Massachusetts.

Socorro Cruz Miranda
("Doña Coco"), mayor
of Comalapa.   ▶

34

Housing construction in
Comalapa. Bricks are made
locally using a recently built
kiln. The homes are being
built collectively by the
people who will live in them.

Bluefields Bay

Fishing on Sunday morning in Bluefields. Bluefields is located on Nicaragua's Atlantic Coast, which has historically been both physically and culturally separated from the Pacific Coast, leading to tensions between the Managua government and indigenous groups such as the Miskito, Sumu and Rama Indians, and the Creole population. These tensions are slowly being resolved thanks to the innovative autonomy project initiated in 1985 which promises new hope for development in the region.

How to Begin 4

"The beginning of every organization smacks of being a one-shot affair, for the simple reason that theorists who fiddle around waiting and delaying until they've got a fullblown across-the-board organizational program are never ready to commence swinging into action."

Nicholas Von Hoffman

You may wonder if it is possible to organize a sister-city project in your community, particularly if you have encountered frustration in past efforts to raise local concern about Central America. "My town is too small to become involved in something like that," is one skeptical comment. "The city council would never go along with it — too controversial," is another. Others worry that their city is too conservative, too apathetic, or too resistant to change. "I tried to hold a demonstration in front of the post office," said a resident of one small town in Wisconsin. "It seemed the logical place because it was our only federal building. I put an announcement in the newspaper, but nobody showed up. It looks like the people in my community are more interested in bowling than they are in peace issues."

Skeptics become believers, however, once they begin to participate in the practical aspects of organizing a drive to collect clothing, food or medicine for their sister city. The same people who would not be caught dead demonstrating in front of a post office often turn out to be generous and eager contributors to a charitable effort. People who love bowling may turn out for a fundraiser at their local bowling alley, and however stubborn city councils may seem, in practice they are far more accessible and often far more responsive to their constituents than politicians in Washington. Moreover, successful sister-city projects have been organized both with and without official approval from their municipal governments. Successful projects have also been organized in small towns and conservative areas.

A sister-city relationship with Nicaragua will be something new for your community, and people who try to initiate changes frequently complain that communities resist change. This is true, but Harold Nix, a professor at the University of Georgia's Institute of Community and Area Development, observes that "it is also true that communities have always accepted and sought change. Understanding that change is a constant process in social groups helps the change agent to ask the right questions." Instead of asking, "What is wrong with these stupid people who refuse, or are slow to accept, my proposed changes?" he recommends asking questions such as: "Is there something wrong with my proposals? Have they been properly explained so that they are understood? How can I improve the relationship between myself and the people who

37

resist my concerns? Are my proposals too costly — economically, socially, or psychologically — for the benefits that I am offering?"

"The kind of changes people frequently resist," Nix says, "are (1) changes not clearly understood, (2) changes they or their representatives had no part in bringing about, (3) changes which threaten their vested interest or security, (4) changes advocated by those they do not like or trust, and (5) changes which do not fit into the cultural values of the community."[1]

As shown in chapter two, there are practical reasons that cities can benefit by developing their own foreign policies. Moreover, the current climate of public opinion is receptive to the sister-city approach. The main task for sister city organizers, therefore, is not to change public opinion, but to win the trust of community members, to explain the sister-city concept, to adapt it to the needs, values and interests of their community, and to ensure that the opportunity to participate in sister-city activities is extended as broadly as possible to a wide spectrum of people within the community.

The ideas in this chapter reflect the experience of a number of U.S.-Nicaraguan sister cities, the advice of Sister Cities International, and some general principles of community organizing that have been developed by groups ranging from civil rights activists to government experts in community development. They focus on how to:

- Assess your community
- Set up a "core group" of organizers
- Find a Nicaraguan city to pair with
- Institutionalize the sister-city relationship
- Publicize your project
- Recruit members and volunteers
- Raise public awareness about Nicaragua
- Obtain funding and other resources for your activities

These suggestions are not written in concrete. Your own insights and knowledge, based on living in your community, must become the basis for your project.

General Guidelines

The following guidelines summarize the "general wisdom" that Nix has identified for groups wishing to initiate new programs in their community:

1) The proposed project should be defined as noncontroversial by indicating its benefits to all groups.

2) An attempt should be made to bridge gaps between important constituencies within the community by (a) enlisting leaders respected by all sides, (b) enlisting support of representatives of all sides, and (c) indicating benefits to all sides.

3) The project initiators should recruit mass support through gaining the support of influential and cohesive organizations in the community. This is often important in gaining the support or cooperation of government officials.

4) Great effort should be expended in gaining the consent and support of potential sources of opposition. According to one researcher, "The most successful community organizers whom I have encountered were extraordinarily skilled at this prime task and spent upward of half of their time at it."[2]

Assessing Your Community

The concept of community has often been praised and even idealized. The word evokes a nostalgic image of friendliness and social harmony, of small town values and neighborly cooperation. Belonging to a community requires neither wealth, inherited status, learning, nor refined manners. The concept of community also suggests moral values: honesty, mutual respect, civic concern, trustworthiness, helpfulness and clean living. "Neighborliness occurs in times of personal and family crisis — birth, death, illness, fire, catastrophe," observe sociologists Arthur J. Vidich and Joseph Bensman. "On such occasions friends and neighbors mobilize to support those in distress: collections of money are taken, meals are prepared by others, cards of condolence are sent." A family whose house has burned may find neighbors organized to aid in reconstruction. Neighborliness also has "institutional supports . . . Ministers and church groups make it a practice to visit the sick in hospitals and homes and to remember them with cards and letters." Other organizations "designate special committees to ensure that remembrance is extended to the bereaved and ill," and during the holiday season, civic groups distribute food and clothing to the poverty-stricken.[3]

These homespun practices are real virtues and potential roots of support for a sister-city project with Nicaragua. But cooperative and harmonious images are only part of the reality of community life. Communities are also havens of gossip, interpersonal feuding, prejudice against "outsiders," and all of the ills of modern society. In addition to cooperation, communities invariably contain conflict and competition between community members with different interests and goals. Storeowners, for example, compete with each other for customers, and other businesses have their own interests to defend, often in conflict with one another. Nix defines community as "a social system whose function it is to manage . . . competition and conflict." A successful community is "not one with complete harmony and consensus, but one whose specialized leaders and group representatives realize that their interdependency requires an organized approach to compromise and a system of conflict management. . . . They meet together precisely because they realize that it requires some coordination and compromise to provide stable conditions within which to pursue effectively their individual goals."[4]

In short, communities contain both internal harmony and internal divisions. Both of these aspects of community life can play a role in enriching your sister-city project. Moreover, a sister city can help to promote greater understanding between different segments of your community. The sistership between New Haven, Connecticut and León, Nicaragua, for example, led to cooperation between affluent New Haven residents and the city's large and mostly poor Hispanic population. "In order to communicate with León, we ran into difficulties with translation and turned to the Spanish churches because of their language abilities," says New Haven organizer Patty Nuelsen. "This was a different sort of relationship for us, where we came to them for help with our problems. It forced us to forego the paternalistic assumption that we were leading the relationship, and they were passive recipients of our help."

The boundaries of your city intersect and overlap with a number of other, nonmunicipal forms of community — communities of people united not by geography but by professional interests, beliefs, cultural and ethnic values, and memberships in diverse organizations. There are also bonds of community that unite families and groups of friends. In assessing your community, begin by identifying as many of these groupings as possible. Determine what ties, if any, you or members of your committee possess or can establish with each group. Also try to identify each group's interests and reasons for existence as a group. Give some thought to the ways in which those interests might become the basis for a sister-relationship with a corresponding group inside Nicaragua.

Also, try to identify the resources which each group within your community might be able to contribute to your project. Different constituencies have different strengths: professionals and businesspeople have money; students have time and access to research materials; retired people have time and often community respect; service clubs, labor unions and other community groups have organizational resources including member lists, money, and ability to mobilize members; churches have moral authority and sometimes have already-organized peace and justice committees; health care professionals have access to medical supplies and materials, often at discount rates.

Like any other organization, a sister-city association needs at least three things: (1) a network of people spread out and in position to reach and mobilize others; (2) continuity; and (3) money. Each group within your community has some of these resources, but few have all three in abundance. It is by uniting the strengths of different groups within your community that your sister-city project will succeed.

Identifying Community Leaders

Obviously, city officials are not the only leaders within a municipality who may be interested in working on a sister-city project. The patterns of leadership and social power within a community are often quite complex. It is important to understand the pattern in your city because support from local leaders can help to spread the word and build support on many levels for your project. "You talk to people through their leaders, and if you do not know the leaders you are in the same position as a person trying to telephone another party without knowing the telephone number," says political organizer Saul Alinsky. Knowing the identity of these natural leaders is knowing the telephone number of the people."5

Unless you live in a very small town, Nix says, several types of leaders probably exist within a local hierarchy. At the top are *legitimizers*, people who have the reputation of being top leaders in the community. They may or may not become involved in a particular community endeavor, but their approval is often necessary in order to obtain the support of the next level of leadership. This second level consists of *effectors*, people who often plan and direct community projects. Effectors tend to be specialized leaders, with expertise in a particular area — public health directors, for example, or school superintendents. The support of these higher-up leaders is particularly important if you wish to obtain official endorsement and support for your sister-city project. Even if it is unlikely that they will help directly, you may wish to touch bases with them in order to answer their concerns and prevent their active opposition.

The third and most numerous type of leader is often called an *activist*. Activists are the active workers and officeholders in community, civic, service and political organizations. Nix describes them as "doers and joiners . . . a means through which to diffuse information, educate the public, and gain support on important decisions already made. Activists also sometimes act to bring public pressures upon leaders higher up."6 Some activists are political activists, but

"I found that in each group I met there was one man who directed the activities of his fellows and whose word carried authority. Without his support, I was excluded from the group; with his support, I was accepted."

William F. Whyte
Street Corner Society

many are simply active in what they consider "community betterment." The support of all sorts of leaders can strengthen your project, but activists will likely become its backbone, contributing most of your volunteer labor, community outreach and other human resources.

Ethnic and Cultural Diversity

In order to have a truly city-wide project, you need to include the participation of all sectors within your community, including minority groups, workers, and poor people. The participation of minority and disenfranchised groups can bring a new dimension to your project. In the first place, their own experience of oppression and discrimination makes it easier for them to identify with the people of Nicaragua. Secondly, they are often more deeply involved and more focused on economic, religious and political struggles that relate to what is happening in Nicaragua. "Ethnic communities often have a resource that most of the Anglo communities don't have, namely national organizations," says Roy Wilson of the Seattle/Managua Sister City Association. "Many of these national organizations have positions on Nicaragua. It may not be their main priority, but it's not something they shy away from."

The Seattle/Managua project is an outstanding example of multi-ethnic, multi-racial organizing. Of its delegations that have visited Nicaragua, 48 percent come from Chicano, Asian, Black, Indian and other non-white communities. Representatives of these communities sit on the Association's board of directors. "One of the benefits that we've found of having a multi-ethnic group is that it tends to sensitize everyone to the fact that all U.S. citizens have things in common with the Nicaraguan population, and at the same time we have things that are dissimilar," Wilson says. "A homogeneous group would tend to generate homogeneous thoughts about another nation or race of people. If these thoughts take the form of unconscious attitudes of superiority or cultural arrogance, it could lead to tensions and misunderstandings."

Minority and disenfranchised groups often experience "ghetto-ization" and subtle discrimination even from well-meaning individuals who consider themselves "enlightened" and unprejudiced. They may not join the project unless an active effort is made to demonstrate that their participation is wanted. "It's a step more than just being 'open' to having them come," Wilson says. "We have actively solicited their support; we've been very up front about it, telling them straight out that we need their involvement. We've hustled money for scholarships for their members to join our delegations to Nicaragua, and maintained a very strict affirmative action policy that we would postpone or cancel a delegation if it didn't have some ethnic balance. Over time that commitment has become known, and now there's trust and faith between us."

The location where you hold your events will affect the nature of the group you attract. A talk at a university auditorium, for example, will be likely to attract academics, students, and some interested middle-class people, but it will not attract workers, chicanos, blacks and poor people. "When we bring Nicaraguans to Seattle, we try to have them speak to their specific peer groups," Wilson says. "When a black Moravian minister came, for example, he preached in black churches. He was also hosted by an all-white suburban Presbyterian church, and during the week he was there, the white church invited a black congregation to their services. It was the first time, according to them, that black people had been inside their doors. I would call that a visible benefit to

"Ethnic communities often have a resource that most of the Anglo communities don't have, namely national organizations. Many of these national organizations have positions on Nicaragua. It may not be their main priority, but it's not something they shy away from."

Roy Wilson
Seattle/Managua Sister City Association

the people of Seattle. One spin-off effect of a multi-ethnic coalition is that it creates more inter-community understanding here at home.

"My sense of it is that a lot of white organizers and activists have a hesitancy to approach the minority community, and that hesitancy creates a stumbling block," Wilson says. "I think it's due to the racism that exists in our country; it's due to ignorance of other people in our communities, and also to fear of failure or fear of rejection. Do the work; don't give up, be humble and honest, and make sure on your monthly calendar that there are meetings with members of the minority community and create a dialogue."[7]

Establishing a "Core Group"

Organizing a sister-city project is different from organizing a political campaign. Political campaigns — elections, legislative lobbying, demonstrations — are short-term projects with definite goals that must be accomplished within a limited period of time. The work of organizing an election campaign, for example, cannot be postponed until the day after voters go to the polls. The people who work in political campaigns learn to function under hectic deadlines, often making short-term sacrifices in their personal lives. Once the campaign is over, they know that they can relax and attend to the things that they have let slide.

The goal of a sister-city association, on the other hand, is to develop continuity and a stable relationship that will last for a long time. Sister-city organizers are real people with marriages and relationships, jobs and children, friends and enemies, and problems with each. They cannot put their own lives "on hold" until the the sister-city project is "over." Instead of overcommitting to extravagant goals, projects must pace themselves based on a realistic assessment of their resources. "We seem to need a project always in sight to keep the interest high, but not so much that it leads to burnout," says Joyce Lobner of the Wisconsin Rapids/Rio Blanco sister-city project.

The first step in ensuring that your sister-city project has continuity is establishing a "core group" of people to share the work of organizing. This group should consist of people who are committed to taking charge and making sure that things get done — planning meetings, sending out letters, making the phone calls necessary to get other people to help with one-time needs such as bringing baked goods to a fundraiser or sitting in at a literature booth. Your core group should include as diverse a representation as possible of the groups within your community. The more members the better, but successful projects have started with only a handful of people.

Many sister-city projects have begun by identifying people who are interested in Nicaragua and forming projects around their professions, having them talk to and stimulate interest among their colleagues. In Seattle, for example, Chris Jasper and Dr. Jeff Hummel began a sister-relationship, titled "Partners for Health," between the private health clinic where they worked and the Acahualinca Clinic in one of Managua's poorest neighborhoods. They launched a campaign to raise supplies and medicines for the Nicaraguan clinic. Initially, the project encountered reluctance from clinic administrators, who feared that it would be too controversial. During the project's initial stages, Jasper, Hummel and a handful of other clinic employees held bake sales every three weeks "to keep the word alive." From this beginning, "things really grew rapidly — more rapidly than we expected. Being health care workers, it's easier to pluck their heartstrings." The clinic administration's attitude softened after the project received friendly coverage in a local newspaper, and one administrator agreed to visit Nicaragua. "She came back a completely changed person and has put incredible energy and resources into it ever since," Jasper said. Within eight months, the project's mailing list grew to 1500 names, and it was receiving so many donations of medical supplies that instead of sending them down in suitcases it became necessary to charter commercial bulk shipping. "We were really overwhelming our sister clinic with all our comings and goings," Jasper recalled. When the quantity of donations became more than the Nicaraguan clinic could absorb, Partners for Health adopted a maternal infant pediatric hospital. Today the project is part of the National Central America Health Rights Network (NCAHRN), with over 50 local chapters and affiliated projects that have sent an estimated $10 million worth of medical aid to hundreds of clinics throughout Nicaragua, as well as bringing hundreds of North American health professionals to Nicaragua to teach and study.

Another way to initiate a sister project is to hold an organizational meeting. Send invitations to members and representatives of the various groups whose participation you wish to solicit. The meeting can be set in conjunction with a report by travelers returning from Nicaragua or you could try to schedule a speaker from Central America. An existing organization in your region may be able to provide speakers or events. Follow-up phone calls are especially helpful in getting good attendance. If you hold such a meeting, plan beforehand to ensure that it moves smoothly. If possible, come prepared with concrete proposals for activities that the people you have invited may wish to undertake. If there is enough interest in your community to carry out more than one activity, you may wish to establish committees and task forces at the organizational meeting. Be sure to collect the names, addresses and phone numbers of people who attend, so that you can contact them later. Pass the hat at this and all public meetings to help raise funds for your activities.

Finding a Nicaraguan Sister City

Many of the first U.S.-Nicaragua sister cities formed as the result of contacts formed by U.S. visitors to Nicaragua. Tim Jeffries of Fairfax, California, for example, organized a sister-city project with the town of Condega after visiting that town and "falling in love with its people and character." Because of the spontaneous way in which these projects formed, some areas in Nicaragua enjoy numerous sister-city relationships, while others have only a few contacts. Nicaragua has 160 cities, and the Nicaraguan government has taken an active interest in ensuring that the benefits of sistering are extended to all parts of the country. Offices of International Relations have been established in each of the country's regions, with duties that include assistance in coordination of sister-city programs.

To facilitate this process, the Nicaraguan government has requested that new groups forming in the United States contact the Nicaraguan embassy as they begin the process of selecting a Nicaraguan counterpart. Going through this official channel is respectful to the Nicaraguans. It helps them keep track of where projects have formed and offers the best distribution of resources to needy cities and towns in Nicaragua. Moreover, the embassy can help to speed things along by seeing to it that correspondence is delivered in a timely fashion (an important detail, given the disruption and delays that often occur in a Third World country, particularly a county torn by war), and by facilitating other aspects of travel and communication.

Write to the official in charge of sister city relations at Nicaragua's embassy to the United States at the following address:

Sister City Coordinator
Embassy of Nicaragua
1627 New Hampshire Ave., N.W.
Washington, DC 20009
Phone: (202) 387-4371

The letter should include the following information:

- The name, address and phone number of your organization and a contact person for your group.

- Is your project officially supported by your municipal government? Attach any relevant city council resolutions, mayor's proclamations or voters' referendums that have passed.

- A brief description of the community you live in: size, economic base, natural resources, physical description, population make-up, etc. This information will help the embassy to recommend an appropriate Nicaraguan community for you to sister with.

- A description of the group or groups in your community that will be participating in the project (numbers of participants, degree of enthusiasm, etc.).

- What type of community you would like to pair with. For example, do you want to pair with an urban town or a rural community? A community on the Pacific Coast or the Atlantic Coast? A village in a war zone? A resettlement village?

- The types of activities you are interested in developing.

Your request will be forwarded to Nicaragua's Department of Regional and Municipal Affairs in Managua, which will recommend a city for you to pair with. Normally, an effort is made to match cities with similar characteristics — university towns, common industries, similar ethnic makeup, geographical setting, etc.

After an initial pairing has been established, send a letter of invitation to the mayor of the Nicaraguan city, introducing yourselves and sending greetings. The letter should propose affiliation and describe what it means. Send both an English and a Spanish translation of the letter. If your project has official status, the letter should come from the appropriate municipal official — most likely your mayor. Include copies of any city council resolutions or other formal measures that have been passed. If you *don't* have official status, be sure to make that fact clear in your letter. One group that visited their sister city went through the embarrassing experience of receiving an elaborate welcome, only to discover that the Nicaraguans "seemed jolted when they found out that we were not representatives of the mayor's office."

Sister Cities International cautions that an answer through the mail may take as long as three months, and warns that there have been cases of ill feelings due to the loss of letters in transit. You may have greater success in reaching the Nicaraguan officials if your letter of invitation is sent by registered air mail with a return receipt requested. Another possibility is to send the letter with a delega-

February 14, 1988

Sister City Coordinator
Embassy of Nicaragua
1627 New Hampshire Ave., N.W.
Washington, DC 20009

Dear Counsellor:

I am writing regarding the formation of a Las Vegas/Nicaragua Sister City Project. We became interested in a sister-city project through the Wisconsin Coordinating Council on Nicaragua. We are also working with the South West Organizing Project from Albuquerque, New Mexico.

The WCCN has told us we should contact you for advice regarding an appropriate Nicaraguan city with which we might be paired. We would like to be paired with an urban area located on the Pacific side of Nicaragua and do not wish to be near a war zone.

Las Vegas is a resort city of more than 600,000 people. We have a four-year university, University of Nevada at Las Vegas, several community college branches and more than 100 public schools. We're located in a high-desert region of Nevada, near Lake Mead and the Colorado River. The city supports a Triple A baseball team and a nationally-ranked university basketball team. Mount Charleston, located less than an hour's drive outside the city, provides winter sports activities.

Known mainly for its legalized gambling, Las Vegas also has a thriving arts community. We have many art galleries, Nevada School of the Arts which provides excellent training in music and dance for young people, Nevada Dance Theatre, two private dance schools affiliated with the Royal Academy of Dance, an opera company, the Las Vegas Symphony, and a wealth of professional artists who perform world-wide and also teach privately as well as in the schools.

Our community consists of educators, business people, writers, health care workers, accountants, attorneys, community leaders, and hotel industry employees, including performers, service workers and management. We have representatives of the Hispanic, Black, American Indian and Asian-American communities, as well as members of various religious backgrounds, i.e. Roman Catholic, Protestant, Mormon, Jewish, Unitarian, etc.

Members of our group are affiliated with the National Education Association (NEA), AFL-CIO, Parent-Teachers Association (PTA), American Institute of Certified Public Accountants (AICPA) and environmental and peace organizations.

We are encouraged by the success of the sister-city projects in the United States and hope to promote friendship and understanding between the people of Las Vegas and Nicaragua through exchanges of people, ideas and projects, thereby promoting goodwill and information in true humanitarian efforts.

We hope to send at least three members of our group to the sister cities convention in June. At that time, we would like to shoot a video documentary of our visit to aid our efforts here in Las Vegas.

Sincerely,

Renee Rampton
President, Las Vegas/Nicaragua Sister City Project
229 Mallard Street
Las Vegas, Nevada 89107

A sample letter to the Nicaraguan Embassy, proposing sister-city affiliation.

tion of individuals from your city to Nicaragua. The Nicaraguan embassy may also be able to help ensure that the letter is delivered and receives attention.

Seeking Official Status

City governments can give official support to U.S.-Nicaragua sister-city projects in a variety of ways. They can initiate contact with a Nicaraguan city by extending an official invitation of sistership. Once contacts have been made and willingness to pair has been expressed on both sides, legislation can be enacted to formalize the relationship. City councils can also be asked to pass symbolic resolutions commemorating and honoring important anniversaries, Nicaraguan holidays, or projects undertaken by your group. Legislation can be enacted either through a city council resolution or through a voter referendum. The following examples describe two ways this process has been carried out:

- The Community Board of New York City's Lower East Side passed a resolution adopting a Nicaraguan sister city simultaneously with another resolution criticizing the use of U.S. tax dollars for military and economic aid to Central America. The resolutions were presented by two community members and supported by petitions signed by 500 people and with a number of organizational endorsements. The project addressed the criticism that foreign policy should not be made on a local level with statistics on cuts in social spending in the U.S., proposals of how money aiding the contras could be used on the Lower East Side, and articulating the real concern that uneducated and unskilled youth from their neighborhood would be prime targets for a draft if the U.S. declared war in Central America.

- Ann Arbor, Michigan modeled its successful April 7, 1986 ballot initiative on a similar effort in Seattle, Washington. The referendum included both a condemnation of current U.S. policy in Central America and provisions establishing a sister city task force. A broad group of individuals and organizations, including the city attorney, was consulted on the resolution wording. Well-prepared lobbying of the editorial boards of both local newspapers and an agreement to involve no city money helped the initiative pass.

Not every official sister city makes these sorts of political statements. "It should be tailored to the respective community on both ends," says one organizer. "In some cases, we may succeed in involving more people by being less political." Roy Wilson of the Seattle/Managua project points out that the sister-city concept was launched in the United States by President Eisenhower, a Republican. "It's not inconsistent with a conservative or a liberal or a progressive point of view to have sister cities, because they're not based on endorsements of one another's politics. They're based on the feeling that it's better to have dialogue and understanding, regardless of whether you share each other's point of view."

If your city government is willing to formally endorse and recognize a sister-city relationship with Nicaragua, clearly you should seek such recognition. Official status will give your project additional legitimacy in the eyes of some people, opening doors that otherwise might remain closed. Moreover, Nicaraguans take official pairings very seriously as an indication of the depth and commitment your community is likely to bring to the relationship. On the other hand, getting involved too quickly and closely with official city institutions can pose a danger for the project. If your municipality decides to take control by appointing a restrictive oversight body, energy and momentum may be tied up in the offices of city hall rather than in the grassroots of your community.

Often, official status is sought after sister-city work has already been carried out. This gives the project legitimacy and acts as a wedge to bring city officials along. Without evidence of such grassroots support, the proposal may be jeopardized in city hall. In one city, for example, organizers developed an impressive compilation of documents, fact sheets and photographs for the purpose of lobbying their mayor and city council. But according to one participant in the sister-city effort, this lobbying campaign began before an adequate base of activities had been developed at the grass roots. "Basically they started with the approach that they would wine and dine the mayor's office and the city council. They figured it would be approved as a matter of course, because the community was progressive, the mayor was sympathetic, and it wouldn't cost him anything politically. But the reality is, no matter how nice a guy the mayor is, you don't get to that office without possessing some pretty sharp political instincts. The mayor and the council could tell how the wind was blowing, and they perceived — correctly — that the proposal was just a piece of fluff. There was no community basis to it, nothing had been organized to give it substance, and the mayor's office played with it for awhile and then just dropped it flat."

While a positive ruling by the city council on a sister-city resolution is useful, it is better to have no judgment than to have a negative one. It may be more important to avoid resistance than to risk a highly visible defeat. Proceed with caution before approaching a governmental body for approval. It helps to begin by discussing your project informally and by contacting people you know, who have friends working with city government officials, or who have attempted similar work before.

Launching a sister city through a local voters referendum has the virtue of reaching the grassroots more directly than a city council vote. On the other hand, ballot campaigns can be time-consuming and may divert resources that you would prefer to use for other purposes. As with city councils, official status should be sought through this approach only if you feel confident of success.

To distinguish themselves from official projects, some unofficial U.S.-Nicaragua city pairings call themselves "friendship projects" rather than "sister cities." There is no hard rule requiring you to do this, but if your city already has official sister-city ties with other countries, choosing a different label may avoid conflicts with these established groups.

If you plan to seek official status, you may wish to use or modify the sample city council ordinance and ballot referendum included in the appendices.

Organizational Structure

Some U.S.-Nicaragua sister-city organizations are informally structured coalitions of community leaders, but the most popular form of organization is that of an association which is formally structured and incorporated under state statutes. Such an association is governed by a board of directors, executive committee, or steering committee which sets policy. This working board is a formal version of the "core group"; its membership should consist of people who are committed to helping raise funds, organize activities, and promote the sister-city relationship within the other groups to which they may belong. Many groups also establish "advisory boards" consisting of respected community members

"Organizing is what you do before you do something, so that when you do it, it's not all mixed up."

Christopher Robin
in A.A. Milne's *Winnie the Pooh*

who lend their names in support of the project. Project Minnesota-León has two advisory boards, one in Minnesota and one in León. In addition to their symbolic role, PML organizer Mary Foster says the advisors serve as sounding boards to "bounce ideas off of."

Adopting by-laws and incorporating are prerequisites to filing for tax-exempt status under Section 501(c)(3) of the Internal Revenue Code. This status is helpful mainly when soliciting contributions from large donors. Tax-exempt organizations are required by law to refrain from "substantial political activity," and the Internal Revenue Service has never clearly defined what "substantial" means. Most sister-city groups have not been hampered by this restriction, however, because it does not prohibit educational and charitable efforts. "Political activity" means lobbying for specific pieces of legislation or campaigning for the election of specific candidates. If your organization chooses to obtain tax-exempt status, you will not be able to use your newsletter to publish congressional voting records or urge members to "vote for Dick Glick in November" or "write your Congressman and tell him to oppose Assembly Bill 666." You *can*, however, describe the effect of U.S. policies in Central America and draw whatever conclusions your analysis demands. Moreover, you can retain tax-exempt status *and* carry out political activities simply by forming two separate organizations, one for each purpose.

To facilitate incorporation and adoption of by-laws, the National Institute of Municipal Law Officers has drafted model documents. These can be obtained from the national office of Sister Cities International, Suite 424-26, 1625 Eye Street NW, Washington, DC 20006; phone (202) 293-5504. (Note: Sister Cities International is officially a "nonpolitical" organization, but it receives a major part of its funding from the U.S. government, and in recent years has not shown much interest in cooperating with U.S.-Nicaragua sister-city projects.)

To involve the maximum number of people and organizations, many projects have committees concentrating on specific activities, such as fundraising, outreach, the arts, education, youth, health, and religion. You may want to create structures to involve groups such as women, hispanic groups, trade unionists, environmentalists, etc. Someone who can translate letters to and from Spanish should be invited to participate, as well as a lawyer who can advise the executive board.

Most local sister-city associations welcome anyone supporting their principles to join and to contribute ideas, attend meetings, and work on local projects. You may want to charge membership dues, with a sliding scale for low-income, student and senior citizens.

Coordinators in Nicaragua?

Some groups, such as Project Minnesota-León (PML), have full-time coordinators from the United States living in their Nicaraguan sister cities. PML's coordinators each receive a monthly salary of $75 per month to cover living expenses, plus an additional $200 per month deposited in a savings account back home. Health insurance is not included among the job benefits. "Medical care is free in Nicaragua, so if I get hurt, I'm taken care of," shrugged Elizabeth Sander, a former Minnesota Senate page who was working as one of the León coordinators when she was interviewed in January of 1987.

PML's coordinators act as news correspondents, sending back letters and photographs describing the progress of the various projects that Minnesota sponsors in León, and indicating specific resources that are needed, such as micromotors for dental drills or lamp bulbs for a hospital's operating rooms. In addition, they act as advance teams and translators for visiting U.S. delegations, scheduling meetings and lining up families to host Minnesota guests in their homes. Sander said she also sometimes "puts pressure on the government, hounding them a little to get us the information we need and so forth."

Those groups that have coordinators living in Nicaragua are enthusiastic about the benefits, claiming that it makes their projects more efficient. Nicaraguans are cautious, however, about the idea of all projects having a permanent person living in their sister affiliate. Seattle/Managua's Roy Wilson says the idea strikes him as "kind of a chauvinistic, big sister/little sister approach. Let's put the shoe on the other foot. How would we like it if the Nicaraguans sent people here to coordinate our activities, deciding on the itineraries for their delegations that come here, setting up all the exchanges? The gringos up here would freak out at the idea. They'd call it intrusive, an intervention."

Despite these concerns, Nicaragua has not actively prevented anyone from acting as a coordinator in their sister city. "The Sandinistas do very little in telling us what to do or what to tell people back in the states," Sander said. "I'm given a free hand here. I've never been told not to do something, and they've never given me information and said, 'You've got to send this back to Minnesota.'"

If your project needs a coordinator in Nicaragua, consider hiring a Nicaraguan. This alternative would satisfy your needs while respecting the concerns of Nicaraguans.

Spreading the Word

New ideas usually go through a series of stages before winning widespread community support. Some people are innovators and adopt new ideas early, while others are more cautious. Moreover, the idea of friendship with Nicaragua has to contend with the constant barrage of confusing, disillusioning and contradictory information about Central America that comes to us through the news media. The overall effect of this information is to instill apathy, hostility and fear in the American people. Measured quantitatively, the images of Nicaragua that reach your community through the mass media are vastly more numerous than the images your project can produce. It may seem that the sister-city concept, which is based upon personal contacts within your community and personal contacts with the Nicaraguan people, is too slow and small-scale to have a significant impact.

In fact, studies have shown that the seemingly slow approach of face-to-face contacts is more effective at shaping attitudes and motivating people to act than the impersonal influence of the media. A picture may be worth a thousand words, but the feelings of a friend are often worth a thousand pictures. Groups that have depended only on the mass media to get people to attend an event generally report very low attendance. It takes time to visit an office or home to sound out a leader or get a neighbor to attend a slide show on Nicaragua, but it is very effective.

Because personal contacts are so important, many sister cities have found that they reached a "take off point" after an individual or delegation from their community visited their sister city. The importance of sending delegations cannot be overemphasized. You should plan to send a group as soon as it is feasible, and every effort should be made to send groups on a regular basis. Delegations serve many important functions. First, they educate the participants in ways that no other forum can. Second, they establish real, personal ties, relationships that can be nurtured through the mail but which are difficult to establish without personal contact. Third, they begin the process of collaboration. Delegations meet with ordinary individuals as well as community leaders in Nicaragua to discuss how counterparts may cooperate. The process of exchange begins with the selection of a project, and there is no better way to assess need and potential than in person.

As you speak to groups in your community, it is important to have specific projects in mind that they can reasonably undertake. There is nothing more futile than working hard on education, only to leave the people with nothing to do and no organization into which they can incorporate themselves. One of the key ways that sister cities empower people is by not only helping them rethink their relationship to Nicaragua, but also enabling them to do something specific and within their means.

A "multi-tiered approach" that includes a variety of projects can appeal to people with different levels of commitment, resources and interest. A simple project might entail sending handmade greeting cards to Nicaraguan children; a more elaborate project would involve raising medical supplies and arranging the details of storage, shipping and delivery. Some projects have been quite complicated, such as a housing project that involved architectural planning, shipment of equipment and materials, and coordination of volunteer construction crews from several states.

For detailed information on how to organize person-to-person delegations between the U.S. and Nicaragua, see chapter five. For information on developing material aid projects, see chapter seven.

Attracting Members and Volunteers

People rarely join an organization only to work on the organization's goals. They join also because the organization is fun, because friends are in it or they want to make friends, because they seek recognition, power, creativity or an escape from boredom.

If you want your sister city project to grow, it is important to keep morale high within the group. Celebrate each of your successes, including the small ones. Hold welcoming receptions when delegations return from Nicaragua. Before sending a shipment of aid, invite the local news media to a ribbon-cutting ceremony. "Everyone works very hard, but at no stage do we allow ourselves to feel that our work is a sacrifice," says John Bevan, who organizes Nicaraguan friendship projects in England. "This is something we have learned from the Nicaraguans. Many of our activities are cultural, and we have had some beautiful and successful concerts with Latin American performers such as Dimensión Costeña, Zínica, and Rubén Blades. Our education events always end in parties. Celebration is a major part of our campaign; we make it enjoyable to do campaigning for Nicaragua."

Celebrations can also increase the public visibility of your project. The Brooklyn/San Juan del Río Coco project held a parade with a marching salsa band and steel drums to mark July 19, the anniversary of the Nicaraguan revolution. "Citizens of Brooklyn seemed warm to the idea as they hung from their window to watch the crowd move down the street, accompanied by drums and a large camouflaged tank with a Ronald Reagan puppet at the helm," reported the Brooklyn community newspaper *The Phoenix*. "A few waved and a few laughed and pointed at the rolling tank as the group slowly moved up Court Street heading toward Carroll Gardens, red balloons waving over their heads and small children in tow, a few carrying their own placards. . . . One elderly man, nodding his head to the drum beats, said in response to the passing stream of people: 'I don't want war either. That's what they're saying.' . . . As marches tend to do, and with a sunny sky overhead, pedestrians intermittently joined in as the group proceeded through Park Slope, and when some dropped out, others picked up where they left off, until the group arrived at its final destination in Prospect Park," where the parade culminated with a picnic and poetry reading.[8]

To recruit volunteers to help with your projects, follow these guidelines:

- *Ask them*. Most people won't volunteer without being asked. This doesn't mean that they don't want to be active.

- If possible, the person to ask them should be someone they know and trust; a friend, a neighbor, a co-worker. But if you cannot arrange for someone else, do it yourself.

- Be sure that new volunteers are welcomed by the leader of the group they will work with. The most effective combination is being asked by someone they already know and being welcomed by whomever is heading the activity.

- Make clear what job you are asking them to do, and be sure it has a definite beginning and end. People do not want to sign up for life, so do not get them to overcommit themselves.

- Ask people to do things they can do well, especially in the beginning.

- Tell each person how his or her job fits in with the rest.

- Let each person know that his or her help is needed.

- Discuss their own goals and how they fit into those of the organization. People have their own reasons for volunteering, and you need to know them in order to lead effectively.

- Ask what *they* would like to know.

- Do these things *in person*.

News Media

At the national level, U.S. news coverage of Nicaragua is dominated by the three major TV networks, a handful of wire services, and a few "leading" publications such as the *New York Times* and *Time* magazine. These media institutions claim to offer objective, honest information about world events, but in practice they tend to function as a sieve through which the "Washington agenda" filters down to the general public. One analysis of news coverage in major newspapers showed that 80 percent of the information about Central America came, not from the region, but from sources in Washington.[9] The White House, State Department and Pentagon ensure that this perspective predominates by holding hundreds of news conferences per year dealing with Nicaragua, supplemented by interviews, background briefings, and staged media events. Information leaks are also used to play reporters off against each other in the competition for "inside information." During Oliver North's tenure in the White House, for example, reporters glossed over his role in the contra supply

"Of course the common people don't want war. Why should some poor slob on a farm want to risk his life in a war when the best he can get out of it is to come back to his farm in one piece? . . . But after all, it is the leaders of a country who determine the policy, and it is always a simple matter to drag the people along, whether it is a democracy, or a fascist dictatorship, or a parliament, or a communist dictatorship. . . . All you have to do is tell them they are being attacked, and denounce the pacifists for lack of patriotism and exposing the country to danger. It works the same in any country."

Herman Goering
at the Nuremburg Trials

Fairfax-Condega Sister Cities
P.O. Box 336
Fairfax, CA 94390
January 7, 1987

For more information call:
Tim Jeffries, 415-456-7433.

FOR IMMEDIATE RELEASE

SISTER-CITY DELEGATION TO VISIT CONDEGA, NICARAGUA

In late January, a 10-member delegation from the Fairfax-Condega Sister City Project will travel to the town of Condega, Nicaragua, near the Honduran border, to further the two cities' cultural and friendship bond, to install a public address system requested by the people of Condega, and to initiate the plans for a sister-city construction brigade to return to work in Condega this fall.

One member of this January's delegation will be Paul Lory, of Seattle, Washington, an 81-year-old ex-Marine who was stationed in Condega in 1928-9 during one of the U.S. occupations of Nicaragua (see enclosed *Mother Jones* reprint, September, 1986). This will be Mr. Lory's first opportunity to fulfill his long-held wish to make peace with the people of Condega, who are once again under attack from our country.

Since its inception in the summer of 1985, making Fairfax the first city in California to be officially paired with a Nicaraguan city, the Fairfax-Condega Sister City Project has sent two delegations, and collected and shipped more than $5,000 worth of humanitarian aid to Condega. With the increasing threat of a direct U.S. invasion of Nicaragua, people-to-people missions of peace and friendship such as this are critically important.

There will be a send-off dinner and party for the delegation on Sunday, January 25th (see enclosed announcement), and Mr. Lory will be available for interviews between January 22-26th.

For more information, call Tim Jeffries, delegation coordinator, at 415-456-7433.

- 30 -

network because North served as a frequent source of news leaks. The national news media is itself a large, powerful institution, which by its nature identifies with rather than challenges the powers that be. "The wire services are influential beyond calculation," observes journalist Timothy Crouse. "The only trouble is that wire stories are usually bland, dry, and overly cautious. There is an inverse proportion between the number of persons a reporter reaches and the amount he can say."[10]

"In the first couple of years I was here," says Judy Butler, a journalist who lives in Nicaragua, "there was an interest, at least on the part of some reporters, to try to write about what they 'saw' in Nicaragua, within the framework of what would be acceptable to their editors. Increasingly, their stories were changed in the States and the reporters started carrying telexes around to show that what got published was not what they had written. Now, they don't even bother. You're lucky, these days, if you can find a journalist sitting around with a beer in the Intercontinental Hotel who will complain that he 'couldn't write what I really saw.' The journalists don't worry about it anymore because their careers are much more important than a little country like Nicaragua, and it does seem that finding a way to say what they actually see is not even in their hands anymore."[11]

At the local level, the rules are somewhat different. Local papers, TV and radio stations usually lack the resources to send their own reporters to cover national and international affairs. Instead, they rely upon networks and wire services, and because their information comes from the national media, they often share its biases. But local papers, especially small ones, are often starved for community news and are the papers most likely to give you consistent coverage. Moreover, local reporters do not have "inside Washington sources" to jeopardize, and may feel more free to write stories that would be considered controversial and risky at the national level. In gathering information for this book, we found excellent coverage of sister-city projects in newspapers such as the *Ann Arbor News;* the Minneapolis *Twin Cities Reader;* the weekly *Bainbridge Review* of Bainbridge Island, Washington; and the *New Haven Register,* to name just a few. Similar coverage was almost nonexistent in the national media.

Good media work can help create a much broader awareness of your group's activities and concerns.[12] A good way to begin is by organizing a media committee within your group, consisting of three to six people who will take responsibility for writing media releases, developing contacts with the media, monitoring coverage that appears about your group, and developing a media kit.

Gathering a list of media contacts should be the committee's first task. You may want to borrow the media list from another group. Initially you want to include the names of reporters and city editors in this list. Try to find out if anyone in your group knows reporters who may be friendly or who have covered groups like yours in the past. As articles on your work are printed, make note of who wrote the story and whether or not it was favorable. Usually the same reporter will be assigned to do future coverage of your group. If the coverage is especially good, the committee may wish to send a note of thanks to the reporter. Over time, cultivating friendly, personal relations with reporters will have a big impact on both the quantity and fairness of the coverage you receive.

News Releases

News releases are used to notify the media about upcoming meetings and events as well as to announce your accomplishments, e.g., "Sister city group raises $3,000 in fund drive." The news release is short and factual, usually no more than one page in length. The first two paragraphs should contain the most important information, sometimes called the "five W's": Who, What, When, Where, Why. This doesn't mean your news release should be dry or neutral in tone. On the contrary, the more interesting the release, the more likely it will be read. Write the release as if you were writing the article. Some reporters may lift sentences, quotes, even entire paragraphs directly from your release.

The release should have the name of a contact person on the top of the page who can be called for more information. You may want to include two names with day and evening phone numbers. Below the contact person comes the release dateline. In most cases this should read: "FOR IMMEDIATE RELEASE." Only if there is a good reason to specify a date should you do so. The newspaper may not have room for your item on a specific date, and will discard it after that date. Below the release dateline, also capitalized, is the headline. As with the body of the press release, write this the way you would like it to read. It should summarize the release and be no more than one line.

While it's important to keep the release to one page, you can include background material with your release. This is very helpful if you are contacting

"How is the world ruled and led into war? Diplomats lie to journalists and then believe those lies when they see them in print."
Austrian Scholar Karl Kraus

newspapers or TV stations who are not familiar with your group. This could include:

- Your brochure
- Fact sheet on Central America
- Fact sheet on your sister city
- List of endorsers
- Photographs (black and white)
- Copies of favorable newspaper articles

This last item is especially important. It establishes your legitimacy as a newsworthy organization.

Releases for daily papers should be sent to arrive about one week before your event. For weeklies and bi-weeklies, call to see what their deadlines are. The day before the event, follow up with phone calls. Ask to speak with the city desk or with the reporter who has covered you in the past. If the paper is unable to assign someone to cover your event, ask if they would like to arrange a telephone interview or would like you to drop by a written report and photographs of the event immediately after it's over. If you send copies of your release to the wire services, AP and UPI, call to make sure that you are listed in their "daybook," the daily listing of newsworthy events each wire service publishes.

Be careful about inviting TV stations if you're not sure about the turnout at the event, or if some people will resent the presence of TV cameras. If the TV stations have a bad experience covering your event, it will be harder to get them to come out the next time.

There are many other ways to get your activities covered in the media. Newspaper surveys show that letters to the editor are one of the most widely read features in the paper. The media committee can distribute a listing of the addresses of the local papers to supporters in order to stimulate such letters. Follow closely the coverage of Central America in your local media. If you see stories that are inaccurate, ask for equal time through an op-ed piece or ask that the paper give coverage to the work your group is doing. Many papers will be responsive to criticism of unfair or "unbalanced" coverage.

When inaccurate coverage appears, don't automatically assume that it reflects a malicious attitude on the part of local journalists. Assumptions derived from the national media may create unconscious biases, which appear in the form of automatic references to Nicaragua's "Marxist-Leninist" or "communist" government, "one-party system," "economic mismanagement," "repression of religion," etc. Likewise, journalists may simply take it for granted that your group is "leftist," "anti-U.S.," "nostalgic for the 1960s," "pro-Sandinista" or "innocent dupes." Part of your objective is to educate journalists, and this is best done diplomatically.

Send out your media package to feature writers and producers of TV and radio talk shows. Let them know your group is available to provide a local angle on coverage of Central America. Develop a list of people in your group who are available for interviews. Your group may be called upon for interviews at times when Central America issues are in the news.

Special preparation should be made when you expect TV or radio coverage. The group may wish to designate two or three spokespersons for the group at any one event. These persons should be well informed about the group, about

To the Editor, *News Tribune*:

Many thanks to the *News Tribune* for Les Orsini's article about our recent trip to Nicaragua. The article was excellent in showing how interesting and varied were our experiences, but readers may have inadvertently received a few wrong impressions: namely, that Nicaragua has a one-party system, that shortages are the result of that system, and that the Sandinista party is dominated by communist foreign governments. These are common misconceptions about Nicaragua, and we would not want to perpetuate them.

I mentioned talking with a leader of the chief opposition party, the right-wing PLI, because we thought Americans ought to know that there *are* opposition parties, and that they are not afraid to talk. (He did not even mind our tape-recording his comments.) But we thought his claim that the party with the most votes — i.e., seats in the General Assembly — should not govern, did not make sense. Who would make policy? Why have an election? Nicaragua has a parliamentary system, and with such a system, the party with the most seats governs until another party wins more seats in an election; that does not constitute a "one-party" system.

In the election of 1984, deemed fair by a large delegation of international observers, the Sandinistas won 66 percent of the vote, and the other parties hold one third of the seats. The other parties represent a broad spectrum from right to left, the Communist party receiving only two seats, and the PLI, nine. We found widespread support for the Sandinistas among all types of people — doctors, church workers, and poor people, and it is not difficult to understand their popularity. They are the central party, and the one party with a proven record of achievements.

We also found *no* evidence that Nicaragua will let itself be dominated by any foreign power — not the U.S., not Cuba, not the Soviet Union. What they crave is independence, and a chance to build their country in peace. They do *not* want a Soviet base, which they feel sure would provoke an American invasion, and make them a battleground between the superpowers.

Finally, the widespread shortage of all mass-produced goods are the direct result of the U.S. embargo, since the great majority of Nicaragua's trade used to be with the United States. They want to trade with us again, and to have good relations with our government, but they consider our demand that they share power with the contras to be totally unreasonable. Would we include in our government a group which was trying to overthrow the elected government by force, with the aid of a large foreign power, through terrorist attacks against our civilians?

Rodney Barker
Newton Highlands

Central America, and be comfortable speaking before cameras. Often an hour of filming will be cut to 30 seconds on the evening newscast and a five minute interview will be reduced to one or two sentences. For this reason it's important to be concise and consistently positive. Some reporters will ask provocative questions in an attempt to get a negative quote to use on the air. The spokespersons may want to roleplay hostile interview questions beforehand. Remember, you don't have to let reporters set the agenda in an interview. Keep in mind the points you want to convey and stick to them.

The spokespersons should not always be the same people. This is a fun and exciting role that should be shared with as many people in the group as possible. The media committee may want to organize a workshop to train members of the group to give interviews and deal with the media.

Internal Publicity

As your group expands, you will develop a list of hundreds of supporters and contacts. Many of these people will be unable to participate in the group's regular meetings but you can stay in touch with them through a regular newsletter. There are periods when your group is less visible in the local media. It's important for your supporters to know there is still a lot happening.

Aim for quarterly or bi-monthly publication to begin with. Your newsletter should include a calendar of upcoming events, news of your sister city, and reports on past activities and events. You may want to occasionally include longer pieces that analyze events in Central America and U.S. policies. Such articles involve a lot more effort than staying with brief news items. As an alternative, consider reprinting articles from other publications.

Check to see if you have people in your group who can draw cartoons, or have skills in photography, graphics, layout and typesetting. Someone in the group may have a personal computer that can be used to print the newsletter and even produce graphics.

You may want to develop symbols to identify your organization. Make sure that during each event you have a large sign displaying your group's name and logo in whatever direction the TV cameras are pointed. Many sister-city logos use images that symbolize the two cities. The Boulder/Jalapa project uses an image of snow-covered mountains; Brooklyn/San Juan del Río Coco uses an image of the Brooklyn Bridge leading into mountain peaks. The logo can be used on stationery, as well as on buttons, T-shirts, banners and bumper stickers.

As soon as possible, develop a brochure. This should be an attractive, professionally printed piece. Your brochure is your case statement: why you exist, what you hope to accomplish, and what you're doing now. It should contain some background information on U.S. policies in Central America, and information on your sister city. A listing of the group's endorsers or the groups making up the sister-city coalition should be listed in the brochure. Include a clip-out coupon that people can send in to get more information, volunteer for work, get on your mailing list, or send with a donation.

A literature committee can also develop one-page informational leaflets to hand out at tables and events. These might cover subjects such as: your sister city, U.S. intervention, an analysis of the Iran-Contra scandal, or Nicaraguan history. A literature committee can also develop a collection of books and pamphlets on Central America to sell at events. This can be an important service in small towns where such literature may not be widely available.

Raising Funds and Donations

Among his other talents, Benjamin Franklin was a skilled organizer of voluntary organizations. His advice for soliciting donations is hard to surpass: "Apply to all those whom you know will give something; next, to those whom you are uncertain whether they will give anything or not, and show them the list of those who have given; and lastly, do not neglect those who you are sure will give nothing, for in some of them you may be mistaken."

Every source of money has one thing in common: you only get money if you ask for it. Asking for donations is not difficult, but many people hesitate to do so out of fear of rejection or reluctance to "beg." Soliciting donations is not begging; it is an invitation for groups in your community to help with a project whose humanitarian value you can easily demonstrate.

"Never doubt that a small group of thoughtful, committed citizens can change the world; indeed, it's the only thing that ever has."

Margaret Mead

Fundraising is one of the primary responsibilities of an organization's board of directors. It should not be left up to a handful of people. Every member of your board should actively work to raise funds.

The following advice for fundraising success is taken from *The Successful Volunteer Organization* by Joan Flanagan:

1) People give to people. Ask in person.

2) The best people you can ask for money are people who already have given money. Keep complete records of your donors.

3) People cannot respond unless you tell them what you want. Always ask for a specific amount or item. Be enthusiastic, optimistic, and bold! You get what you ask for!

4) People who ask for money become better givers. People who give money become better at asking for it.

5) People want to back a winner. Be proud of your project, what you do, and how you do it. Success breeds success!

6) More people means more money and more fun. Find a job for every volunteer. Make it more fun to be on the inside and participating than on the outside and looking in.

7) People want recognition. Send thank-you notes![13]

Fundraising projects do not always involve asking for money directly. The examples below illustrate some of the approaches you or your organization's board of directors might take:

- Direct mail campaign: The Minneapolis/St. Paul Nicaragua Solidarity Committee raised $6,000 with a mailing to 1500 supporters. They attribute success to: a focus that would appeal to donors (they chose medical aid); well-researched information about the contra war's effect on the health of the Nicaraguan people; a list of what specific health care items could be purchased for each donation unit ($1 would buy 300 aspirin, $5 10 serum donations for diarrhea, etc.); and a list of incentives to encourage large donations (a donor of $10 would receive a bag of Nicaraguan coffee, etc.).

- Acquire mailing lists for your organization. If you belong to another group, perhaps you can arrange an exchange. Ask all your friends to give you the names of 10-15 people they think would like to join.

- Bowl-a-thon: Some groups have raised thousands of dollars through this method, which requires only a few dollars in overhead expenses if bowlers rent their own shoes and pay for the game. Sign up bowlers in advance, and call to remind them a few days before the event; use follow-up calls if necessary to collect the money. Award prizes for the bowler with the highest score and the person who brought in the most money. The same approach can be used for bike-a-thons, dance-a-thons, walk-a-thons, etc.

- Beans and rice dinners: Many committees put on one-shot or weekly dinners. For 65 people, soak 24 C. pinto beans and 26 C. rice in the morning. Brown rice cooks in a 350 degree oven in an hour; white rice cooks faster and will look better cooked with some chopped carrots. To each 12 C. dried pintos which have been soaked and cooked, cook in oil 1 large onion, chopped, minced garlic, 3 T. cumin, 1 tsp. chili powder, and 1/2 tsp. cayenne. Serve with cole slaw or lettuce salad, corn tortillas warmed in the oven, a cold drink, and Nicaraguan coffee. Charge $10 per person.

- Set up a memorial fund in honor of someone in your sister city. In some cases, this has been done in remembrance of victims of the contra war.
- Poker party: Get your gambling friends together. Charge $5 to get in, and ask that a percentage of each pot go to your organization. Individuals win, and so does the organization. You can charge extra for refreshments, or include one or two glasses of something with the price of admission. (Note: watch the laws in your community on this one; in some places it is illegal to gamble, even in your own home.)
- Honoraria for speaking engagements.
- Sell shares: Boulder/Jalapa built a pre-school by selling "shares" in the building at $5 per square foot.
- Rummage sales.
- Raffles.
- Recycle newspapers.
- Hold a "dog show" benefit. Participants "vote" for best dog at 50 cents/vote.
- Set up a challenge campaign. Identify a donor who will give $5 for every $25 others give, or will match every $10 gift up to 10 gifts. For added suspense, make this challenge during a fundraising event: "For the next five minutes, Bob will give $5 for every new member that joins the sister-city association."
- Phone-a-thon: Have the people in your group pool the names of people you think would like to join, and call each of them. If you are shy about asking your own friends for money but not afraid to ask people you don't know, trade names with someone.
- Teach a seminar on a topic you know: knitting, organic gardening, gourmet cooking, dog grooming. Charge $25-35 per person.
- Conduct a volunteer canvas. For one evening, take a bunch of literature to all the neighborhoods around you and ask for money at the door. Be sure to comply with city and county ordinances.

In addition to money, you can ask for donations of goods and services. If you are organizing a project to send supplies to the health clinic in your sister city, for example, write to local doctors and companies in the health field, explaining the nature of your project and asking if they would be willing to contribute any of the items on a list which you attach to the letter. Send the letters to the director of public affairs of each company, and follow up a week later with phone calls.

If merchants can't donate something outright, ask them to offer discounts on the items you need; then buy them yourselves as a group, or urge individuals in the community to buy them for you. The latter approach is particularly attractive to businesses, because it provides them with a marketing tool to attract customers. Offer to trade advertising in your newsletter in exchange for donations or discounts.

Sometimes donations that are inappropriate for your sister city can be "traded" through a creative public event into resources that you *can* use. In Madison, Wisconsin, for example, a local brewery offered coupons for free beer in exchange for each baseball donated to Nicaraguan Little Leagues. In Boulder, Colorado, several top fashion salons participated in a charity fashion show to raise funds for construction of a Nicaraguan preschool.

In-kind contributions are another potential source of support that you can solicit. In-kind contributions can include office space, administrative support, use of staff time, copying machine, computer, etc.

If your group has IRS 501(c)(3) non-profit status (see the section on "Organizational Structure" above), most expenditures made in behalf of your activities should be tax-deductible, including transportation to and from meetings, cost of overnight lodging, unreimbursed postage, long distance phone calls or telegrams, membership and meeting registration fees, cost incurred in hosting Nicaraguan visitors, etc. Volunteer time is not tax-deductible, but can be recorded as a "gift-in-kind" at an appropriate hourly rate on your annual report. If you apply for foundation grants, it is important to have such documentation in order to present a full picture of the scope of your activities.

I was shocked
like a good child of
   the north
shocked at the bare
   and dusty
setting of bleakness
shocked at the walls
forlorn walls
cobwebbed, cracked and
   peeling walls
walls without pictures
without comfort
I was shocked . . .

61

. . . *like a good child of*
    the north
looking for love in walls.
Finding love instead
in the land
      in the word
made flesh.

"Land of the Potters,"
the Chorrotega called
   Condega.
Land of the clay,
of the soft, smooth
loving clay
      with
burning eyes.
Eyes like black pearls
that know the meaning
of touch.
Know that skin is velvet.
Know that the warm
   moment
of the hand on the arm
is the joy of sunsets.

We of the north who touch
   at a distance
who caress the soul
with floral designs
and bright swatches
of framed beauty
know touch like a
   camouflage,
a commodity,
a negotiated settlement.
But in Condega
touch and laughter
   are awake
—rising in a revolution
   of love.

I found in Condega
smiles that touch and
    tickle,
smiles that paint the day
with brilliant colors
and fill the drab spaces
with shades of tenderness.

In Condega,
Land of the Potters,
smiles and spirits and
    fingertips and eyes
wrap around the bread and
    the soil
the corn and the heart
—rising in a revolution
                of life.

Marja Eloheimo, Marin County
(Fairfax-Condega) Sister City
Project, Fairfax, California

Coming Face to Face 5

Like any tourist, Kim Esterberg came home to Bainbridge Island in the state of Washington with lovely stories — of swimming in the moonlight, sharing watermelon with new friends on a ferry ride, laughing at the antics of a broken-down jeep on which he was a passenger.

But Esterberg's trip was not just a vacation. It was also a pilgrimage. He carried relics from his home island to introduce it to Nicaraguans: a Bainbridge Island Arts Council calendar; pictures of a class at Wilkes Elementary and another at Commodore Middle School; and photos of Winslow Way, the Walla Walla ferry, Father Donald Conger of St. Cecilia's Roman Catholic Church, and Pastor Scott Huff of Seabold United Methodist — little slices of Bainbridge life. And he took two "sister relationship" proclamations, one signed by 90 people from Bainbridge and another for the Nicaraguans to sign and return. With assistance from the Seattle-Managua Sister City Association, he was on a quest to find a Nicaraguan sister island for Bainbridge.

Esterberg's request caught the Nicaraguan Office of Municipal and Regional Affairs (DAMUR) by surprise. He had asked ahead of time for an island to pair with, but they replied that they were used to city or county sister relationships, and that islands are not political entities.

"My response was that I didn't see that as a problem," says Esterberg, "because our own island is not a political entity either. But I felt we would have something in common geographically. Bainbridge residents have a strong sense of community, and my suspicion was that Nicaraguan island-dwellers would, too. And that turns out to be the case."

DAMUR found him an island, in Lake Nicaragua. Ometepe is about twice the size of Bainbridge, with two volcanic mountains distinguishing its skyline. Of the things that Esterberg brought with him, the islanders were most impressed with the picture of the Bainbridge ferry. Their island had a population of 24,000 people and only 27 trucks, and they were amazed to hear that a ferry existed capable of carrying 200 cars.

Esterberg in turn was amazed at the poverty he saw throughout the island. He asked an Ometepe resident: What was the one thing the United States could do for them? "I was thinking: They need everything. But he answered that the one thing is, 'respect that we have a country.' "[1]

"What we see now is like the dim image in a mirror; then we shall see face to face. What I know now is only partial; then it will be complete. . . . Meanwhile these three remain: faith, hope and love; and the greatest of these is love."

I Corinthians 13:12-13

Why Make the Trip?

A one-week tour of Nicaragua typically costs between $1,000 and $1,500, including expenses for travel, food and lodging. When you consider that $1,000 is more than the yearly income of most Nicaraguans, and that it can be used to pay the shipping expenses for roughly $25,000 worth of donated tools or medical supplies, you may feel that travel to Nicaragua is an extravagance and a waste of resources. In fact, however, person-to-person visits and exchanges are an absolutely vital aspect of sister-city organizing. Face-to-face contact transforms your sister city from an abstract concept into a living experience for people in your community. "When you meet people firsthand, the perspective changes and you forget political rhetoric," says Mary Foster of Project Minnesota-León. Paul Kranz of California says his project to provide electrical generators for Nicaraguan hospitals has grown because of "the one-to-one basis of it, the fundamental aspect of which is concrete contact with the people of Nicaragua. It makes you more credible, because you've seen it with your own eyes, and you can talk on a real first-hand basis about what you're doing."

If your group intends to carry out large or long-term material aid projects such as building a school or health center, you may find it necessary to have at least one person visit Nicaragua on an extended basis to coordinate your work. But "technical coordination" is not the most important reason to visit Nicaragua. Experienced organizers have found that material aid projects which originate in the United States without consultation with Nicaraguans tend to fail, either because they are impractical or because they don't fit in with Nicaraguan cultural expectations and desires. "Don't plan very elaborate projects before you go there," advises Lee Cruz of New Haven, "and shut up and listen to the people about what they want to do and what their needs are."

Nicaraguans consider delegations an important way of presenting themselves directly to the American people, bypassing the tendency of the government and news media to interpret and distort their situation. "The best thing that can happen is that a delegation comes down and sees the reality here and what Somoza has left us, and reports these things to people back in the United States," says Juana Escobar Tellez, a nurse in Malpaisillo, which has a sister-city relationship with Pittsfield, Massachusetts.

Visiting Nicaragua has transformed the attitudes of some North American travelers. Brent Shirley, the mayor of Port Townsend, Washington, toured his sister city of Jalapa in January of 1986 and returned "impressed by the Nicaraguans and confused by my country's approach to that country." In a letter to President Reagan, Shirley stated, "I am generally known as a political conservative, and I support much of what your administration proposes. But after spending two weeks in Managua and Jalapa, I can not understand why this nation has imposed an embargo and openly supports the 'contras.' . . . What I saw was a people attempting to build a country, to establish economic opportunity, freedom from want; they have a great desire to develop friendly relations with the United States. This impression was gained from our delegation's purposeful and successful attempt to meet and talk with peasants of the country."[2]

Visits to Nicaragua also produce a "multiplier effect" when the visitors return home and describe their experiences to friends, neighbors and relatives. Carolyn Kenney, an organizer of the Wisconsin Rapids/Rio Blanco sister city project, says her interest in Nicaragua began in 1983 when she visited two relatives in Kansas City, both of whom had been to Central America. "They shared their

"I am generally known as a political conservative, and I support much of what your administration proposes. But after spending two weeks in Managua and Jalapa, I can not understand why this nation has imposed an embargo and openly supports the 'contras.' . . . What I saw was a people attempting to build a country, to establish economic opportunity, freedom from want; they have a great desire to develop friendly relations with the United States. This impression was gained from our delegation's purposeful and successful attempt to meet and talk with peasants of the country."

Brent Shirley
mayor of Port Townsend, Washington

perspective, and it was very eye-opening," she recalls. "It was the first time I had talked to anyone who had been down there, and as I began asking more questions, it brought out convictions and feelings I had held for a long time but never acted on." According to Alan Wright, "People who visit Nicaragua start to get involved in the process of what's happening there, and eventually the process starts to involve a community. The more people you send down, the more people want to go."

This "sense of community" bridges the gap between people's private lives and the public roles they play. In public spheres of work, politics and civic life, people adopt functional roles which reflect only part of their human personality. A store check-out clerk, for example, treats customers in polite but impersonal terms and avoids emotionally intimate exchanges. "In the public sphere," observes author Harry C. Boyte, "there is respect, accountability, goal-oriented behavior. Meetings properly start on time. Strategies are developed. Leaders are those who get results. . . . There is a constant process of testing, refinement, and improvement in techniques, skills, and abilities." But there is also a tendency for people to regard each other as means to ends, disregarding the intrinsic worth and significance of each individual. By contrast, "In one's private life — shared with family, close friends and neighbors — belongs much of . . . the 'organic roots' of things: love, intimacy, play, informality. There are no agendas. Behavior is not primarily aimed at achieving things. One seeks reciprocity, sharing, ties nourished and sustained over time through daily experience."[3]

Friendships of this type do not develop instantly; they require the accumulation of numerous small memories and interactions. They begin through face-to-face contact.

Getting There and Back[4]

Trips to Nicaragua, tailored to a variety of individual schedules, interests and abilities, can be arranged in any of the following ways. To find the sponsoring organizations mentioned here, see the directories at the back of the book.

- Join a work brigade, picking cotton or coffee, planting trees for environmental restoration, or helping in the construction of a hospital, school or other facility. (See the section on "Work Brigades" in chapter seven.)

- Many groups sponsor educational tours of Nicaragua. Some are general-interest tours, covering diverse topics and offering the opportunity to meet with Nicaraguans from a wide range of backgrounds and political perspectives, such as government officials, opposition figures, religious leaders, peasants and business executives. Other tours focus on a particular interest, such as the arts, medicine, farming, or education. Two progressive travel agencies, Marazul Tours and Tropical Tours, are good at arranging group and individual trips to Central America. The Wisconsin Coordinating Council on Nicaragua (WCCN) organizes tours with a sister-city emphasis that are open to participants from throughout the United States.

- People with technical skills in areas such as economics, computers, agriculture and mechanics visit Nicaragua, usually for periods of a month or longer, to share their skills by offering training and consultation. Many such visits are arranged by the organizations TECNICA and Science for the People.

- The organization "Witness for Peace" sends delegations that maintain a continual presence of U.S. citizens in Nicaraguan war zones, in order to "share with the Nicaraguans in their daily lives, including the dangers they face from U.S.-directed war." Short term delegations typically spend two weeks working and praying in areas that have suffered from contra attacks. They also interview political and religious leaders representing a wide spectrum of viewpoints, as well as survivors and relatives of people killed, kidnapped and wounded. Upon returning home they report their experiences to the media, their congressional representatives, church and community groups. Witness for Peace also organizes long-term teams that spend eight months or more in Nicaragua, working systematically to document contra attacks and the implementation of the peace process. The purpose of Witness for Peace is "to develop an ever-broadening, prayerful, biblically based community of United States citizens who stand with the Nicaraguan people by acting in continuous nonviolent resistance to U.S. covert or overt intervention in their country" and to "mobilize public opinion and help change U.S. foreign policy."

- Spanish language classes are available in Managua and Estelí. In addition to language instruction, they include lessons in Nicaraguan history and culture, as well as meetings and interviews dealing with a variety of topics, including the political situation. For details, contact NICA or the Casa Nicaragüense de Español (CNE).

- Academic research can be expedited through the Latin American Studies Association (LASA).

- Many people visit Nicaragua as journalists, both professional and amateur, full-time and part-time. If you intend to pursue this option, bring letters of assignment from the newspaper, radio, TV station or newsletter for which you will be reporting. If possible, bring copies of materials in which you are listed as a contributor or an editor. Be sure you know the exact address, phone number, and size of circulation or audience of your sponsor. You also need to bring two small (1x1$^{1}/_{2}$") photographs if you intend to apply for government press credentials. The cost when applying for credentials is currently US$25. Apply at the International Press Agency in Managua or the Casa de Gobierno.

- You can visit Nicaragua as an individual, even hiring a personal guide/translator. Alternately, you can join a tour and make arrangements to stay on after it has ended. This approach has the advantage of providing you with a guided introduction to the country before you have to start fending for yourself, which can be a valuable and relatively painless way of learning, not just about Nicaraguan political issues, but also about the inconveniences with which people — including tourists — must contend in an underdeveloped country that has been impoverished and disorganized by years of war. If planned in advance, extending your stay should incur no additional airplane expense, and other expenses inside Nicaragua are usually minimal. (Note: In early 1988, Nicaragua undertook major economic reforms including currency devaluation which sharply increased tourist prices. Before traveling to Nicaragua, obtain current information from a knowledgeable source.)

After the U.S. attempted to restrict travel to Nicaragua by closing down Nicaraguan consular offices around the United States, the Nicaraguan government expedited procedures by allowing U.S. citizens to apply for visas at the Nicaraguan airport. Non-U.S. citizens, however, must apply for a visa at the

Nicaraguan embassy in Washington, D.C., *before* traveling to Nicaragua. Visitors to Nicaragua receive a 30 day visa and renewal is a hassle, so apply several days before your expiration date if you intend to stay longer. Nicaraguan authorities will be more likely to approve a visa extension if you work through a Nicaraguan institution — a church, school, union, government office. Get a letter from that institution requesting an extension, explaining why it should be granted and what you plan to do during your time in Nicaragua.

If you will be returning alone instead of with a delegation, you should confirm your return flight 72 hours in advance, and make a point of arriving at the airport at least two hours before departure time. Bring US$10 and 50 Nicaraguan cordobas to pay the airport exit tax. While waiting for your plane to board, you can shop for gifts at the airport's duty-free store.

It is *not* true that most Nicaraguans know enough English that you can get by without knowing Spanish. If you are not Spanish-speaking, make sure your trip includes arrangements for an interpreter.

The national Nicaragua Network in Washington, D.C. has a helpful pamphlet with advice on travel to Nicaragua. Another useful travel book on Central America is the *South American Handbook*, published annually by Trade and Travel Publications, Ltd., which provides information about hotels and transportation and also contains brief descriptions of many cities. Look for a copy at your local library. Friendship City Projects of Boulder, Colorado sells a "Destination Nicaragua" packet for $5 which contains useful information about traveling to Nicaragua, either alone or with a group.

Some travelers to Nicaragua have experienced harassment by U.S. customs officials, including confiscation of notes, personal address books and other items. These have been returned after legal appeals, but materials that you wish to keep private should remain in your pockets, not in your luggage. The Movement Support Network of the National Lawyers Guild has a booklet detailing your rights, and is a good source of legal assistance if you have trouble.

As of this writing, there are no legal restrictions to prevent U.S. citizens from traveling to Nicaragua. In the event that such restrictions are imposed, the National Lawyers Guild and the Center for Constitutional Rights may be of assistance. When travel to China was banned during the peak of U.S.-Chinese hostilities, many U.S. citizens found ways to circumvent the restriction, and in the process contributed to an eventual improvement of relations.

Getting to Your Sister City

Before organizing a delegation to your sister city, you should seek advice from a group that has already organized several trips on its own. The following groups are experienced and willing to help: On the west coast, the Seattle-Managua Sister Cities Association; in the west, the Boulder/Jalapa Friendship Cities Project; in the midwest, the Wisconsin Coordinating Council on Nicaragua; on the east coast, the New Haven/León Sister Cities Association. For your first visit, you may prefer to simplify the task of making travel arrangements by signing on to a tour sponsored by someone else.

There is no guarantee that you will be able to get from Managua to your sister city, particularly if it is located on the Atlantic Coast or a war zone. You can improve your chances considerably by contacting the Nicaraguan embassy *at least* a month before your visit. They can help obtain the necessary permission papers, but you should count on coming up with your own means of transportation. Airplanes to the Atlantic Coast are rare and usually booked full a month in advance. Buses are overcrowded to the point of overflowing, except for buses that have been reserved by a tour group. If the gasoline shortage is not severe, taxi and jeep drivers can be hired for long excursions at a price of around $50 per day (a very rough estimate; the price fluctuates), but these arrangements can only be made after you arrive in Nicaragua. Be sure to agree with the driver about the rate beforehand. Some drivers may ask to be paid in dollars rather than cordobas. Strictly speaking, this is black market activity, which is illegal and can result in jail or being barred from Nicaragua. Taxis are hard to catch on the street, but they can be found at the Intercontinental Hotel or rented from the Carlos Fonseca Taxi Co-op located in the same neighborhood. Rent-a-cars are usually available at the Intercontinental and at the Managua airport.

Another approach to transportation is available by contacting a local U.S. chapter of the group "Bikes Not Bombs." They will provide a boxed bicycle, free of charge, which you can take on the airplane for an excess baggage fee of about $30. Upon your arrival in Nicaragua, they will assemble it in their workshop for you to use during your stay. After you leave, the bicycle will be distributed for use by Nicaraguans. They also rent bikes in Nicaragua at reasonable rates.

Nicaragua is a poor country suffering from shortages of skilled labor as well as other realities of a country at war. Sometimes this leads to inefficiency and bureaucratic hassles. During your brief stay in Nicaragua, you will want to see and do as much as possible, and you may feel frustrated if you encounter obstacles and delays. Persistence will sometimes help to overcome these obstacles, and there are cases when determined appeals have opened doors that would otherwise remain closed, but avoid rude or pushy behavior. Nicaragua is not your country, and your sister city project will fail if Nicaraguans come to regard you as an unwelcome nuisance rather than as a friend. Remember, whatever frustrations you encounter are only a sample of what Nicaraguans themselves must deal with on a constant, long-term basis. Also, bear in mind that what appears to be "inefficiency" may have other causes.

"Americans easily forget that many of those problems, big and small, are the direct result of the contra war," writes Zachary Sklar, who visited Nicaragua in 1984 to help pick coffee and described his experiences in an issue of *The Nation* magazine. "Just how easily, I realized on the day we left La Lima for home. The farm's truck dropped us in the city of Matagalpa, where another truck was to have met us. But it was nowhere to be found. For eight hours we waited as UNAG officials searched for some means of transportation to get us back to Managua. Bored and irritated, some of us complained, just as Nicaraguans do, about the bumbling Sandinista bureaucracy. When a truck arrived, we heard the explanation for the delay. That morning the contras had burned down seven private haciendas and one coffee storage plant to the north, near Yalí. . . . The truck scheduled for us had been commandeered to help transport the eight dead and seven wounded."[5]

Trip Tips

Personal Safety. Many people have exaggerated fears of the danger involved in visiting Nicaragua. Outside the war zones, Nicaragua is one of the safest countries in Central America with respect to political and criminal violence, and in fact is safer than many cities in North America. John Mahon of Gainesville, Florida, who joined a delegation to his sister city of Matagalpa in December of

1986, recalls that "When I left the U.S., some well wishers seemed sad because I was going into grave danger. But I walked the streets of Managua and Matagalpa in the dead of night, with a pocket full of money, free of threats, free of insults, free, so far as anyone could tell, even of curious notice."[6] Over 80,000 U.S. citizens have visited Nicaragua since the 1979 revolution, and only one has been killed — Ben Linder, who was working in an isolated section of the northern war zone when he was targeted and attacked by contras.

Unfortunately, in 1987 Nicaragua's sharply deepening economic crisis led to an increase in the number of instances of robbery and theft-related assault. It is no longer advisable to walk the streets of Managua "in the dead of night." You should also guard against pickpockets (particularly on public buses), room break-ins and other types of theft. Carry small valuables with you, and keep your suitcase locked. Don't leave your possessions unattended in public places.

War-related precautions are particularly advisable when traveling between cities. If you travel in a war zone, check with the army to make sure contras are not active along the roads you intend to travel. Accept whatever advice they offer; neither they nor you have anything to gain by creating North American "martyrs." Travel only during the daytime; don't get caught on the road after nightfall, when contras find it easiest to attack.

Health. A big problem in travel to any foreign country is stomach trouble. The best non-prescription preventative is liquid Pepto-Bismol, taken as directed. Discuss prescription drugs with your physician before your trip. The antibiotics Bactrim DS or Septra are commonly recommended to treat diarrhea, but should not be taken as preventatives. Lomotil is a strong medicine and should be used only in emergencies, e.g. long bus rides or severe cramps.

Water and ice in Managua are safe to drink, but elsewhere you should stick to soda, beer or bottled water (ask for "Ensa"). Bring a plastic water bottle and iodine-based tablets for purifying water; a flavoring powder such as Tang may improve the taste of treated water. Avoid leafy vegetables which have not been cooked, greasy foods, clams, oysters and marinated fish.

No immunizations are required for travel to Nicaragua, but it would be wise to see a doctor two weeks before you go, and make sure you have up-to-date immunizations for tetanus, malaria and typhoid. A shot of gamma globulin just before you go may reduce the risk of hepatitis. If you use any other medication (including allergy and cold medicine), bring along a sufficient supply to last for the duration of your stay. Bring copies of any medicine prescriptions.

In case of illness while in Nicaragua, you can use the free public health system (which is overworked and sometimes undersupplied) or the private system, which is generally faster and sometimes better. Take along claim forms from your insurance company; get them filled out in English and the bill in dollars.

Money. Upon arrival at the Managua airport you will be required to exchange $60 for Nicaraguan córdobas. Dollars can be exchanged for córdobas at most banks, but you cannot change córdobas back to dollars, so only exchange what you expect to spend. Nicaraguan economic conditions in 1987 and 1988 included an inflation rate of over 1,000 percent and a growing black market, with many Nicaraguans anxious to trade their currency for dollars at rates higher than the official rate. While this "survival strategy" is understandable, it undermines the Nicaraguan economy still further; it is also illegal and can get you arrested or expelled from the country. Don't do it.

Even first class hotels in Nicaragua often don't accept credit cards. If you want to take travelers checks, Citibank is recommended since they can be refunded to you in Nicaragua if they are lost or stolen. All of the other companies require you to return to the States before you are refunded. Usually it is best to simply bring cash.

Clothing. Take colored clothes with at least some cotton (white gets dirty quickly). Bluejeans tend to be hot and uncomfortable, as are heavy boots. There are no laundromats, so bring hand washable clothing. Bring a change of clothing for each day of your tour.

Nicaraguans dress informally, but neatness and cleanliness are important. Avoid outlandish or ragged clothes, tattered shoes and sandals, and don't wear shorts, cutoffs or tank tops in public places — they offend local sensibilities. Straw hats are for the beach, not for public meetings. Out of courtesy to Nicaraguans, women should wear bras. Men should get a haircut and shave or keep their beards trimmed. "Quite often internationalists are stereotyped as being dirty hippies, because there are a lot of those people walking around," says one North American living in Nicaragua. "Nicaraguans sometimes say to me, 'You look so neat and clean. Why can't those other people be more like that?' "

What to Take. You will be allowed 66 lbs. of luggage on your flight to Nicaragua. Overweight charges beyond that that amount average around 85 cents per pound. Due to Nicaragua's economic crisis, you may be unable to buy common items such as soap, toilet paper and camera film. Conditions may change, so check with someone knowledgeable before going. The following items are among the things to bring:

- A passport valid for 6 months after the departure date of your stay in Nicaragua. Also bring copies of all important documents, and keep them separate from the originals.
- First aid kit, including disinfectant, bandaids, clear medical tape, tweezers, thermometer, aspirin
- Spanish-English dictionary and traveler's phrasebook
- Toilet paper, soap, shampo/conditioner, toothpaste, shaving items, tampons
- Insect repellent
- Sun screen and lotion, chapstick
- Sunglasses and hat with visor
- Poncho and galoshes if you are visiting during Nicaragua's rainy season (May through December).
- A large beach towel and a small towel to carry with you (bathrooms almost never have towels)
- Swim suit
- Moist towelettes for washing your hands and face (water service is cut off two days a week in Managua, and similar conditions prevail elsewhere)
- Alarm clock or alarm wristwatch
- Plastic bag for soiled clothes (bring extra plastic bags — they come in handy)
- Bedsheets (not necessary if your stay is in a hotel)
- Flashlight with batteries

- Vitamins with minerals
- Camera. 35mm gives superior photos; slides taken with a cheap camera will not. Film and batteries are almost impossible to find, so bring enough to last through your entire trip. Pack your film separately and have it inspected rather than x-rayed at the airport. Please be advised that it is illegal to take photographs of military installations and government buildings in Nicaragua.
- U.S. stamps. The fastest way to get a letter home is to ask a returning traveler to post it for you when he or she gets back to the states. One convenient way to locate U.S. citizens is to attend the demonstration which the Committee of U.S. Citizens Living in Nicaragua (CUSCLIN) conducts at 7:30 a.m. every Thursday in front of the U.S. embassy in Managua.
- Portable sewing kit
- Spare eyeglasses and your prescription
- A cardboard tube (for bringing back posters)

Do not bring into the country any illegal drugs, firearms, explosives, knives or sharp scissors. If you attempt to bring olive drab, khaki or camouflage army clothing or similar army-issue items (canteens, etc.), they will be confiscated by customs. You will not need a sleeping bag unless you are joining a work brigade. Bring a backpack only if you plan on a lot of traveling and hiking. Backpacks can be awkward to transport in vehicles, easy to rob out of, and may mark you as a "hippy."

Since cargo shipments to Nicaragua are slow and cost money, most delegations hand-carry suitcases full of donations, such as medicines or school supplies. The National Central America Health Rights Network (NCAHRN) or the National Nicaragua Network can tell you what kinds of donations are generally needed, or they may ask you to carry supplies which they have already collected.

You may also want to bring photographs, posters and other mementos from your home city, along with gifts of friendship for people in your sister city. If you take gifts for children, consider giving them in some collective way, such as to a school or orphanage. If you give them out randomly on the street, you will never have a moment's peace and you will encourage the habit of begging from rich foreigners. This habit should be discouraged, because it psychologically perpetuates an unhealthy "rich country/poor country" relationship between the United States and Nicaragua.

For additional information on what types of material aid to take, see chapter seven.

True Contact or a Guided Tour?

Opponents of the Nicaraguan revolution argue that delegations to Nicaragua come back with distorted impressions created by deliberate Sandinista manipulations. According to author Paul Hollander, this manipulation has "two major components: first, the strengthening of favorable attitudes among visitors by 'ego massage,' that is, by making the tour a pleasant experience both physically and psychologically, by attending to the needs of the visitors and catering to their self-esteem. Such treatment creates or contributes to a sense of obligation or indebtedness toward the generous host; it also helps to stifle or defuse critical sentiments. The second major component of political hospitality is the screening of reality, the controlled presentation of what there is to see. . . . Political

"The concept is simple, but it requires a lot of work. We need to work hard to rise beyond the neo-McCarthyism of our society and simply promote friendship."

Gary Handschumacher
Boulder/Jalapa Friendship Cities Project

hospitality seeks to minimize chance encounters and experiences and generally succeeds in excluding unfavorable impressions." Hollander claims that most North Americans who visit Nicaragua are "predisposed political tourists" who experience a "guided tour" of Nicaragua, not the reality. In order to carry off this facade, "Security agents pretending to be photographers, journalists or relatives of people in the region to be visited frequently join the delegations. . . . Using advance notice, [the Interior Ministry] sends teams of people to be on the routes used and in the localities to be visited. These are called 'casual encounter' teams . . . pretending to be local residents. . . . They describe alleged contra atrocities and the benefits of the Sandinista revolution."[7]

Your own experience in Nicaragua should provide adequate evidence with which to test these allegations. Actually, the charges raised by Hollander apply to conventional vacation tours more than they apply to study tours of Nicaragua. Authors Alister Mathieson and Geoffrey Wall observe that commercial tourists "are controlled in their movements directly by tour operators or indirectly through the location of required services, such as accommodation, restaurants, entertainment and recreation facilities. . . . Regardless of how ancient or complex the destination culture, it is reduced to a few recognizable characteristics, such as arts and crafts, dance, music, buildings and special functions or ceremonies, and is promoted as a commodity. . . . The tourist sees the country or destination visited in terms of its superficially picturesque, predictably 'exotic' or 'typical' aspects, and experiences local life highly selectively and episodically." Instead of real cultural experiences, tourists experience staged "attractions": "For example, it is not uncommon to see regular hourly concerts of native dances in Hawaii, or to be able to experience a fire-walking display every evening in Fiji, or to see mock wedding ceremonies in Tunisia. The staging of contrived experiences is a way for the traveler to remain out of contact with foreign peoples in the very act of 'sightseeing' them. They keep the natives in quarantine while the tourist in air conditioned comfort views them through a picture window." Moreover, the relationship between tourists and their native hosts leads to unequal and unbalanced experiences, both because the tourist has more money and leisure time, and because a "tourist's stay in one destination is usually short. . . . Tourists often consider the meeting fascinating and unique because the host is frequently of a different nationality or culture. The hosts, on the other hand, may see it merely as one of many such superficial relationships which are experienced throughout the course of the tourist season. . . . As the tourist has a low customer loyalty, seldom returning to destination areas, the interaction between hosts and guests normally occurs only once and has little opportunity to progress beyond a superficial level."[8]

Sister cities seek to establish relationships that go beyond the shallow encounters common to conventional tourism. For this reason, sister-city delegations should plan beforehand with the expectation that their visit will not simply be a one-time experience. They should seek personal contacts with the Nicaraguan people as the first step in a long-term process of mutual exchange and cooperation. The following suggestions may help:

• Select tour participants who are influential in your community and who will help promote the sister-city project after their return. In addition to announcements and advertisements directed at the general public, extend personal invitations to your community leaders. The best delegations are those

"When we send our delegations, we want to have the most unusual, surprising mix of people who probably would never be together otherwise."

Kathy Engel, Madre

which represent the ethnic, religious and economic diversity of their home communities, as well as a range of political viewpoints. Roy Wilson of the Seattle/Managua Sister City Association says his group makes a special effort to send those "who are not convinced." According to Kathy Engel, executive director of the women's organization Madre, "When we send our delegations, we want to have the most unusual, surprising mix of people who probably would never be together otherwise."

• Prepare beforehand by studying. Some groups, such as the Boulder/Jalapa Friendship Cities Project, conduct a series of detailed educational seminars with each delegation before it travels to Nicaragua, explaining Nicaraguan history and Latin cultural perspectives as well as providing logistical information. They also sell informational packets to groups wishing to conduct similar seminars. Other groups, however, prefer a simpler approach. "We have a single preparatory meeting before each delegation leaves, but we think it's more important to provide practical travel information — what to pack, what to bring — than to study Nicaraguan history," says one organizer of delegations. "Most people who visit Nicaragua are busy people, and if we had more than one preparatory meeting, I don't think they'd show. Most delegates already have some sense of Nicaragua in their minds, some sense of what they want to learn there. That sense may be based on misconceptions, but the fastest and best history lesson they could get is not out of some book or seminar, but out of their first two days in Nicaragua."

• Many groups organize "participant led" delegations, in which delegates themselves meet with organizers in the planning stages to help shape the itinerary.

• Study tours are inevitably packed with numerous interviews and meetings, but most tours also schedule some "free time" during which delegates feel free to strike out on their own. In addition, it is usually possible for individual delegates to separate from a part of the tour and rejoin the group later. Travel is not restricted in Nicaragua, except where dangerous.

• Some delegations stay with Nicaraguan host families rather than in hotels. While this can pose logistical problems for large groups, it gives participants an intimate picture of daily life in their sister city. They become accustomed to eating rice and beans, to noisily playing children, and to barking dogs and roosters crowing long after they have gone to bed. Nicaraguans are particularly touched when North Americans demonstrate a willingness to share in their lives. "It's an experience of people coming and staying even though we have only minimal conditions to offer them," says Fidel Zambrana of rural León. "These people see that we don't live in the center of town, that we have poorer homes, and yet you don't see dismay or surprise in their faces. Rather than disliking where they are, they have a sincere interest to help us. The most beautiful thing we've experienced since the beginning has been the sincerity and the goodwill towards us."

• Have long-term goals in mind when you visit your sister city. Before your departure, prepare a written list of specific things you want to accomplish. If your group includes people interested in education, for example, plan to meet with local schools and school officials to learn about their situation and to find out how you can work with them in the future on particular projects.

• Check Nicaraguan holiday times before planning your trip. Major holidays, such as Holy Week, the Christmas season, and the month of July when Nicaragua celebrates the anniversary of its revolution, can severely limit your ability to carry out your intended itinerary. U.S. citizens are welcome to come and join the holiday festivities, but study tours may have difficulty.

• Meeting people from your sister city can be an exciting and emotional experience, but try to be sober-minded in describing your project to Nicaraguans. Be honest and detailed in describing your group; specify the number of people involved, their areas of interest and abilities. Don't get carried away with exaggerated optimism. When talking to Nicaraguans, it's better to underestimate rather than overestimate what your group is able to accomplish. People in Third World countries sometimes have an inflated notion of U.S. wealth and can be misled by unrealistic promises of what you are able to provide in the way of material resources. Avoid raising false hopes, as these can lead to disillusionment and misunderstandings. Your efforts will be appreciated, even if your group only consists of two or three people.

• After returning to the U.S., your group may want to give a public report on your trip. Invite the news media, and have several members of the delegation describe their experiences and impressions. Travelers to Nicaragua can do public education after their return through a variety of methods: giving slide shows; speaking to schools, colleges, and civic associations; appearing on radio and television; writing articles for professional journals; writing to members of Congress and the President; starting personal newsletters or contributing to your group's newsletter; sending journals of their experiences to everyone on their Christmas lists; starting local lecture series and educational workshops; and, of course, leading new trips.

• Finally, avoid any attitudes of superiority or cultural arrogance during your visit. Think of your relationship with Nicaragua as a mutual friendship, not as a "charitable gesture" on your part. When you adopt a sister city, the Nicaraguans are also adopting *you*. As the relationship unfolds, you should expect to find that it consists of Nicaraguans helping you as much as you help them. You may have material resources to offer, but they can offer inspiration and ideas for your community. They can give lessons on how to organize food banks, how to unionize, or how to teach, because those are things that they have done in their own country.

Unfortunately, the worst cases of cultural insensitivity are, almost by definition, unconscious. For most North Americans, coming to terms with the reality of life in the Third World requires making a conscious effort to avoid imposing preconceptions and the agenda of our own culture onto theirs.

The following behaviors are definitely inappropriate:

—Photographing people without their permission, particularly in situations of emotional stress or during religious ceremonies. (Usually people do not object to having their picture taken, but if in doubt, ask.)
—Moralizing or lecturing to Nicaraguans about their family practices, religious or other deeply held beliefs.
—Using the term "American" to refer to people from the United States. Latin Americans (not to mention Canadians) think of themselves as Americans too.

—Passing out gifts to children without consultation with their parents.

—Ignoring local rules or authorities.

—Bringing food or beverages into a church or cathedral.

—Casual sexual advances. What seems like innocent flirtation to you may be construed more seriously by Nicaraguan cultural standards, and can lead to hurt feelings.

—Talking about non-English speaking Nicaraguans in their presence, in a way you wouldn't if they understood English.

—Promising to write a letter or send people pictures you've taken of them, but never following up.

—Wearing clothes inappropriate to Nicaraguan customs. (See "Clothing" section above.)

Bringing Nicaraguans to the United States

When Wayne Ostlie, corporate executive and Republican, read the letter from Alba Reyes, he began to question the wisdom of opening his home to the 18-year-old Nicaraguan electronics student and Sandinista firebrand. "Some of her political comments, like calling Ronald Reagan a 'fascist pig,' really had us concerned," he said. "We didn't know if she'd show up waving a machete or something." But by the end of Reyes' week in the Ostlies' home in Lino Lakes, Minnesota, such fears were completely forgotten. "We found out she was a really neat, friendly person — a good sport. I'd like to see her go to the University of Minnesota and spend more time here," Ostlie says.

Such testimonials were typical from the church and school group members who sponsored the October 1986 youth exchange program organized by Project Minnesota/León. Nine students, ages 12 to 20, were selected by Nicaraguan school and community groups for the exchange.

"I had some real problems with the idea at first," admits PML organizer Mary Foster. "We were worried whether people would see this as a political exploitation. But our real goal of just making personal contacts with people in Minnesota seemed to come though. These kids were such wonderful communicators and so resilient that I think it went better than anyone could have hoped."

A three-week whirlwind of activities took the young Nicaraguans from the Iron Range to State Capitol receptions, from Halloween and election eve parties to appearances at church group and Rotary Club meetings, and from hayrides to rollerskating. . . . These young ambassadors spoke mainly of friendship. Luisa Fernández, 12, who plays a flute donated by PML in the León municipal band, charmed her way into the hearts of students at Woods Academy in Maple Plains. With the aid of a school yearbook, she had memorized the names and faces of most of her fellow sixth and seventh graders before their first meeting.

"Why should I be frightened of coming here?" she asked. "Gringos are such pretty people."

"The kids, especially a couple of boys, just loved her," said Spanish teacher and host Tamara Rossburg. "And my daughter her age misses her already. I'd hear lots of giggling from their bedroom late at night."

from "A Cultural Exchange" by Jon Kerr
Twin Cities Reader, *November 19, 1986*

"When you meet people firsthand, the perspective changes and you forget political rhetoric."
Mary Foster, Project Minnesota-León

Bringing a Nicaraguan delegation to the United States is a great way to establish face-to-face contacts between Nicaraguans and large numbers of people in your community. In addition to short-term visits, Nicaraguans have visited their sister cities through educational exchange programs, tours by music groups, and exhibition baseball games. Your group will have to raise the travel expenses for

Nicaraguans you bring to the United States. In order to share expenses and maximize the value of their visit, you may want to organize a travel itinerary that takes them to other communities in your region.

In order to obtain a visa at the U.S. embassy in Nicaragua, Nicaraguans need a formal letter of invitation that contains the following information:

- Airfare is paid for by the sponsor, as well as housing, meals and expenses.
- Date of flights and flight itinerary.
- Exact travel itinerary in the United States, including activities they'll be involved in.
- Address and phone number where they will be staying each night.
- Address and phone number of each sponsoring organization.
- Purpose of the trip.
- Return date, including flight itinerary.

In addition to sending the invitation to Nicaragua, submit a copy to the Nicaraguan embassy in Washington, D.C. Once the invitation is received, it can take up to three weeks to be processed by the United States embassy. Nicaraguans also need time to procure an exit visa by Nicaraguan immigration.

A number of Nicaraguans, including Nicaraguan President Daniel Ortega, have been forced to abandon plans to travel in the United States after experiencing difficulty in obtaining U.S. visas. "There's a general tendency to not want Nicaraguans here," says Seattle/Managua's Roy Wilson. "After experiencing a number of visa denials, we finally bit the bullet and hired a lawyer. In addition, we generate a political movement around anyone's visa application. We get our governor's office and our mayor and whoever in the community — a university president or doctor — and we publicize it so there's knowledge in the community of what's happening."

In many cases, travel arrangements have proceeded smoothly, but you should plan intended visits well in advance, allowing time to deal with unexpected obstacles. Your U.S. Senator or Representative may be able to assist if immigration officials appear to be dragging their feet on a visa application.

Some problems involving visits by Nicaraguans to the United States have arisen due to lack of communication and lack of mutually agreed-upon goals and objectives. It is essential to communicate early your goals and objectives to the mayor's office in your sister city. Three months is a minimum amount of time in which to begin that communication. It is not enough to simply set up an itinerary and ferry Nicaraguan guests from one appointment to another. Nicaraguans who visit the United States may be unfamiliar with North American weather and customs, and may experience "culture shock" comparable to what North Americans experience upon visiting the Third World. In addition, they are on the spot to represent their country under conditions that may include challenging and even hostile encounters. In order for them to cope and communicate effectively, they should be briefed beforehand so they know something about the persons they are meeting with and why they are meeting.

Follow-through is also very important. Keep track of any commitments and prospects for future outreach that arise during the visit. It should be your responsibility to centralize that information and make sure it isn't lost or forgotten in the shuffle.

Ocotál in northern
Nicaragua, sister city to
Hartford, Connecticut.

Shortages of all types of
teaching supplies result in
creative solutions to many
problems. Here, friends share
a chair at the Elvis Diaz
Romero High School in
Managua, sister city to
Seattle, Washington and
Madison, Wisconsin.

Teaching people in
Nicaragua to read and write
has been a major program of
the new government. The
1980 volunteer literacy
campaign reduced the
country's illiteracy rate from
54% to 12%. Adult education
classes, like this one at a
farmers' cooperative near
Estelí, continue the literacy
program.

Soldiers at a rally in Managua.

A bridge on the Pan ▲
American Highway near
Estelí, damaged in a 1985
contra bombing.

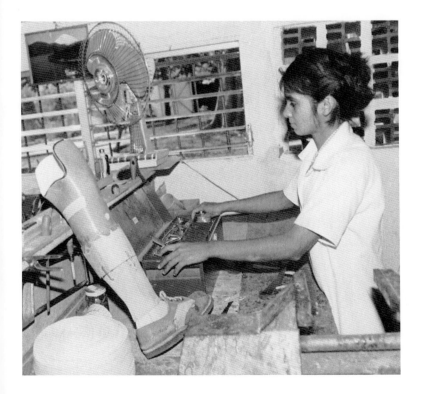

The Erasmo Paredes Herrera
Prosthetics Factory for the
construction of prosthetic
devices for people who have
lost limbs, usually due to the
war. The program is sup-
ported partly by the International Red Cross which has
helped develop designs using
locally available materials.

◀

Rally in the "Plaza de la ▲
revolución", Managua,
January 22, 1988.

Jaime Chamorro, editor of *La
Prensa*. An outspoken
opponent of the Nicaraguan
government, he complains
about instances of
government censorship and
says his paper is struggling for
democracy and freedom of
speech. *La Prensa*'s critics say
the newspaper's acceptance
of over US$300,000 from the
U.S. government amounts to
treason, and compare its
activities with the CIA's use
of the newspaper *El Mercúrio*
in its psychological destabilization campaign against the
government of Salvador
Allende in Chile. ▶

Enrique Bolaños of ▲
COSEP, the anti-Sandinista
businessmen's association.
U.S. delegations to Nicaragua
frequently meet with representatives of COSEP and
other opposition figures.

Monimbó, Nicaragua

Sorting coffee beans at a
factory near Matagalpa, sister
city of Gainesville, Florida. ▶

88

At the annual poetry festival held in Ciudad Darío to honor Nicaragua's national poet of the nineteenth century, Ruben Darío. ▶

A woman prepares lunch in her kitchen in the Francisco Jardín Valley near Managua. ▼

At an artisans' collective in
Estelí, Salvadoran refugees
create hand crafted items for
sale.

Friends In Need 6

"I was among people whose basic value was to help others, to better humankind, and it helped me to realize that there are other people with this value."

Liz Diaz
Providence/Niquinohomo
Sister City Project

"The point is, I matter here," says Doug Murray, a safety inspector for the Nicaraguan Ministry of Labor, in *Where Is Nicaragua?* by Peter Davis. "In Nicaragua I feel unseparated, after a long time, from the part of myself I value most. I think the reason all of us are down here is that there's nothing going on for us now at home, and no prospects, no way to make ourselves felt in our own society. We've become strangers there. . . . Whatever part of the national character is dominant in the United States now — rolling back everything progressive, telling other countries what kind of government they're going to have — doesn't seem to include me. You get your degree and bang away at some meaningless job for a few years, or a teaching position where you feel alienated from your own subject, and you finally get so frustrated you just have to get out. You come down here and immediately your attention quickens, your energy begins to come back to you, you regain a little credibility with yourself. Meanwhile, when you read what people read in American papers every day about this so-called Leninist police state, you wonder why the invasion didn't come a year ago. You know they're not awake yet to any of the realities of life in Central America. You think to yourself, 'My God, what can I do so the folks back home won't sleep through this one?' "[1]

U.S. attitudes toward the Third World seem, on the surface, paradoxical. On the one hand, the people of the United States send billions of dollars each year to overseas charitable causes, and although attitudes about most aspects of U.S. foreign policy tend to vary with the times, surveys of public opinion consistently show a deep concern about the plight of needy people in other countries. According to one recent survey, eighty-nine percent of the American people feel that "wherever people are hungry or poor, we ought to do what we can to help them."[2] Only five percent feel that fighting world hunger is "not important." Eliminating world hunger and poverty rank far ahead of "protecting American business abroad," and even ahead of "defending our allies' security" or "matching Soviet military strength" as an international concern.[3]

Simultaneously, however, the public's attitude toward *government* foreign-aid programs has been thoroughly negative since at least the early 1970s, when pollsters began taking surveys on that question. When asked to volunteer their views of "the two or three biggest foreign-policy problems facing the nation

Four out of five Americans believe that military aid "lets dictatorships repress their own people," and five out of six believe that it "aggravates our relations with other countries" and "gets us too involved in their affairs." . . . Fifty-seven percent of the American people believe foreign-assistance projects should be financed by voluntary contributions, not taxes.

today," respondents regularly identify "reducing foreign aid" as one of their top concerns.[4] According to the Gallup polling organization, a sharp difference has emerged between the attitudes of the general public and the attitudes of individuals that pollsters designate as "opinion leaders" — prominent heads of business, the professions, the news media and labor union officials. Although over 90 percent of these leaders support foreign economic aid, the general public favors such aid by only a thin margin. Most people see foreign aid as helpful to the economies of recipient countries, but not to the United States. Moreover, they perceive it as benefiting the rich more than the poor; they doubt that it prevents communism from spreading; and 75 percent feel that it gets the U.S. "too involved in other countries' affairs."[5]

Support for foreign aid rises significantly when citizens believe the aid actually helps the people for whom it is intended, but many people have begun to question whether government foreign aid is being wisely spent. "We hear so much about projects that fail, initiatives that go sour," said ABC News anchorman Harry Reasoner in a 1974 broadcast. "Failures have become a regular part of everybody's newscasts, and there's a kind of high tide of cynicism washing the last few blooms of hope out of our country's great heart. . . . While the American government might send billions of dollars through official channels to South America, our cynical hearts tell us that all but a few of those billions of dollars probably go for stateside administrators' salaries. And the remaining few bucks might buy a Spanish-language pamphlet on 'How to Chew Gum.' "[6]

Opposition to foreign economic aid is particularly strong among people who describe themselves as conservatives. "The American government's efforts to bring relief, prosperity, and security to impoverished peoples in other countries have gone seriously wrong," writes author Nick Eberstadt in the June 1985 issue of the right-wing magazine *Commentary*. "Far from contributing to the goal of self-sustained economic progress in the low-income regions, our funds are instead being directed to a tragic extent into the construction of barriers against such progress and in some cases may actually be paying for the creation of poverty."[7] In the September 1986 issue of the conservative monthly magazine *USA Today*, James Bovard argues that "Our foreign aid has made life more pleasant and entertaining for government bureaucrats in poor countries. However, it has done little to promote the production of wealth, to breed political responsibility, or to encourage people to help themselves."[8]

Public support for foreign military aid has fallen even more sharply than support for economic aid. Although military aid to foreign countries still receives the support of a two-to-one majority among U.S. leaders, roughly the same majority within the general public *opposes* military aid. Moreover, four out of five Americans believe that military aid "lets dictatorships repress their own people," and five out of six believe that it "aggravates our relations with other countries" and "gets us too involved in their affairs." Increasingly, the people of the United States are coming to believe that aid to foreign countries should come from private rather than public sources.[9] According to a poll taken for the Overseas Development Council, 57 percent of the American people believe foreign-assistance projects should be financed by voluntary contributions, not taxes.[10]

Private aid agencies do in fact have some advantages over government agencies. According to John D. Lange, a U.S. Treasury international expert, "The field staff of private agencies live in the remote rural areas of less developed countries with the victims of underdevelopment and share their problems and aspirations. They tend to know more about what is culturally possible and whom to support in a rural community because they know their religious and social mores and motives." Private groups also find it easier to experiment and innovate than government bureaucracies.[11]

Most importantly, however, citizen-based aid tends to focus on human concerns and needs, whereas the government's primary concerns are political. In recent years, moreover, U.S. citizens have learned of outright corruption, sometimes on a massive scale, by governments that receive U.S. aid. Food aid has been diverted for military purposes; in other cases, local merchants have bought up donated food and resold it at inflated prices to their starving countrymen. Aid of this kind has not transformed antidemocratic economic control by a few into a participatory, democratic process for change. In fact, say many critics, this politically-motivated foreign aid has reinforced the primary cause of hunger and poverty — concentration of control over food-producing resources in a few hands. By bolstering the large landowners, the military, and the other forces that block change, it has made brutal, bloody confrontations even more likely.

The History of U.S. Aid

Prior to the Second World War, private citizens provided almost all U.S. foreign assistance.[12] As early as 1793, private secular agencies in the United States helped refugees and other disaster victims in Santo Domingo. In the 1820s, U.S. citizens sent aid to the Greeks during their war of independence, and in the 1840s, Americans sent over $1 million to the Irish during their famous famine. Later recipients of American private generosity have included countries such as Russia, India and China.[13]

It was the Marshall Plan for reconstruction of postwar Europe that first mobilized a national consensus in support of foreign aid as a major government activity. Led by President Harry S. Truman, the Marshall Plan poured over $13 billion into Europe and coincided with an economic revival across the continent. Truman believed that a centralized effort was necessary for the plan to succeed, and in 1946 he issued a directive "to tie together the Governmental and private programs in the field of foreign relief."

Government-sponsored "development assistance" to low-income countries began in 1949, modeled after the Marshall Plan. In the early 1950s, these programs enjoyed the overwhelming support of large constituencies including church, farm, labor and women's organizations. The Marshall Plan had seemingly demonstrated that it was possible to marry the goals of economic development, humanitarian assistance and U.S. geopolitical strategy, and on the basis of this assumption, government programs grew dramatically. Although private and voluntary organizations today still send an estimated $2 to $3 billion worth of aid overseas each year, the federal government is responsible for the great bulk of U.S.-sponsored aid, much of it delivered through the "Food for Peace" program of the State Department's Agency for International Development (AID). Since World War II, the United States government has distributed over $150 billion in economic aid to foreign countries.[14]

These postwar programs emerged in the heyday of America's international power, and they embodied the optimism of that period, a time when it was easy for U.S. citizens to see themselves as "protectors of the free world" and to imagine that people in "little countries" around the world, including Latin American

"Foreign aid consists of taking money from poor people in rich countries and giving it to rich people in poor countries."

former Congressman
Clarence Long

countries like Nicaragua, loved and looked up to them. North Americans tended to think of Latin America in particular as a sleepy, picturesque region with exotic people and customs. "Managua, Nicaragua" even became the title of a popular song of 1947 that romanticized its subject as a "city of amor" located "between the Carribean and Pacific shore" — a "beautiful town" where "you buy a hacienda for a few pesos down."[15]

The *real* Nicaragua, however, was quite different from this pleasant fantasy. Thirty-five years before "Managua, Nicaragua" was written, an occupying army of U.S. Marines had landed in Managua, disarming the Nicaraguan population and crushing all opposition to the country's U.S.-backed government. In 1927, the Marines established, officered, equipped, trained and financed the Nicaraguan National Guard, whose chief, Anastasio Somoza García, made himself dictator by arranging the murder of his most prominent opponent, General Augusto C. Sandino. The year the song was popularized by Guy Lombardo and his Royal Canadians, Somoza used a rigged election to ensure the victory of his official candidate for the presidency. Under his rule, Nicaragua became what journalist John Gerassi described in the early 1960s as "by far the worst" country in Central America:

> It is so poor and rundown that one corner of Managua's main square, where Congress, the cathedral, the tourist headquarters, and the oligarchy's club are located, is an empty lot. Along main Roosevelt Avenue are a few stores and a hotel or two, the swankiest of which (the Gran Hotel) is an ugly, hot, wooden monstrosity that, except for its swimming pool, would compare adversely with a dozen Times Square roach dens.
>
> The only impressive buildings are located on top of a hill at the other end of Roosevelt Avenue from main square. There stand two huge palaces: the President's and the National Guard commander's. Around them on one side are officers' quarters, barricades, fortifications, checkpoints, and fences. In back, after a hundred-foot precipice, is a small lake where Managua's womenfolk gather, coming from the far side, to wash their clothes. And between the military installations and the lake, on the only exposed flank, is, appropriately, the United States Embassy complex.
>
> Aside from these buildings, Managua and the rest of Nicaragua is a filthy, year-long-hot, depressing hovel where only high military officers and a few well-connected oligarchs can escape the misery around them by flocking to the plush air-conditioned country club which, though not a military but a private club, is guarded by soldiers. But then, the whole country is run by soldiers — for the Somozas.[16]

Somoza and his sons ruled virtually unchallenged in Nicaragua until 1979, during which time they routinely used armed force to break strikes and assassinate political enemies. Peasants were cruelly tortured. During their 45 years in power, the Somozas accumulated wealth estimated at $400 to $500 million. Meanwhile, half the country's population was illiterate. One in three infants born to poor Nicaraguans died before the age of one. Eighty percent of the population had no running water. More than 20,000 Nicaraguans suffered from advanced tuberculosis. The country had one doctor for every 2,000 people.

For those government officials within the United States who understood what was happening in Nicaragua, however, these sordid aspects of the Somoza regime were less important than Somoza's willingness to place his country at the service of United States "foreign interests." Although the first Somoza openly admired Hitler, he quickly joined the Allied cause when the United States entered World War II. In the 1950s, Nicaraguan territory was used to train people for the CIA-sponsored overthrow of Guatemala's government, and Nicaragua served again as one of the U.S. staging bases for the Bay of Pigs invasion of Cuba in 1961. In addition to these political and military favors, the Somozas opened Nicaragua up to U.S. financial interests. At one point over 90 percent of Nicaragua's exports went to the United States. The picture of a U.S. ambassador was printed on Nicaraguan currency, and United States corporations owned a sizeable percentage of Nicaraguan property. "Somoza is a son of a bitch," said President Franklin D. Roosevelt, "but he's *our* son of a bitch."[17]

But although cynicism and even callousness circulated within high government circles, the majority of the American people were more naive than cynical, just as it was naiveté about the Third World, not selfishness, that led soldiers like Philip Caputo to enlist in the Vietnam war. "We went overseas full of illusions, for which the intoxicating atmosphere of those years was as much to blame as our youth," Caputo writes in his book, A *Rumor of War*. "War is always attractive to young men who know nothing about it, but we had also been seduced into uniform by Kennedy's challenge to 'ask what you can do for your country' and by the missionary idealism he had awakened in us. America seemed omnipotent then: the country could still claim it had never lost a war, and we believed we were ordained to play cop to the Communists' robber and spread our own political faith around the world. . . . We carried, along with our packs and rifles, the implicit convictions that the Viet Cong would be quickly beaten and that we were doing something altogether noble and good. We kept the packs and rifles; the convictions, we lost."[18]

From the mid-1960s to the early 1970s, South Vietnam received the bulk of U.S. economic aid. By 1966, Vietnam was receiving over 43 percent of the government's worldwide development grants, in the form of projects such as the "strategic hamlet" and "civilian relocation" programs. While labeled "humanitarian," they in fact served military objectives and contributed to a growing "credibility gap," as U.S. citizens became aware of contradictions between official descriptions of these programs and their reality in practice.[19]

This change in awareness is one of the major barriers that has prevented President Reagan's personal popularity from translating into public support for the contra war against Nicaragua. Reagan has described the contras as "the moral equivalent of our founding fathers," and in public speeches, he has frequently and passionately denounced the Sandinistas for turning Nicaragua into "a second Cuba, a second Libya," a "totalitarian dungeon," a "Soviet beachhead in Central America." He has accused them of supplying weapons to terrorists, smuggling cocaine, persecuting Jews, building secret prisons, and beating Catholics in the streets for attending Mass. But no set of events and no level of presidential pleading has managed even to dent the roughly two-to-one majority by which the American people consistently oppose aid to the contras. At the peak of Reagan's popularity in April 1986, shortly before Congress voted in favor of $100 million in contra aid, a *New York Times/CBS News* poll showed that only one in four Americans supported such aid, while sixty-two percent opposed it. "Even those who approved of the way Mr. Reagan was handling his job as President — a very strong 64 percent of the total — rejected aid to the contras by a margin of 52 to 35 percent," the *Times* reported. "Those who described themselves as conservatives opposed it by 57 to 30 percent and

"Opposition to aid for the contras crossed all political, ethnic and regional and socio-economic lines. No demographic group favored it."

New York Times/CBS News poll
April 1986

Republicans by 51 to 36 percent. . . . Opposition to aid for the contras crossed all political, ethnic and regional and socio-economic lines. No demographic group favored it." And "when a suggestion was made to include American personnel in the aid, the survey showed support for American involvement dropping sharply. The 25 percent who favored funds to the contras fell to 16 percent when asked whether they would favor American military advisors if the money 'did not work.' Then, if advisors 'did not work,' they were asked whether they would favor sending United States combat troops. Only 10 percent said yes."[20]

Disillusionment and Discovery

Unfortunately, however, opposition to contra aid is often motivated by feelings other than friendship for the people of Nicaragua. One recent analysis of public opinion revealed that Americans today hold extremely negative feelings about Central America. They perceive the region as a "jungle" — hot, dirty, foreign, impenetrable; full of poverty, hatred, corruption, disease and killing. Most Americans picture contras and Sandinistas in almost identical terms: "unshaven," "sweaty," "dark," "Spanish-looking," "a bandoleer of ammo," "wearing fatigues," "militaristic," "jungle gypsies." Neither side in Nicaragua seems worthy of their concern; instead, they worry about the cost to taxpayers and the danger of U.S. involvement in "another Vietnam."

These concerns have reinforced an isolationist attitude among some Americans, who express bitterness in their belief that "we're always trying to be the good guys and then people kick us in the face." Many people simply believe the United States should concentrate its energies and resources on solving problems at home. "If I hear Nicaragua mentioned one more time, I'm going to scream," said one caller to a radio program in 1987. "Why should I care? We need to take care of our own people before we worry about what's happening all over the world."

But the war in Central America has also produced a sort of "Vietnam syndrome in reverse" for those U.S. citizens who have joined the movement for friendship with Nicaragua. Rather than retaining their rifles and losing their convictions, U.S. citizens are returning from Central America with their convictions strengthened and their idealism renewed. "My trip gave me tremendous hope that people under all kinds of circumstances were still able, in some form or another, to do the best that they could," said Martin Lepkowski of West Kingston, Rhode Island, who visited Nicaragua in July, 1987. "What I saw empowered me, because I saw how people had to live and still they survived."[21]

Only God and political ideologues can predict with confidence what type of society will eventually emerge as a result of the Nicaraguan revolution. Critics point out that the Sandinistas have at times censored news media and jailed political opponents. On the other hand, the revolution has stimulated a flowering of traditional culture, with a massive and highly successful literacy campaign and popular workshops to teach dance, poetry, painting and other forms of expression; and years of revolutionary struggle have made the Nicaraguan people so outspoken in criticizing their government that many observers wonder whether the country is even capable of returning to the atmosphere of sullen silence that characterized political discourse under Somoza.

Economically, Nicaragua is in a severe crisis; on top of the billions of dollars in disruptions and damage caused by war, it has suffered from a U.S. trade embargo and from a sharp drop in international prices for its major export commodities. In 1987, the country's inflation rate reached 1,800 percent, and shortages of basic staples such as rice, beans, cooking oil, eggs and toilet paper were commonplace. In 1988, the government began a number of dramatic economic reforms, devaluing the national currency by a ratio of 1,000 to 1, and even these desperate measures seemed inadequate to stem the crisis. And yet Nicaragua is also blessed with abundant physical resources: fertile soil, beautiful countryside, valuable minerals, and volcanos capable of generating enough geothermal electricity to supply the entire region of Central America. With time, an end to the war, hard work, and wise policies, Nicaragua could conceivably become an economic miracle.

"In Nicaragua one feels an intense participation in the country, not just because life is poor and elemental, but because the country is caught up in an effort to overcome its marginality," said William Warren of Providence, Rhode Island, after visiting his sister city of Niquinohomo. "The hopelessness one typically feels when faced with relentless poverty is replaced by a kind of wild hope that this country might be able to dig its way out, to challenge the partnership of exploitation and atrocity that has maintained the chasm of privilege throughout Central America."[22]

But with the war consuming over half the national budget, Nicaragua's "survival economy" has no surplus for long-term developmental projects. "Frankly, the only way out we have right now is international cooperation," said Maria Teresa Illescas, the former director of international relations for the Managua mayor's office. "We look at the sister-city relationships as really crucial, and as one of the ways that we can develop from underdevelopment."

Groups working to assist Nicaragua have discovered that their assistance makes a real difference. "You experience great joy when you close up a truck loaded with 20 tons of supplies that you know will help the people in your sister city," says Brooks Smith of Central New Jersey, which has a sister relationship with Nicaragua's Masaya region. And even small contributions can solve some of the pressing problems caused by Nicaragua's inability to obtain spare parts for machinery purchased in the United States. "Sometimes a factory has to stop producing for lack of a single part," said former Managua Mayor Moisés Hassan. "Machinery will go out of whack because of oil filters, for example."

Many North Americans and Europeans have been attracted to Nicaragua precisely *because* the country is passing through a social transformation. The old rules that governed life under Somoza have fallen, and new rules have not fully established themselves. As they search for solutions to their problems, Nicaraguans are often willing to innovate and experiment with ideas that other countries might pass over.

In the field of agriculture, for example, the high cost of insecticides and problems with environmental contamination have attracted North American ecologists who are interested in developing alternatives to chemical pesticides. The U.S.-Canadian Group for New Agriculture has been sending technicians to Nicaragua since 1981. In León, they are exploring the possibility of producing industrial quantities of *bacillus thuringiensis*, a bacteria that destroys certain crop-damaging pests, while an entomologist is testing the use of ants to control pests. In Managua, a soil specialist is working on a program to partially replace plowing with other methods of cultivation and weed control. "Students, peasants, state institutions, the government — everyone is really interested in these projects, pushing for them to work," said Kathy Savoie, an ecologist from Michigan.

Her group has carried out similar projects in Mexico and Costa Rica, but despite the enthusiasm of the peasants involved in those projects, they encountered indifference among people with the ability to apply the new techniques on a large scale. "That's how it is in the United States, also," Savoie said. "You can probably get funding for any project, but there are few opportunities to put it into practice. It's frustrating. We could be doing these investigations somewhere else than in Nicaragua, but they would be simply academic studies."

Another group called Bikes Not Bombs (BNB) began in July 1984 when Carl Kurz, a bicycle mechanic, decided to combine his interest in Nicaragua with his belief in bicycles as an environmentally sound means of transportation. Nicaragua has no oil reserves and has to import both fuel and vehicles from other countries, and as a result, the country's economic crisis has created enormous transportation problems. Kurz noted that bicycles provide up to 85 percent of the transportation in India and Asia, and argued that "if the Nicaraguan government promotes the bicycle in a mass-transportation campaign, then they wouldn't have to rely on imports of petroleum or vehicles.

"Transportation takes place in a social, economic and political and cultural context," Kurz said. "All too often people who make decisions about developing transportation systems in the Third World are those who are rich and powerful. In Central America only 13 out of 1,000 people can afford an automobile, but the World Bank, the American Institute for Development and other institutions are constantly pushing the concept of motorized transportation because the major auto industries are looking to the Third World and Latin America as a potential future source for 60 to 70 percent of their profits. In Nicaragua, poor people now participate in decisions that affect their lives, but they are still affected by lack of access to information about alternative technology concepts. I felt that if they had the right information, they would see the advantages of adopting a mixed-mode transportation system incorporating different methods of transportation, an affordable system that would give all sectors of the population access to mobility."

Largely through word of mouth, Kurz and co-founder Michael Replogle succeeded in establishing Bikes Not Bombs chapters in California, Massachusetts, Colorado, Minnesota, and Washington, D.C. In January and February of 1985, a crew of mechanics representing the various chapters assembled and donated their first shipment of 110 bikes to representatives of Nicaragua's teachers' and health care unions as a means of delivering education and medical services to Nicaragua's countryside. Since that time, dozens of Bikes Not Bombs chapters have formed throughout the U.S., Canada and England, and have sent over 1500 bicycles.

"Along the way, someone gave us the idea of having each group that solicits bikes from us send a letter to the Nicaraguan Ministry of Transportation to show how demand for bicycles is growing," said Paul Martin, a Boston bike mechanic who served as coordinator of the group's Managua workshop. The Bikes Not Bombs campaign began to receive repeated coverage in the Nicaraguan news media, attracting demand for bicycles and repair services far in excess of what BNB could offer from its own resources. In June of 1987, Transportation Minister William Ramirez visited the BNB shop, accompanied by a news media entourage, and used the occasion to announce that Nicaragua would import 50,000 bikes over the next five years as a way of reducing its dependency upon imported petroleum.

Begun as a project that made outright donations, BNB is shifting now to providing developmental aid, helping to create a bicycle industry in Nicaragua that will make it possible for Nicaraguans to purchase their own bikes at affordable prices. Donated bikes are sold to Nicaraguan organizations for considerably less than the prices for which most bikes sell on the Nicaraguan black market, and money earned from sales is used to cover the costs of a bike assembly and repair shop in Managua, which provides jobs for several Nicaraguan residents. In 1988, Kurz was making plans to open up additional shops, including one in Estelí and another under the sponsorship of the New Haven/León Sister City Project, in which emphasis would be put on training Nicaraguans as well as refugees from other parts of Central America.

"We started as a handful of people with the dream of sending a small donation of bicycles to aid health and education efforts in Nicaragua," Kurz said. "That dream has broadened. We are expanding into a vital logistical network of assembly and repair shops, and we are creating the first mixed-mode transportation system on the American continent."

◀ José Francisco, an employee at the Bikes Not Bombs workshop in Managua. Bikes Not Bombs promotes alternative technology solutions for Nicaragua's transportation problems.

Carl Kurz discusses the impact of recent government economic reforms on employee salaries and benefits with workers at the Bikes Not Bombs shop. ▼

A disabled war veteran ▲
performs leg-strengthening
exercises as part of his
rehabilitation at the Aldo
Chavarria Rehabilitation
Hospital in Managua.

Walter John Chilsen,
Republican State Senator
from Wausau, Wisconsin,
hugs a child at the Rolando
Carazo Zeledón Orphanage,
which receives contributions
through a "godparent
project" sponsored by the
Ecumenical Refugee Council
of Milwaukee. Senator
Chilsen became concerned
about U.S. policy in
Nicaragua in part because of
his daughter Liz's experiences
in her first visit there. ▶

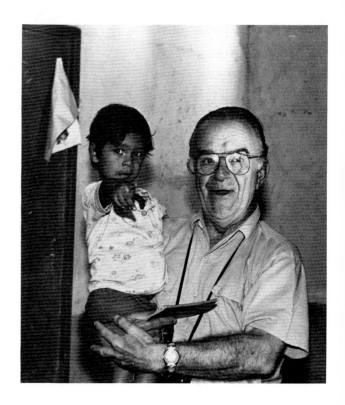

102

This dental clinic and ▶
supplies were donated to
the health center in Barrio
Riguero, Managua by
Medical Aid to Nicaragua
of Milwaukee.

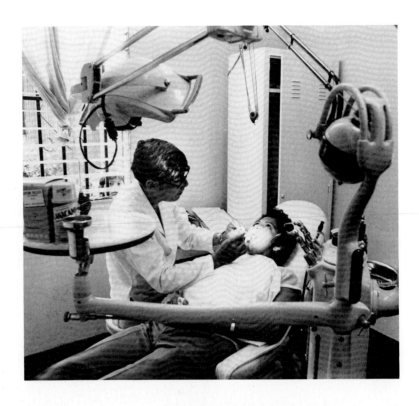

Raymond Daffner, a
TECNICA volunteer from
Connecticut teaching
computer programming to
Fidel Campos, Mario Gonza-
lez and Gabriel Gailán in
Managua. ▼

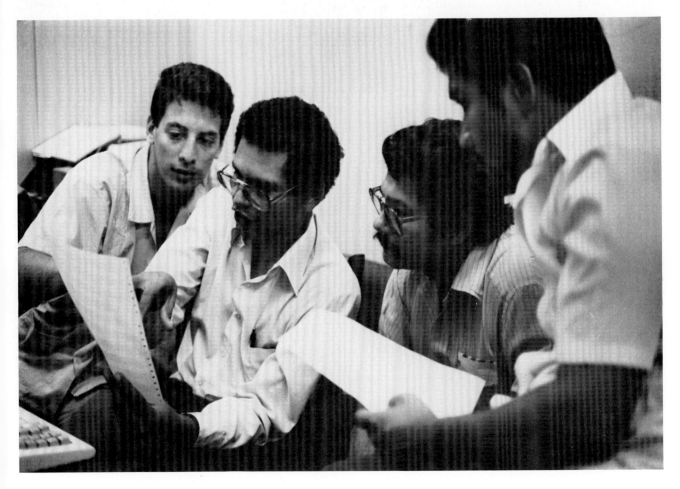

In Malpaisillo, health clinic
nurses rely upon supplies
from their sister city of
Pittsfield, Massachusetts.

Helping Hands 7

Over 600 organizations and thousands of individuals throughout the United States are actively working on projects to help the people of Nicaragua. Sometimes highly imaginative, these projects come in all sizes and address a variety of concerns. Nursing home residents have donated individual bars of soap, and computer professionals have installed entire data processing systems. School children have sent crayons and note paper; churches have sent Bibles; in Georgia, a group called PJs for Peace and Justice has sent pajamas, hoping to give some comfort to children in the midst of war; in San Francisco, gay and lesbian people organized a project called "Condoms Not Contras" which sent thousands of contraceptives to promote safe-sex campaigns. Economists, librarians, welders and architects have all found ways of contributing their skills, both as workers and as teachers.

"Not everyone has the same degree of commitment and interest in Nicaragua," says Elizabeth Sander of Project Minnesota/León. "We try to have a multi-tiered approach, with a variety of projects that enable people to become involved at their own level."

Since its founding in 1984, Project Minnesota/León has sent over $600,000 worth of material aid to León, through projects such as the following:

- Medicines, supplies, spare parts and teaching materials to a hospital and teaching center affiliated with the León university.

- Supplies for a rehabilitation center where former prostitutes are taught sewing and tailoring skills.

- Dental supplies, spare parts and teaching materials for the university dental school.

- Sports equipment and financing for library books at the LaSalle Technical Institute; sports materials and supplies for an elementary school.

- Playground and educational supplies for handicapped children at a special education center.

- Educational and crafts materials at a delinquency prevention center, which offers positive direction for "high risk" children.

- Books and supplies for story and art workshops at the León public library.

"If we just go up to people and start talking about 'imperialism' or 'the contras,' it doesn't mean a lot. But when you tell them that Nicaraguan women don't have sanitary napkins, they immediately understand what the blockade means, and you don't need to use statistics."

Phil Westman, Tools for Peace, Canada

- New or used musical instruments, supplies and sheet music for the León Municipal Band.
- Financing for the final stage of constructing housing for 38 families who were flooded out of their previous homes.
- Chemicals, supplies and tools for the regional Water Department to use in testing the quality of drinking water.
- Swimsuits and supplies for the León swim team.
- Toys, diapers and supplies for city and rural child care centers.
- Supplies for regional recreational events to benefit war orphans.
- Financing for improving León's park facilities and the "Arlen Siu" zoo.
- Seeds and other supplies for primary school children to use in raising gardens, learning basic agricultural skills and improving their diet.
- Medicine and supplies for the "El Jicaral" rural health center and four satellite health posts.
- Recreational and school supplies for the "San Martín" elementary school in Nagarote.
- Financing for a well and pump for the "Cristo Rey" agricultural cooperative and the surrounding rural community.
- Sewing machines, fabric and other supplies for a women's sewing collective in the village of Malpaisillo.

Sander has no illusions of transforming the Nicaraguan economy through these projects. "We have no intention of developing Nicaragua. In the first place, we're just not capable of doing that," she says. "The purpose of all our projects is to make personal connections. For example, within the water testing project we have pen-pal relationships between water technicians in Minnesota and technicians in León. Our main concern is with educating people back home. I don't want to be the person who sees to it that the Nicaraguans get cement for their housing project. I want to be the link who establishes connections between the people in Nicaragua and people in the United States. Material aid is a way to establish that connection, not an end in itself. But unfortunately, the needs of the people here are so great that sometimes the educational aspects get forgotten in the effort to meet those needs."

General Guidelines

International aid organizations recommend the following principles for material aid projects in Nicaragua and other Third World countries:

- Listening to the Nicaraguan people is very important, and listening to the appropriate Nicaraguan *institution* is very important also. A project should have a Nicaraguan institutional counterpart, such as a hospital, school, church or municipal government. This contributes to the continuity and permanency of a project, helps to guarantee accountability, and ensures that it will benefit an entire community of people rather than isolated individuals.
- Use appropriate technology, local materials and labor as much as possible. Imported materials are sometimes helpful and necessary, but projects should not promote dependency on imported aid.
- Be sure to solicit feedback and evaluation of the project's results.

"$7.40 will buy two six-packs of Rainier beer. But it could also be used to send 200 4"x4" sterile gauze sponges to Acahualinca Clinic in Nicaragua. With $10 you could take yourself and a friend to go see 'Top Gun.' But that ten spot will also purchase 100 tubes of Neosporin antibiotic skin ointment to send to our sister clinic. Two people could enjoy a night on the town for $50. But with the same money they could eat steak at home and still send 400 3ml syringes to Hospital Fernando Velez Paiz to aid pediatric burn patients."

Seattle/Managua Sister City flyer

- Provide a mechanism to train Nicaraguans to carry out the program, and a mechanism for maintenance of donated materials.

If this is your first material aid effort, you will want to begin with a small project that has clear, concretely defined objectives and easily attainable goals that can be accomplished within a short time period. Seeing a project to quick completion provides important positive reinforcement to both U.S. and Nicaraguan counterparts, and provides a solid base for growth.

Donations

It is important to evaluate the needs of the Nicaraguan people prior to shipping supplies, as the experience of Burlington, Vermont demonstrates. Through its highly successful sister city relationship with Puerto Cabezas on Nicaragua's Atlantic Coast, Burlington has sent several major shipments of donations. Early in the relationship, however, problems arose after a local hospital underwent renovations and donated large quantities of surplus medical equipment to the project. "We raised $250,000 in medical equipment and shipped it down in March of 1986," said Burlington resident Bob Scott. "When it arrived, our biggest question was whether the old wooden structure of the Puerto Cabezas hospital could handle the weight of all our equipment. One of the most expensive pieces of equipment was a gas sterilizer, which was almost dumped because it didn't match their technology. We had to look for a way to convert it to steam before they could use it."

Roy Wilson of the Seattle-Managua project advises groups to avoid the "rummage sale" approach where "people go out and find second-hand or surplus supplies that aren't specifically asked for. Face-to-face communication has made our material aid campaigns more efficient. Medical people here in Seattle have spearheaded drives for very specific pieces of medical equipment for hospitals in Nicaragua, which Nicaraguans themselves have determined that they need."

On the other hand, your project may have easy access to supplies which, though inappropriate for your sister city, are desperately needed somewhere else. Several "interest-affiliated" networks function on a national basis that can help identify needs and match them to your available resources. These include health networks such as the National Central American Health Rights Network (NCAHRN); the Let Nicaragua Live Campaign which focuses primarily on helping war refugees; Oxfam America, which focuses on the problem of hunger by sending agricultural tools and supplies; and "godparent projects" which invite sponsors to adopt Nicaraguan orphans with a monthly pledge of $10 or $20. For details and addresses, see the directory of interest-affiliated groups at the back of this book.

It is also important to make sure that sister programs don't create a situation of privilege for some communities while others go without. This problem can arise if you try to bypass existing channels that identify needs and set priorities. The mayor's office in your sister city is one such channel; the national government of Nicaragua is another.

The most important aspect of a material aid project is its educational value and the friendships it engenders across cultures. Include information about yourselves with your donations — photographs, letters, maps, descriptions of your city, school or workplace. "We even send pictures of the packaging parties. It helps make our process more clear to the Nicaraguans," says NCAHRN's

Chris Jasper. Also include envelopes, paper and postage so the Nicaraguans can write back.

In Port Townsend, Washington, donations were collected from elementary, junior high and high-school students as part of an extended study project in "contemporary world problems" taught by Port Townsend teacher Jim Roberts. After learning about their sister city of Jalapa through class study and independent research, high school students themselves became "teachers for a day" by speaking to students in the lower grade levels. They passed out large clasp envelopes to each younger student, which the intermediate and grade school students decorated with crayons and felt-tip pen drawings and then stuffed with pictures and information about themselves, their families and Port Townsend, in addition to gifts of school supplies.[1]

"It's neat to see kids learning. They really take it in and listen," said high school student Joe D'Amico after his experience as a teacher. "If these kids learn to grow up and care, maybe the next generation will turn out better so more people will like each other. Our educational system doesn't help you get along with other countries; we just learn how to be the best, instead of helping them."

"The children were so excited to have the opportunity to do something for less fortunate children that we were amazed. Every envelope was filled to bursting and beautifully decorated on the outside," said teachers at the Grant Street School, in a letter commenting on the project.[2]

Roberts said he made a conscious effort to "keep it real apolitical and focus on the humanitarian issue." But some groups use material aid to make a political statement by piling packages of collected donations in front of their congressional district office before shipping. Sometimes this has included civil disobedience, such as a "pack-in" at a local office.

Shipping

The simplest way to send general humanitarian goods to Nicaragua is to work through the Quixote Center, an independent, Catholic-based social justice organization situated near Washington, D.C. The Quixote Center coordinates a nationwide campaign called "Quest for Peace," which began in 1984 after the CIA bombed oil storage facilities in Nicaragua's port city of Corinto. "Peggy Healy, a religious sister from the United States who lives in Nicaragua, asked if we could organize some sort of relief effort," says Quest coordinator John Kellenberg. "We got together boxes of medical supplies and hand carried them down. Since then, we've shipped over $50 million worth of supplies." Quest for Peace also conducts a national tally of U.S.-Nicaraguan humanitarian aid projects, which succeeded in matching the $100 million in military aid sent by Congress to the contras during the 1986-87 period.

For a list of items that can be sent through Quest for Peace, see the section below on "What to Send." The following guidelines hold for all donations:

- Careful sorting, packing and labeling of donations is crucial. For each box in a shipment, label all six sides in large letters, stating the contents and numbering the boxes (i.e., 1 of 10, 2 of 10, 3 of 10, etc.). Be sure to put your return address, including name and phone number, on the boxes.
- Donations of small items should be in bulk quantities.
- Equipment of different types should be boxed separately for ease of distribution in Nicaragua. Test all machinery to see that it is in working order prior

to shipping. Include any accessories needed for operation, such as extra paper, spare parts, etc. Likewise, each piece of machinery should be accompanied by instructions and repair manuals, in Spanish if available.

- Nicaragua uses 110 Volt, 60 Hz electricity, the same as is standard in the United States. If you send electrically-powered equipment, it may be helpful to include a power surge suppressor (available for $10-$15 in most hardware stores) to avoid damage caused by uneven current.

- Money to cover shipping costs should accompany any donations that you wish to send.

The Quixote Center currently sends one 20-ton seagoing container (measuring 40'x8'x8') to Nicaragua every week. They provide one possible channel through which you can ship general types of donations. Due to the large number of groups contributing, however, they are swamped with requests and do not usually have the time or resources to direct specific donations to specific locations such as your sister city. Quixote organizers have advised sister cities to develop their own network for transporting and distributing supplies, and a number of projects have already established shipping channels and warehouses. The Center can help put you in touch with such a group in your region. Even if you decide to ship aid on your own, the Quixote Center can provide useful advice. Their address is: 3311 Chauncey Place, #301, Mt. Rainier, MD 20712; phone (301) 699-0042.

Whatever channel you use, it will be your group's responsibility to pay for the shipping expenses associated with your donations. These costs currently amount to roughly $450/ton, or $3.50 per cubic foot.

One very simple way to transport small donations is to hand-carry them in your luggage when you visit Nicaragua. Good items for suitcase donations are medications, bandages, small equipment like a microscope, centrifuge or slide projector, and surgical tools. If you decide to carry goods, follow these rules:

- Prepare a comprehensive list of everything and carry it with you.

- Give a copy of the list to the Nicaraguan Embassy at least 20 days before the trip (so they can help get the goods through customs).

- State the name of the recipient organization on the package and clearly label it as a donation.

- If you are carrying a large stock of goods, it is preferable to work with a contact from the recipient group in Nicaragua who can meet you at the airport.

- Insist on staying with the goods at all times. If the suitcase must be left in customs or if the baggage arrives late, save the luggage claim check and be prepared to go back the next day or send someone back for the luggage.

Residents of Boulder, Colorado found another simple but creative way of transporting donations: they loaded up an old truck and drove it down to their sister city of Jalapa. This turned out to be quite an adventure, due to the physical and emotional toughness of driving long distances along unfamiliar roads. Before making the trip, Boulder organizers contacted Mexican consular officials in the United States in order to obtain official endorsement for the trip and arranging for pre-approved and stamped truck inventories. In addition, they received a letter of assistance from a Mexican customs official which helped avoid the necessity of bribing police and other officials along the way.

"The needs in León that they first presented to us were a steamroller and a convention center. We told them, 'Those things are very important, but a sister-city committee is usually not able to transport a steamroller or build a convention center.' Through communication with Nicaraguan groups, we tried to develop a very long laundry list, with the Nicaraguans' understanding that just because it's on the list doesn't mean it's going to come to pass. We used the list to give ourselves as many options as possible in approaching different sectors of the community."

Alan Wright
New Haven/León Sister City Project

Due to the Reagan administration's economic embargo against Nicaragua, some goods cannot be sent directly, and the embargo has virtually ended all forms of commercial transportation originating from the United States. So far, the embargo has not been used to block the shipment of most humanitarian goods, but you may wish to check with an experienced group before sending items about which you have questions.

One way to deal with the difficulty of transportation is to simply send money. While this form of aid might seem to take away from the popular dynamic of gathering donations within your community, it can be very effective aid, particularly in regions which are directly affected by the war. In the first place, war-related inflation has multiplied the value of U.S. dollars in relation to Nicaraguan currency. Secondly, donations of material goods take several months to gather, package and transport, by which time the priority of needs within a community may change as a result of the disruptions caused by war — sudden destruction of property, unexpected refugees with unplanned needs. Money may seem less "personal" than other types of donations, but it provides a means of responding quickly to the often desperate situations which arise.

What to Send

If your group is just getting started and hasn't had a chance yet to visit your sister city or identify its specific needs, you can still begin helping the people of Nicaragua. Several U.S. groups serve as shipping channels for items that are in general short supply throughout Nicaragua. If contributed through a non-profit organization such as Oxfam America or Quest for Peace, both cash contributions and in-kind donations of material aid are tax-deductible. (Note: If you intend to take a tax deduction, the IRS may require an independent appraisal or other documentation of the fair-market value of donated items.)

In a single afternoon, you can put together a package of school supplies that will equip 20 Nicaraguan students for four months. Fill a box with the following items: 80 pencils, 20 pencil pouches, 80 pieces of chalk, 3 chalk erasers, 20 boxes of crayons, 10 felt markers, 7 rulers, 1 box thumbtacks/push pins, 5 small pairs scissors, 40 spiral composition books, 200 sheets of 8 1/2"x11" construction paper, 10 sheets of poster board, 3 rolls masking tape, 3 rolls of shelf paper (for book covers), 3 wall maps of the world/Western hemisphere; 3 Spanish-to-Spanish dictionaries, 1 pencil sharpener, 5 rolls assorted crepe paper, and 2 picture magazines (such as National Geographic). Seal the box shut and send it, along with a $10 donation to defray shipping costs, to the American Friends Service Committee School Supplies Campaign, 1501 Cherry Street, Philadelphia, PA 19102. The value of your contribution will be tax-deductible.

The following items can be sent through the "Quest For Peace" campaign of the Quixote Center (see "Shipping" above):

Medicines. Analgesics; anesthetics (local and general); antiarrhythmics; antibiotics; anticoagulents; anticonvulsants; antidiarrheals; antiemetics; antifungal cremes; antihistimines; antihypertensives; antiinflamatories; antimalarials; antiparasitics; antispasmotics; antitoxins; bronchodialators; diuretics; expectorants; eyewash; ferrous sulfate; florinated steroid cremes; gastrointestinal; hormones; hydrocortisone cremes; immunizations; mercurochrome solution; skin ointments; TB and mantoux tests; vaginal creams/suppositories; Vitamin E oil; vitamins.

Medical Supplies. Adhesive tape, any size; alcohol; arteriogram syringes and needles; bandaids; batteries for opthalmoscopes; betadine; blood pressure cuffs; blood tubes; catgut; catheters; clinic scales/bathroom scales; crash carts; disposable gloves, both sterile and nonsterile; doptone; EKG machines; endotrachial tubes; epidural kits; fetascopes; feverstrips; file boxes; foley catheters; gauze—any size; hemoglobinometer; hemolysis sticks; ice bags; incubators; infant scales—prefer spring and hook; instruments for minor surgery—clamps, forceps, scalpels, suture holders; intravenous catheters, solutions, tubes; laryngoscopes; lumbar puncture kits; masks; measuring tapes; nasogastric tubes; obstetrical forceps; opthalmascopes; otoscopes; peroxide; scissors; specimen containers; speculums; splint and cast supplies; stethoscopes; suction tubes; suture; syringe needles; syringes—3, 5, 10cc; thermometers; thoracentesis; urine dip sticks; wheelchairs; X-ray film, developer, fixadent. *NOTE: See "Medical Aid" section below for shipping guidelines.*

Educational Supplies. Pencils and pens; notebooks and binders; crayons and markers; rulers; paper—all kinds; thumbtacks; paper clips; scissors; glue; rulers; chalk; children's books in Spanish.

Tools. pliers; wirecutters; screwdrivers; wrenches; hammers; rubber boots; saws; screws; nails; wire; electrical wire; tape — all kinds; batteries — all sizes; pocket calculators; drafting and surveying tools; drills and drill bits.

Clothing. Send clothes appropriate to Nicaragua's weather, which is warm and frequently rainy. In general, only summer and fall weight clothing is needed. Particularly useful items include: any type of children's clothing; house dresses for women; shoes (Nicaraguans are generally smaller than North Americans: Men's—size 9 and under, Women's—size 6 and under); pants, T-shirts, and shirts; blankets; fabric, needles, and thread. All clothing *must* be in good condition — good quality, clean, and mended. Sort your clothing into three categories: men's, women's and children's. Pack the clothing tightly into boxes and tape them shut. Write "Men's Clothing," "Women's Clothing" or "Children's Clothing" on the outside of the boxes.

Investigate local clothing companies. Often they have excess fabric, thread, or clothes that they may want to donate for a tax deduction.

Sending Agricultural Supplies

The following list of items has been developed in close cooperation with Nicaraguan farmers, and represents their most urgent and specific needs. In the past, these items have been shipped through Oxfam America. All items to be shipped must be of durable quality and in first-rate condition. Please don't send broken or worn-out equipment.

Hand Tools. Spaces, shovels, pick-axe heads, eye-hoes (no handles), hand saws, sharpening files, axes (prefer double-bit), fencing tools and staples, sharpening files (3/4" knife, 1/2" triangular, hacksaws and pruning saws, hammers and wrenches (all sizes), screwdrivers (flat and phillips), tap and die sets, mechanics' tool kits, chainsaws, spare chains and files.

Irrigation. Water pumps (all sizes, diesel and 110V electric), hoses, tubing and ring clamps, aluminum pipe with couplings, sprinklers with connectors, PVC tubing with sleeves and cement, 55 gallon drums (with tight lids).

Livestock Supplies. Horseshoes (pony to mid-sized), 1½" horseshoe nails, hoof rasps, milk cans, (5, 10 gallon and larger), stationary forage choppers, veterinary tools (e.g., syringes and needles, forceps, stomach pumps, suturing needles, clamps, catgut, scalpels, scissors, stethoscopes, gloves, nosegrips.

Office and Training Supplies. Typewriters (manual and electric), mimeograph machines and supplies (stencils, ink, correction fluid), electrostencil machines, bond paper, desk supplies (tape, staplers, staples, rubber bands, whiteout, pens, pencils, erasers, etc.), solar calculators and small desk calculators with tape, 35mm cameras with flash and film.

Pest Management. Backyard garden sprayers (with good nozzles, gaskets, and hoses), synthetic or rubber boots, face masks and gloves.

Tillage and Transport. Rotortillers and hand cultivators, tractors (diesel only), tractor drawn implements, harrow discs and bearings, trucks and pickups (prefer diesel), flat drive belts (2"-4" wide, all lengths), fasteners and gum, tractor and truck tires and tubes, forklifts, welders, hydraulic jacks, solderless electric connectors.

Sending Donations of Medical Aid

The National Central American Health Rights Network (NCAHRN) coordinates shipments of medical aid nationwide. Their address is: NCAHRN, 853 Broadway, Suite 416, New York, NY 10003; phone (212) 420-9635. NCAHRN offers the following guidelines for sending medical donations:

- Careful sorting, packing and labeling of donations is essential. It is also crucial to evaluate the usefulness of each item before sending.
- Contact NCAHRN for the address of an office in your region through which you can ship donations.
- Boxes must be conspicuously numbered (example: 1 of 5, 2 of 5, etc.) and labeled with the contents listed in Spanish on the outside.
- Two copies apiece of an inventory form (available from the NCAHRN national office) and a bill of lading in English and Spanish listing all the parcels in the shipment by number must accompany each shipment. Send a third copy on to the NCAHRN national office which will assist in the Quest for Peace national tally of all material aid sent.

Medicines. The items listed on pages 110-111 above are in general need throughout Nicaragua and can be shipped through Quest for Peace. For information about other needs, contact NCAHRN. The following guidelines apply to all donations:

- Expiration dates must be at least nine months (but preferably two years) from the day they are to be shipped.
- Different medications should be boxed separately for ease of distribution. If they must be mixed, sort them by type of drug (i.e., analgesics, anti-hypertensives).
- Donations should be in bulk quantities (i.e., a minimum of a few thousand tablets). Smaller quantities can be hand-delivered to an individual clinic.
- Generally, medications most needed in Nicaragua are those used most commonly. There is no great need for the latest state-of-the-art pharmaceutical product that is little known in Nicaragua.

- Physicians' samples are not appropriate unless sorted into larger quantities. Their packaging is bulky, they come in small quantities and may not be a priority item.

Equipment and Supplies. Unless specifically cleared by a health organization in Nicaragua or by NCAHRN, medical equipment should not be sent. When collecting supplies, keep in mind durability and appropriate simple technology. Glass syringes, for example, are more valuable than plastic disposables.

Medical Textbooks and Journals. All medical, nursing and technical textbooks should be the last or next-to-last editions. While materials in Spanish are best, texts in English are widely used at medical schools and on the Atlantic coast. The most helpful English language materials are those with pictures and graphics. Health journals should be sent if they are major journals in general and specialty fields, runs of two years or more, and from the last five years. Books and journals should be packed in sturdy boxes that are small enough to be easily carried.

Work Brigades

Thousands of "brigadistas" from the United States and Europe have visited Nicaragua to help plant and pick crops, build homes, schools, playgrounds, health facilities and streetlight systems, and to carry out environmental restoration projects.

The national Nicaragua Network and the Environmental Project on Central America (EPOCA) organize environmental brigades, and Nicaragua Network also organizes cotton- and coffee-picking. These are perhaps the easiest brigades to join, because participants only need to bring work clothes and their willing hands. Construction brigades are more complicated and require organizers to deal with the fundraising and logistical aspects of acquiring materials such as cement, steel, and tools. Precisely for this reason, however, construction brigades may experience a more intensive education in Nicaraguan realities, and the results of their labors are more visible and lasting. Construction projects are also, by their very nature, geographically specific and therefore make excellent community-to-community projects. Groups that have organized construction projects include Architects and Planners in Support of Nicaragua (APSNICA), the Ann Arbor-Managua Initiative for Soil Testing and Development (A^{2}MISTAD), and the Vecino Project of Cambridge, Massachusetts.

"Clearly the most successful activity of our group has been the construction in Niquinohomo of a functioning eight-room health clinic," says Merle Krueger of the Providence-Niquinohomo sister-city project. "Forty-two Rhode Islanders participated in the original construction in the summer of 1986, and 13 more went down in summer 1987 to do some follow-up work on the building. This was successful because it got so many people involved directly with the people of Nicaragua, and because it generated a great deal of positive press including an article in the *New York Times*." As a permanent monument to the work of the Providence volunteers, appreciative Niquinohomo residents named the clinic "La Providencia."

The clinic project began after several Rhode Island residents visited Niquinohomo in 1985 and learned that the existing clinic building, although structurally adequate, was nearly bare of supplies. "The equipment consisted entirely of one examining table, two adult scales, one infant scale, a refrigerator, two or three stainless steel pans and a couple of posters showing how to prevent intestinal parasites," said Providence resident Richard Walton. "That's it. Not even the most basic medical equipment or medicines. I could see how the parents of Niquinohomo and surrounding villages were almost desperate for the establishment of a real clinic."[3]

Sister-city organizers in Providence committed themselves to a fundraising campaign, intending to first equip the existing clinic and then work toward a new building in a year or two. "My notes innocently read, 'Find out how to build a hospital,' " recalls organizer Bill Warren. For advice on methods of tropical construction, the Providence group turned to the Vecino Project in Boston, which had built a 2-building clinic in Estelí that summer. Through fundraisers including a highly successful bowl-a-thon, they raised the $18,000 needed to buy cement, gravel, steel reinforcing rod and other supplies. Posters and newspaper ads attracted several dozen volunteers from Providence to participate in construction brigades that went down to Niquinohomo in a series of two-week work shifts. Before departure, the brigadistas held a "dress rehearsal" by building a tool shed for the Providence Community Garden. In addition to sharpening their construction skills, this increased the visibility of their project and received favorable media coverage.[4]

"I don't like to have the feeling of always being against something. Here was the chance for us to do something positive," said James Pfeiffer, a 26-year-old printer who served as construction coordinator.[5] For Robert Currier, a 68-year-old retired professor of music, participation was "a much more touching experience than I expected. It left me with a feeling of accomplishment, and of how much people working together can do." He also enjoyed Niquinohomo's rural beauty: "At four o'clock the roosters begin to go all over town. It's really a different kind of music, because it's got depth. You hear them at distances, further and further away, a repercussive sound like something out of Berlioz."[6]

"On the critical side, we were damn fools to think we could do this in six weeks," Warren admitted. "Things move slowly in poor countries with little infrastructure at war, and you can count on delays and shortages."[7] In addition, many of the brigadistas experienced diarrhea as a result of drinking contaminated water. But on the positive side, the Providence group developed a sense of cooperation and warmth, both among themselves and with the people of Niquinohomo, who worked alongside them in building the clinic and treated them with what Walton described as "incredible hospitality."

"These people came with a tremendous amount of enthusiasm, and they've been a great example to us," said Gilberto Lacayo Bermúdez, a Nicaraguan engineer who assisted with the project. "It's a beautiful gesture. You can imagine the social impact in a town of 25,000 of 45 foreigners coming in for two months and living with local families."[8]

Technical Exchange

In addition to scarcity of material goods, Nicaragua suffers from a shortage of trained personnel. Under Somoza, less than half of the country's population even learned to read, and only a tiny minority had access to the training necessary to become an architect, engineer or doctor. In many cases, equipment and computers stand idle or are underutilized because there are no trained operators. The shortage of repairpersons and spare parts also means that hospital equipment, farm machinery and other important tools are unserviceable. In the pro-

"One problem is that we have needs in the United States, and then we have the reality of Nicaragua. Sometimes we use charity as a way of satisfying our needs, one of which is a need to feel useful, rather than the needs of people here. In our project, we have moved away from just taking clothing and giving it away, and towards more creative ways of using those donations to promote sustainable development. We take clothing and we go into the community, and they sell the clothing at a very inexpensive cost. The proceeds then go into a local community development project which pays people to dig wells and things like that."

Lee Cruz,
New Haven/León Sister City Project

fessional and managerial fields, many important positions are currently held by inexperienced persons who have never had formal training. The universities are unable to provide adequate education because of a shortage of faculty.

"It's no good to bring in equipment if there aren't sufficient repair and maintenance shops. And this problem isn't limited to spare parts. It ranges from not knowing how to change the water or oil in a vehicle to letting it burn up out of neglect," said Henry Ruíz, Nicaragua's Minister of International Cooperation. "One of our headaches is the lack of a qualified labor force. You can't give a piece of equipment worth $40,000 to someone just because he has the strength to drive it. If this person enjoys mechanics, he has to be trained. But the technical institutes do not have enough space."[9]

Jerry Messick, an emergency medical technician from Oklahoma working in Nicaragua, described the human consequences of Nicaragua's underdevelopment: "One day we received an accident case, a young man who had fallen off a pickup truck and been hit by another. He had head, chest and possible abdominal trauma. The laceration of the head was sutured and we began intraveneous fluids, and a tube was placed in the trachea to allow him to breathe better. We put him in the ambulance without oxygen, as we do not have a portable tank, and lost one of the I.V. lines in the process due to the lack of training in moving patients. Then came a wait. Since there is only one ambulance, we had to wait for another patient who also had to be sent to Managua.

"By the time we got to the emergency room, his blood pressure was very low, and I was covered with blood as the ambulance lacks even enough gauze to reinforce dressings. Inside, we asked for resuscitation equipment, but the poorly trained staff had to search to find it. I had to ask for a device to breathe the patient but there was no oxygen to hook the bag to. By the time the doctor arrived to examine the patient, he pronounced him dead.

"This patient might have been saved if the correct equipment had been available," Messick said, "but in addition to the shortage of supplies, there is also a need for more expertise among health workers. In light of the shortage of trained medical personnel, international volunteers can help."

Over 1,000 U.S. citizens currently live in Nicaragua, working in fields including computer maintenance and programming, auto mechanics, water purification, law, social work, the cultural arts, and agriculture. In addition to teaching and giving of themselves, they have often been inspired by Nicaragua's ability to innovate and cope with difficult circumstances.

"Nicaragua's network of volunteers is one of the outstanding features of its health care system," said Laura Berger, a nurse from Madison, Wisconsin who observed that system at a community health center in her sister city of Managua. "Volunteers donate their homes as health posts; they help monitor health conditions in their neighborhood, provide limited health education, serve in immunization campaigns, and serve as a contact between the community and professional health care providers. It's a truly amazing, comprehensive approach that offers lessons to the rest of the world, including the United States. I have spent six years helping low-income people in the U.S. to obtain health care, and although this is one of the richest countries in the world, I have seen our system stumble repeatedly over obstacles that Nicaraguans surmount every day. Our material wealth, if shared, could be of enormous benefit to the people of Nicaragua. But they also have a wealth—of wisdom and creativity—to share with us."[10]

A number of the interest-affiliated groups listed in the back of this book organize technical assistance programs in their area of interest. In addition, many professional and technical exchanges are organized by TECNICA, a nonprofit, independent organization based in the San Francisco and Silicon Valley area. TECNICA volunteers donate two weeks or more of their time to work in Nicaragua, training Nicaraguan technicians and professionals, solving technical problems that are beyond the capacity of existing experts in Nicaragua, recommending and installing appropriate technology, and promoting cross-cultural understanding. Each volunteer is assigned to a "job placement" in an agency or organization, and works Monday through Friday with his or her Nicaraguan counterparts.

The following list is a partial catalogue of needs for which TECNICA is seeking volunteers:

agronomists; computer professionals, including IBM 360, 4331, System 34/36 and PCs; microcomputer users and instructors; computer and electronics repair technicians; electrical engineers; diesel mechanics; automotive mechanics and engineers; welding instructors; telephone engineers and technicians; industrial electricians; two-way radio engineers and technicians; marine biologists; medical equipment technicians; economists; statisticians; boiler repairpersons, instructors; agricultural experts; translators; mechanical engineers; HVAC engineers; machinists; sheet metal technicians; textile machinery technicians; bankers knowledgeable in deposits, transfers, import-export documentation, international banking; geologists knowledgeable in seismology and vulcanology; soil engineers; concrete pump technicians; electronic composition and editing system design; energy auditors; industrial safety engineers; telecommunications technicians knowledgeable in antenna control, digital telex, automated systems; data transmission and switching experts; science instructors; construction engineers; civil engineers: earthquake-proofing; alternative energy technicians: windmill repair; insurance experts; draftspersons.

The Science for Nicaragua Committee of Science for the People, based in Massachusetts, has organized a teacher placement program at the college level, in conjunction with the Nicaraguan National Council of Higher Education. They place teachers in fields including agriculture, animal husbandry, computer science, ecology, engineering, forestry, medicine, physics, statistics and mathematics. In addition, Science for Nicaragua is looking for donations of reference books and subscriptions to professional journals, and for university graduate departments willing to provide full financial support to Nicaraguan professors seeking advanced degrees.

The North American Farm Alliance has organized a rather unique technical aid program, which aims to help farmers in the United States as much as their counterparts in Nicaragua. A cooperative dairy project in the Boaco area, northeast of Managua, has set aside land for North American farm families who have lost their farms through foreclosure. They hope to attract farmers with skills to help increase milk production by introducing technology scaled to the needs of the cooperative and small- and medium-sized producers living nearby. Eric Holt-Giménez, a resident of Sacramento, California and a director of the Agricultural Exchange Project, said the project has the potential to increase milk production in the Boaco area by at least five-fold within five years by incorporating improved cultivation practices, soil conservation, veterinary services, and genetic improvement. Beyond these practical goals, the project provides an opportunity for educational exchange.

"This will also attempt to serve as an example of how farmers can begin to set their own production agenda in the Americas and how relationships between people of the First and Third World countries needn't be exploitative," Holt said. "This project also demonstrates the fact that the interests of North American farmers and the people of Nicaragua and the Third World are very closely related. As farm prices drop in the United States, commodity prices drop on the international market and in the Third World. Everybody gets hurt. As we are able to combat these policies in the U.S., and are able to build a stronger farm movement there, the Third World will benefit as well."[11]

Trade

Contributions of material, labor and technical advice can provide significant benefit to the people of Nicaragua, but in the long run Nicaragua needs to develop a healthy, self-sufficient economy. This requires, for one thing, normal trade relations with other countries of the world, including the United States.

Prior to the contra war, the U.S. was Nicaragua's number one trading partner. A number of groups, including the New Haven/León Sister City Project, had begun exploring the possibility of additional city-to-city trade relationships, but those initiatives had to be curtailed when President Reagan outlawed trade with Nicaragua on May 1, 1985, under a "state of emergency" declaration that "The policies and actions of the government of Nicaragua constitute an unusual and extraordinary threat to the national security and foreign policy of the United States."

Some groups, however, have found ways of legally continuing to trade. One approach is to buy Nicaraguan products which have been reprocessed in another country. Nicaraguan coffee, for example, is roasted and ground in Holland or Canada and then sold in the United States.

One group, Trade for Peace, Inc., of Madison, Wisconsin, has openly defied the embargo by importing and selling Nicaraguan postage stamps, handicrafts, and unroasted coffee. This trade, amounting to only $3,500 in sales during the group's first three years, has been largely symbolic, comprising what Trade for Peace founder Leonard Cizewski called "nonviolent civil disobedience." In April 1988, however, Trade for Peace received a notice from the U.S. Justice Department threatening criminal prosecution, imprisonment and a fine of $50,000. In response, groups around the United States began to explore the possibility of setting up their own Trade for Peace projects, challenging the government to crack down on them as well.

In late August of 1988, U.S. customs officials entered Cizewski's home with a search warrant, seizing Trade for Peace merchandise and records along with other Central America-related documents. Prosecution seemed likely.

For Ann Arbor, Nicaragua Becomes a Reality 8

"Come to think of it, I don't know what's similar about Ann Arbor and Juigalpa," said Kurt Berggren. "Juigalpa's got about thirty thousand people — Ann Arbor's four times that size. Juigalpa's a cattle and farming town — that definitely wouldn't describe Ann Arbor. We do have a few things in common, though. When Candido Vallecillo, the mayor of Juigalpa, was up here, I took him to the season opener between the Yankees and the Tigers. He *loved* it."[1]

Berggren, an Ann Arbor civil rights attorney, was explaining to a writer for the *New Yorker* magazine why the Ann Arbor Sister City Task Force, of which he was a member, had decided to buy a garbage truck for Juigalpa. The interview took place aboard the truck, which Berggren and his friends, Kip Eckroad and Tom Rieke, had volunteered to drive from Ann Arbor to Juigalpa, a distance of some 4,500 miles.

"It's what they wanted. The people of Juigalpa told us, 'Boy, what this city really needs is a garbage truck,'" said Eckroad.[2]

Residents of Ann Arbor began to explore the possibility of a sister-city relationship with Nicaragua in early 1986, and in April, voters approved a city resolution endorsing the idea by a nearly 2-to-1 margin. By September a formal relationship had been established, and in November, Eckroad, Rieke and Berggren joined the first Ann Arbor delegation to visit Juigalpa, along with the mayor, a minister, a state assemblyman, a nurse and several reporters.

Juigalpa is located in the region of Chontales, a war zone. Transportation is difficult, and although U.S. citizens had passed through Juigalpa on the way to other places, few had spent significant time there. "You could say that this was the first opportunity for the people of Juigalpa to have contact with the people of the United States," said Mayor Vallecillo, who was impressed by the delegation's eagerness to meet the people of his community. "They did not stay at hotels and merely tour the city. They stayed with people in their homes. The mayor of Ann Arbor and his wife stayed in a very humble home, so that he could experience personally the realities of life here."

Berggren's first impression as the delegation's bus pulled into Juigalpa was "hundreds, maybe thousands of people standing along the road to greet us, some carrying candles. We marched into town to a big hall, a union meeting place. A band played music, and there were speeches."

Allison Downing, an Ann Arbor native, served as the group's translator. She had lived in Nicaragua since 1985, working as a music teacher and violinist with Nicaragua's National Symphony Orchestra. For her, the delegation's visit was "a meeting of two homes. . . . Tears were in my eyes when that little group — representing my home, my history — marched into Juigalpa to shouts of 'Long live Juigalpa! Long live Ann Arbor!' and sang the song composed by Ann Arborite Dave Vayo especially for that meeting."[3] The song proclaimed:

> No one is an island
> The suffering of one will hurt us all
> We must stand together
> For if we don't each one of us will fall.
> People of Juigalpa, now that we've joined together
> In our breasts there burns a common flame
> And now that we are family
> The blood that courses in us is the same.[4]

" 'No one is an island . . . We must stand together' . . . I sang those words from the heart," Downing said, "because my solitary voice had never been enough to communicate all the pain and joy in Nicaragua to folks at home." Earlier that year, two of the brothers in the Nicaraguan family she lived with — "shy teenage boys who used to practice English with me" — had joined the army to fight the contras, and Downing had "wanted to call home, call for help, but no one at home had ever seen those boys' faces before." Now, seeing the interaction between the Ann Arbor delegation and their Juigalpan hosts was "like watching a sprout push aside the earth."[5]

Ernestine Rodriguez Spruce, who had been Downing's junior high school nurse, was one of the delegates. "I think the thing that struck me the most is how stark everything was," Spruce said after seeing Juigalpa's hospital. "It was a far cry from a U.S. medical facility with computers clicking away. The entire hospital was very hot, with no air conditioning, and very dark. In the kitchen, it was so dark that I asked if they had any lights. They turned them on, but explained that they usually keep them off because if the bulb burned out they might not be able to get a replacement." She was particularly moved after seeing a 6-year-old girl who had been injured in a contra attack. "Beside her stood her father, a poor, barefoot peasant, with helplessness and despair on his face as he made awkward attempts to comfort her. It was in the pediatric ward that I realized the full significance of the hospital in this war-torn zone."

In the Chontales region, the war has claimed the lives of over 2,000 people. The region is sparsely populated, with only 2,700 of its 20,800 square kilometers accessible by road. Peasants, who traditionally live dispersed in the mountains, are most vulnerable to attack, and the war has caused many of them to flee to the cities. "Our priority for development is the countryside, the very rural areas," said Martha McCoy, a Nicaraguan official in Chontales. "This presents us with a real contradiction, because it is in the rural areas that the contras are affecting us the most." In order to slow the flight into the cities, the government had set up rural settlements where peasants can live together for mutual protection, but travel between cities and settlements was still dangerous. "The problem isn't safety in Nueva Guinea," McCoy said. "The problem is getting to Nueva Guinea, because of the danger of ambushes along the road. Likewise with the road to Rama."

And likewise with the single-lane dirt road leading to Comalapa, a small village about 30 miles from Juigalpa, where a jeep was ambushed by contras on the last day of the Ann Arbor delegation's visit. The attack took place at approximately 7 a.m., and was close enough to Comalapa that village residents heard the gunshots and, having no telephone, radioed for help to Juigalpa. The delegation heard about it later that morning, and several members hitched a ride with a jeep that took them to the scene.

"It was a very isolated road, leading through wooded hills," said delegation member Gregory Fox. "The car was machine-gunned and then burned, with most of the occupants still in the car. We got there about 1 p.m., six hours after the attack. The bodies had been removed, but the car was still smoldering. There were soldiers standing around, as well as the wife of Alfonso Nuñez, the man who was the apparent target of the attack. She was there with her two kids. She had a look in her face like she'd been expecting this."

Nuñez, 45, was a local peasant leader and long-time Sandinista. He was a co-founder and regional director of UNAG, the national union of small farmers and ranchers, which was headed nationally by his brother, Daniel. The attackers had shot him over 100 times.[6]

The only victim of the ambush who survived long enough to describe it was the driver, 26-year-old Ramón Hernández, who was interviewed by *Ann Arbor News* reporter Tom Rogers before dying of his wounds. From his hospital bed, Hernández said he had been carrying the only weapon in the jeep, a revolver. Most of the others killed in the attack had been hitching rides with Nuñez into Comalapa. They included: Norman Eli Duarte Talén, 31, of Comalapa, leaving a wife and two children, ages 3 and 1$\frac{1}{2}$; Alfredo Miranda, 33; 23-year-old Santos Calero from the neighboring village of El Naranjo, who left behind three children ranging from an infant to a 6-year-old; Armida Enríquez of Juigalpa; and 66-year-old Juana Duarte, who had taken the ride into Comalapa so she could visit her son.[7]

The attack had one other eyewitness. Twenty-six-year-old Martín Flores had been riding along the road in a motorcycle when a peasant flagged him down and said he was hearing gunshots. Flores left the road, climbed a hill and saw contras surrounding Juana Duarte, who was still alive and lying wounded in the road. He had watched, helpless to intervene, as they picked her up and threw her back into the burning vehicle.

The visitors from Ann Arbor attended funerals for victims of the ambush. Rogers reported that at the funeral for Nuñez, "his family, including his sons, 3$\frac{1}{2}$ and 2, took its last long look at him. Blood had oozed through the afternoon's stitches to dot the clean white shirt family members had provided for his burial. One of Nuñez' sons pressed his soft hand against, then scratched the hard glass that kept him from touching his father."[8]

"The trip was an extraordinarily important and emotional event in my life," Berggren said later in an essay for the *Ann Arbor News*. "I remember the members of the Christian base community we visited and their little cinderblock meeting house. For hours we sang songs with them, talked about our thoughts, experiences, and feelings and exchanged hugs. . . . I remember the U.S. Embassy official we met and his confusion when one of us asked what the contra policies were for dealing with poverty and the needs of the people." He also remembered that while the delegation was being treated to a farewell dinner on their last evening in Juigalpa, "a wake was being held across the street for one of the victims of the contra attack. Tom Rieke and I went over to watch the wake, and I became concerned that the music from our celebration was bothersome to the family of the murdered woman. I was told no, that everyone believed life had to go on, and it would be totally inappropriate for me to say anything about cutting down on our festivity."[9]

Before returning to Ann Arbor, the delegates asked Candido Vallecillo for a list of Juigalpa's needs. He told them that in addition to garbage trucks, the city needed equipment for a university under construction, and refrigerators for storage of vaccines and other medicines in Juigalpa's health centers. They gave him $1,500 to buy the refrigerators, and later raised another $1,500 for transformers to provide electricity in Juigalpan homes. A campaign to buy the garbage truck became the focal point of their activities. They raised $22,000 and bought a Haul-All Model 12, the model Vallecillo had suggested. It was a small truck by U.S. standards, but equipped with a diesel engine and manual transmission suited to hauling garbage on Juigalpa's hilly streets.

"Kip and Tom and I didn't know each other before joining the delegation to Nicaragua, but we shared common values and became friends," Berggren said. "When we learned that Juigalpa needed a garbage truck, we had joked about driving the truck down, but we really hadn't expected that we were actually going to do it. Then Kip's research revealed that it would cost another $10,000 to ship it to Juigalpa. All of a sudden it became clear that driving it ourselves was the best way to go, both economically and in terms of the personal touch."

Inside the cavern of the truck's compactor, a hammock and a lawn chair were installed for the benefit of the travelers as they alternated between rest and driving. Signs were painted on the doors, with the words "Tren de Aseo Impulsado por Amistad" — "Garbage Truck Propelled by Friendship." The evening before departure, hundreds of people attended a ceremony at city hall, signing messages of friendship on banners to be carried with the truck.

The U.S. leg of the trip turned out to be the easiest. Bill Finnegan, the *New Yorker* writer, had flown into Ann Arbor the previous evening and rode with them to Cincinnati, where they dropped him off at the airport. They stopped for pre-arranged rallies and press conference in several cities along the way, and arrived Friday evening at the U.S.-Mexico border crossing at Laredo, Texas.

"Nobody hassled us on the U.S. side of the border, but when we pulled into Mexican customs, they wouldn't let us through," Berggren said. "The head customs official had gone home, and they told us we'd have to come back the following day to get his permission." Undaunted, the truckers rented a room at a Laredo Holiday Inn and spent the night contacting "customs brokers" to take care of paperwork they had been told they needed. After learning of the nature of their trip, a sympathetic broker prepared the documents free of charge. The following day, however, the Mexicans still refused to let them through.

"We just decided we'd get in the truck and drive south on US 83, which is the route that goes right along the border," Berggren said. "We stopped at every border crossing along the way, trying to get through. There were five border crossings. The U.S. customs people didn't do anything to impede us other than act nasty and rude, but we'd cross over the river and negotiate with the Mexicans for a half hour or so, and each time, we were turned down. A couple of times it looked real good. At one stop, the Mexican officials told us to leave the truck, walk into town, have beer or something and come back in two hours, and it would be taken care of; but when we got back, someone higher up had said no. After the first day and a half of batting our heads against the wall, we honestly believed that we weren't going to be able to get in, and we were trying to figure out what to do. We were thinking we'd ship it from one of the port cities, or just drive it back to Ann Arbor and call it a failure. We were really quite depressed at that point."

The good news was that the truck's difficulties had created interest back home. The *Ann Arbor News* began running a daily map charting their progress. At the *New Yorker*, Finnegan had written his story but was waiting to release it until they reached Juigalpa. He began calling Kathy Eckroad or Anne Berggren on a daily basis with word that the *New Yorker* staff was "rooting for you."

The last chance to cross the border was in Brownsville, where they arrived on Sunday evening. Again, the Mexican officials were pleasant but turned them down. The drivers rented another room and contacted a friend of Eckroad, who knew a customs broker for a large company in Brownsville. On Monday, they made contact with the broker, who said he would try to help and suggested that one of them should go talk to the Mexican consulate. Eckroad left, returned an hour later and ordered everyone to pack up fast. "We threw everything into the truck and headed for the border," Berggren said. "There was no time even for brief explanations. The customs agent had done something, but we never knew what, and Kip had found his way through the bureaucratic maze. By this time our unsuccessful attempts had taken us over the Rio Grande about 12 or 14 times. When we finally made it across the border, we were elated. We thought the trip was going to be pretty easy after that."

At Mexico City, however, a message was waiting at their hotel: "Tell them to give up. They'll never make it. If the Guatemalans don't seize their truck, the guerrillas in El Salvador or the contras in Honduras will blow them away."[10] The message came from a Michigan businessman, claiming to have extensive experience in Central America, who had read about them in the newspaper and phoned Kip Eckroad's wife. "The message upset Kathy, and it didn't make us feel any better either," Berggren said. "We also learned from the morning papers that two bridges had been blown up in El Salvador on the Pan American highway, the route we had been planning to take."

Undeterred, the truckers held a news conference in Mexico City and pushed on towards Guatemala. They had another day's delay due to visa problems, but got through, and arrived in Guatemala City to find the hotels packed with vacationing Salvadorans and visitors arriving in anticipation of upcoming peace talks between the presidents of Central America. They telephoned home and learned that Ann Arbor was in a state of suspense over their saga. In a single morning at a farmer's market, Berggren's wife and others had sold $400 worth of commemorative "garbage truck" T-shirts. "It was a popular item," said Gregory Fox, one of the sellers. "A lot of people had read about the truck in the paper. They would come up and ask, 'Do you think it's going to get through?' "

The crossing into Honduras turned out to be the easiest hurdle of the journey, thanks to a hotel clerk that Eckroad befriended who knew the Honduran ambassador. She called him directly and got advice that enabled them to pass through customs in less than an hour. In order to bypass the blown-up bridges in El Salvador, they decided to take an alternate route through Honduras, following the path taken by a truck from the Boulder/Jalapa sister city project some months earlier. This meant abandoning the Pan-American Highway during the rainy season and spending two days on muddy roads that Sara Lee, one of the

"I contemplated the irony of our journey. Oliver North and company had orchestrated a complicated, secret plan to supply arms to the contras hiding in the hills outside of Juigalpa without encountering a single truculent border bureaucrat. Yet a simple garbage truck, promising to reduce the spread of disease from uncollected garbage, had drawn the scrutiny of officials of five countries."

Tom Rieke
from "The Road to Nicaragua,"
Car and Driver magazine

Boulder drivers, describes as "coils of potholes that wind on roller-coaster paths through some pretty incredible mountains." Parts of the road were paved; other parts were one-lane dirt paths, some of which had been washed away by the rain. "It was a tough road," Berggren said. "I would say probably we averaged 20 miles an hour at best. We were really creeping, and then we'd have army people stopping us at checkpoints every 30 or 40 miles to try to intimidate us."

In Tegucigalpa, the capital of Honduras, they took a room in the Hotel Honduras Maya. The city was full of serious, crew-cut men from the United States. "Everyone seemed to be on edge," Rieke observed in an article about the trip that appeared in *Car and Driver* magazine. "In the Hotel Maya restaurant, planners and consultants whispered about reorganizing the contras. In the lobby, American women exchanged stories about the sick Honduran children they were adopting. [Graffitti] on downtown walls decried 'Yankee Garbage' — the human kind — while government posters threatened: 'Communism is Illegal! Communism Destroys Your Family!' A few days earlier, near the airport, the Nicaraguan foreign minister had barely escaped assassination."[11]

Ironically, the Nicaragua border delay turned out to be the worst they had encountered since Mexico. Instead of proceeding directly to Juigalpa, they were required to first visit Managua, where they spent half a day completing paper-work and getting permission to import the truck. In keeping with weather that had prevailed throughout their trip, it was raining on the evening of August 5 as they pulled into Juigalpa, where Rito Siles Blanco, the city's new mayor, waited to greet them. Candido Vallecillo had been appointed to a different government position but was also waiting, along with several reporters. They celebrated at a restaurant, while the mud-covered truck was taken away to be washed and pre-pared for the official welcoming ceremony.

The event was held the following morning in Juigalpa's central market. In front of hundreds of spectators, Eckroad, Berggren and Rieke attached banners to the truck with the names of the two sister cities and messages of friendship from Ann Arbor. "A lot of hugs could be seen in the crowd," Berggren said. "The truck's operation was demonstrated, and the first shovelful of garbage was thrown into the bin as cameras recorded the action. A historic moment!"[12] By coincidence, Ellen Rusten, one of the 17 members of the original Ann Arbor delegation, was in Juigalpa that day escorting a dozen members of the First Baptist Church of Ann Arbor.

"The most memorable remark was by Hernán Sotelo, the regional education minister," Berggren recalled. "He said the garbage truck did not impress him very much—what *really* impressed him was that the three of us drove it 4,500 miles from Ann Arbor to Nicaragua. He promised that the story of our driving the garbage truck to Juigalpa will forever be a part of the school curriculum as an example of people caring for each other despite governments and politics and war."[13]

"It was extremely moving," said Candido Vallecillo. "People felt very emo-tional about it. The difference between the United States government and the people of the United States was absolutely clear."

U.S.-Nicaragua Sister Cities 9

Arizona

Tucson/Santo Domingo Sister City Project

Contact: Mark Mayer & Molly Moore
921 E. 7th Street
Tucson , AZ 85719
Phone: 602-325-5531 or 602-623-5371

Tucson/Santo Domingo, Chontales Department, Region V. Development of water purification and distribution systems. Economic and cultural parallels: both cities are historical centers for mining and cattle production. Founded: 2/88.

California

Arcata/Camoapa Sister City

Contact: Stan Henerson
P.O. Box 1042
Arcata , CA 95521
Phone: 707-822-3442 or 707-822-7130

Arcata/Camoapa, Boaco Department, Region V. Built birthing clinic; sent school bus; dental project. A diverse coalition including 4-H club, churches, businesses, politicians, doctors, professionals. Founded: 5/86. Official — city council.

Berkeley/León Sister City Association

Contact: Rebecca Cohn-Vargas
   & Jill Friedman
P.O. Box 1004
Berkeley , CA 94701
Phone: 415-549-1387

Berkeley/León, León Department, Region II. A cooperative effort between the city of Berkeley and the Nicaraguan Information Center (see listing under Interest Affiliated Groups). Worked on Mayor's Initiative for Peace in 1988. Founded: 7/86. Official — city council (8/86).

Fairfax/Condega Sister City Project

Fairfax/Condega, Estelí Department, Region I. See Marin/Condega Sister City Project.

Fresno/Talpaneca Sister City Project

Contact: Nancy Marsh & Pam Whaler
4777 North Arthur
Fresno , CA 93705
Phone: 209-442-0488 or 209-226-0477

Fresno/Telpaneca, Madriz Department, Region I. Founded: 6/88. Official—city council (6/88).

Marin/Condega Sister City Project

Contact: Tim Jeffries
P.O. Box 336
Fairfax , CA 94930
Phone: 415-456-7433

Marin County/Condega, Estelí Department, Region I. Delegations; construction to install streetlights and a PA system; slides of Nicaragua by professional photographer Tim Jeffries available for loan. Brigade rebuilt houses destroyed by contras. (Formerly Fairfax/Condega Sister City Project) Founded: 3/85. Official — city council.

Muir Beach/San Juan del Sur Sister City Project

Contact: Gerald Pearlman
270 Pacific Way, Box 296
Muir Beach , CA 94111
Phone: 415-383-5997

Muir Beach/San Juan del Sur, Rivas Department, Region IV. Installed pipes to help extend water service to a barrio of San Juan del Sur; helped with restoration of a local school. Provides support to the Nicaraguan Windmill Repair Project. Muir Beach and San Juan del Sur are both beach communities. Official — Community Services District Resolution.

Arizona
Tucson

California
Arcata
Berkeley
Fairfax
Fresno
Marin County
Muir Beach

Nicaragua/Pomona Valley Project
Contact: Jeff Johnson,
	Project Coordinator
390 W. La Verne Avenue
Pomona , CA 91768
Phone: 714-593-9651

Pomona Valley/Quilalí, Rivas Department, Region IV. Participated in Veteran's Peace Convoy in 1988. Making video. Founded: 7/86.

Sacramento/San Juan de Oriente Friendship Project
Contact: Peter Feeley
P.O. Box 163078
Sacramento , CA 95816
Phone: 916-456-2616

Sacramento/San Juan de Oriente, Masaya Department, Region IV. Founded 1988.

San Rafael del Corazón Sister City Project
Contact: David Mayer or Joan Runyon
P.O. Box 13434
San Rafael , CA 94913
Phone: 415-459-0966

San Rafael/San Rafael del Norte, Jinotega Department, Region I. Projects include water purification, sewage treatment. Founded: 1985. Official — city council (1/88).

Willitz/El Escambray Sister City Project
Contact: Janet Brown
P.O. Box 1641
Willitz , CA 95490

Willitz/El Escambray, Region VI.

Colorado

People to People Peace Brigade
Contact: Elaine Schmidt
	& Michael J. Higgins
P.O. Box 5115
Greeley , CO 80631
Phone: 303-351-1890 or 303-352-7765

Sister barrio project: Al Frente de Lucha, Greeley/Barrio William Diaz Romero, City of Managua, Managua Department, Region III. Helping build a daycare center and clinic. Founded: 10/87.

Boulder/Jalapa Friendship City Projects, Inc.
Contact: Sara Lee
P.O. Box 7452
Boulder , CO 80306
Phone: 303-442-0460

Boulder/Jalapa, Nueva Segovia Department, Region I. Constructed a preschool. Drove a truckload of material aid from Boulder to Jalapa. Provides regional coordination and advice to sister-city projects in the western U.S. Founded: 1984. Official.

Connecticut

Hartford/Ocotal Sister City Project
Contact: Jan Baker
30 Arbor Street
Hartford , CT 06106
Phone: 203-236-1295 or 203-242-8620

Hartford/Ocotal, Neuva Segovia Department, Region I. Delegations, material aid, hospital supplies. Founded: 1984.

Milford Sister City Project
Contact: Mary Malarky & Mrs. Michael Drummy
40 Hawley Avenue
Milford , CT 06460
Phone: 203-874-4229

Milford/Esquipulas, Matagalpa Department, Region VI. Founded: 10/87.

New Haven/León Sister City Project
Contact: Alan Wright
965 Quinnipiac Avenue
New Haven , CT 06513
Phone: 203-467-9182

New Haven/León, León Department, Region II. Experience in most areas of sister-city work: delegations, collecting and shipping aid, developmental work in fields including day care, construction, literacy. Advises sister-city projects in the northeastern U.S. Founded: 2/84. Official — city council & mayor.

Norwalk/Nagarote Sister City Project
Contact: Scott Harris
P.O. Box 962
South Norwalk , CT 06856
Phone: 203-227-1307 or 203-846-8324

Norwalk/Nagarote, León Department, Region II. Delegations, material aid, cultural exchange. Priority is a sports facility and school band equipment. Developing a film project to document the lives of children in both sister cities. Working with librarians in the U.S. to provide Spanish books, office supplies, materials for Nagarote's new public library. Founded: 3/86.

The Grange/San José Sister Project
Benedictine Grange
W. Redding , CT 06896
Phone: 203-938-3689
West Redding/San José.

Delaware

Newark/Nicaragua Sister City Project
Contact: Teri Foster & Bruce Gibson
102 Kirkcauldy Dr.
Elkton , MD 21921
Phone: 302-454-1947 or 302-368-8250
Newark/San Francisco Libre, Managua Depart-
ment, Region III. Building a two-room addition
to a secondary school. Has sent tools and a brick-
making machine, and a refrigerator for a health
center. Producing a show of Nicaraguan art.
Founded: 1/87.

District of Columbia

Washington, DC/Bluefields
Sister City Project
Contact: Hillary Stern & Keith Williams
Box 11099, Cleveland Park Station
Washington , DC 20008
Phone: 202-462-8848 or 202-232-6789
Washington/Bluefields, Zelaya Sur, Special Zone
II. Emphasizes link between Bluefields and
Washington's black community. Works jointly
with Witness for Peace. Founded: 1985.

Florida

Gainesville/Matagalpa
Sister City Program
Contact: Harriet Peacock
        & Susana Picado
P.O. Box 1323
Gainesville , FL 32602
Phone: 904-375-7724 or 904-371-0654
Gainesville/Matagalpa, Matagalpa Department,
Region VI. A university community; has sent
delegations to Nicaragua. Has video, based on
first delegation's visit to Matagalpa. Gainesville's
program is run by the city commission, with the
city clerk serving as coordinator. Founded: 6/86.
Official — city council (1/87).

Port St. Lucie/Corinto
Sister City Project
Contact: Richard Broughton
1117 SE Stewart Road
Port St. Lucie , FL 33452
Phone: 305-335-0281
Port St. Lucie/Corinto, Chinandega Depart-
ment, Region II.

Georgia

Athens/Chaguatillo Sister City Project
Contact: Christopher Debarr
575 1/2 Waddell Street
Athens , GA 30605
Phone: 404-549-4416 or 404-353-0796
Athens/Chaguatillo, Matagalpa Department,
Region VI. Working on a street theatre play
about the history of Central America. Does a
workshop on Latin American poetry for high
school students. Founded: 3/86.

Idaho

Moscow Sister City Association
Contact: Mary Voxman
1118 King Road
Moscow , ID 83843
Phone: 208-882-1009
Moscow/Villa Carlos Fonseca, Managua
Department, Region III. Works through Sister
Cities International. An ambulance project
helped win community support: Founded: 12/85.
Official — city council (8/86).

Indiana

Indiana/Río San Juan
Sister State Project
Contact: Bill & Judy Ney
524 Buckingham Dr.
Indianapolis , IN 46208
Phone: 317-283-9493 or 317-283-3057
State of Indiana/Río San Juan Department,
Special Zone III. Shipment of material aid; sever-
al brigades have worked in Los Chiles on projects
including building a school. Founded: 9/84.

Bloomington Sister Cities International
Contact: Russell Salmon
P.O. Box 100
Bloomington , IN 47401
Phone: 812-336-1319
Bloomington/Posoltega, Chinandega Depart-
ment, Region II. One of a few U.S.-Nicaragua
sister-cities organized through Sister Cities
International. Official (5/88).

Kansas

Manhattan Friendship Cities Project, Inc.

Contact: Julie Coates
719 Osage Street
Manhattan , KS 66502
Phone: 913-539-7767

Manhattan/Nindirí, Masaya Department, Region IV. Construction of a library. Experienced with direct mail. Sponsoring a photojournalist to do a video documentary for broadcast on Kansas public television. Founded: 6/85. Official — city council.

Topeka/Matagalpa Sister City Project

Contact: Rev. Jim Richards
817 Harrison Street
Topeka , KS 66612
Phone: 913-233-9601 or 913-272-4348

Topeka/Matagalpa, Matagalpa Department, Region VI. Relationship with tractor plant near Matagalpa. Founded: 1/87. Semi-official (approved by mayor).

Maine

Belfast/San Nicolás Sister City Project

Contact: Warren Greeley
Plummer Hill
Brooks , ME 40921
Phone: 207-525-4403

Belfast/San Nicolás, Matagalpa Department, Region VI.

Bucksport/La Trinidad Sister Cities Project

Contact: Melissa LaLonde
P.O. Box 40
Bucksport , ME 04416
Phone: 207-469-2155

Bucksport/La Trinidad, Estelí Department, Region I. Remains apolitical as an organization. Experienced in fundraising. Founded: 10/86.

Maryland

Casa Baltimore/San Juan de Limay Sister City Project

Contact: Dick Ullrick
& Rev. Gretchen Van Utt
St. Johns of Baltimore
27th & St. Paul Streets
Baltimore , MD 21218
Phone: 301-366-7733 or 301-547-2689

Baltimore/San Juan de Limay, Estelí Department, Region I. Interfaith project; two full-time volunteers in Limay. Founded: 7/85.

Massachusetts

Amherst/La Paz Centro Sister City Project

Contact: Faythe Turner
& Meryl Fingurdt
P.O. Box 363
North Amherst , MA 01059
Phone: 413-253-7934 or 413-253-2962

Amherst/La Paz Centro, León Department, Region II. Official town committee. Started a drive to raise $20,000 for an ambulance. A university town appealing to students. Official — by representative town meeting (5/87).

Brookline/Quezalguaque Sister City Project

Contact: Elizabeth Wyon
& Maxine Shaw
P.O. Box 1394
Brookline , MA 02146
Phone: 617-277-0069 or 617-277-7867

Brookline/Quezalguaque, León Department, Region II. Projects include building a health clinic. Both cities have similar names: Quezalquaque is an indigenous word meaning "Stony River"; Brookline used to be named "Muddy River." Founded: 9/86. Official — by town meeting (6/87).

Concord/San Marcos Sister City Committee

Contact: Al Armenti
& Gene Sheftelman
32 Wildwood Dr.
Carlisle , MA 10742
Phone: 617-369-3779 or 617-369-2596

Concord/San Marcos, Carazo Department, Region IV. Experience in making sister-city relationship official through a direct town meeting. Sent dental clinic to San Marcos. Official — town meeting (4/86).

Lexington-Waspán Sister City Committee

Contact: Marcia Butman
& Ellen McDonald
50 Bridge Street
Lexington , MA 02173
Phone: 617-861-6154 or 617-863-8959

Lexington/Waspán, Zelaya Norte Department, Special Zone I. Expertise in speaking Miskito and other indigenous languages of Nicaragua's Atlantic Coast, including Rama and Sumu. Founded: 4/88. Official — town meeting.

Amigos en Paz

Contact: Phyllis Vecchia
   & Wendy Ward
P.O. Box 2529
Vineyard Haven , MA 02568
Phone: 617-627-3918

Martha's Vineyard/Solentiname, Lake Nicaragua, Special Zone III. A sister-island project, based on both islands' similar interests in arts and culture. Founded: 1/88.

New Bedford/Telica Sister City Project

Contact: Dawn Blake-Thomas
   & Erica Bronstein
c/o Labor Education Center
Southeast Massachusetts University
North Dartmouth , MA
Phone: 617-999-8007 or 617-994-3050

New Bedford/Telica, León Department, Region II. Official — mayor.

Newton/San Juan del Sur Sister City Project, Inc.

Contact: Betsy & Rodney Barker
49 Woodcliff Road
Newton Highlands , MA 02161
Phone: 617-482-4900 or 617-244-6949

Newton/San Juan del Sur, Rivas Department, Region IV. Contributed to Veterans Peace Convoy. San Juan del Sur has a wonderful beach, ideal for delegations that want to include vacation time in their itinerary. Founded: 3/87

Berkshire-Columbia AMISTAD

Contact: James Moran
306 West Street
Pittsfield , MA 01201
Phone: 413-445-5246

Pittsfield/Malpaisillo, León Department, Region II. Supplying clinics and schools, sending delegations.

Worcester/Comalapa Sister City Project

Contact: Lucy Candib
   & Richard Schmitt
65 Tory Fort Lane
Worcester , MA 01602
Phone: 617-757-0814 or 617-754-6070

Worcester/Comalapa, Chontales Department, Region V. Material aid emphasis on health care/medical supplies. Educational presentations to church, civic and senior citizen groups. Plans to bring a woodworker from Comalapa to visit Worcester. A small project in a conservative, Catholic community. Founded: 9/86. Official — city council (9/87)

Michigan

Ann Arbor/Juigalpa Committee

Contact: Gregory Fox
P.O. Box 8198
Ann Arbor , MI 48107
Phone: 313-663-0655

Ann Arbor/Juigalpa, Chontales Department, Region V. Donated and drove garbage truck to Juigalpa; current projects include an experimental composting waste disposal system. Founded: 4/86. Official — ballot referendum (4/86); mayor; city council resolution.

Detroit/Bluefields Sister City Project

Contact: Margaret Baylor
18653 Lauder
Detroit , MI 48235
Phone: 313-548-1430 or 313-835-1154

Detroit/Bluefields, Zelaya Sur, Special Zone II. Establishing relations with Black churches.

Kalamazoo/Acoyapa Sister City Project

Contact: Alexandra Chaplin
   & Tom Small
2502 Waite Avenue
Kalamazoo , MI 49008
Phone: 616-381-4946 or 616-349-8559

Kalamazoo/Acoyapa, Chontales Department, Region V. Founded: 1987.

Minnesota

Project Minnesota/León

Contact: Nancy Trechsel
7455 S. Lake Sarah Drive
Rockford , MN 55373
Phone: 612-477-6366

State of Minnesota/León Department, Region II. A well established project, with a wide variety of projects. Paired with the entire region of León. Staff includes two full-time coordinators in Nicaragua. Main emphasis is educating people of Minnesota. Sends a high school delegation each year, plus adult delegations. Strongly "nonpolitical." Founded: 9/84.

Montana

Friends of Rivas

Missoula contact:
Laurie Mercier & John Torma
P.O. Box 7666
Missoula , MT 59806
Phone: 607-721-4700 ext. 30 or 406-728-0272
Helena contact:
Andrea Bateen
P.O. Box 11
Helena, MT 59624
Phone 406-458-9686
Helena and Missoula/Rivas, Rivas Department, Region IV. Founded: 1/85.

New Jersey

Bergen/Rivas Sister County Project

Contact: Sal Piazza & Dorothy Pita
300 Winston Drive, Apt. 1721
Cliffside Park , NJ 07010
Phone: 201-837-7929 or 201-224-7750

Bergen County/Rivas Department, Region IV. Part of New Jersey statewide network. Publicly opposes the war in Central America through regular vigils on the Washington bridge, overlooking traffic between New Jersey and New York. Founded: 7/86.

Central Jersey/Masaya Friendship Cities Project

Contact: Brooks Smith
525 East Front Street
Plainsfield , NJ 07060
Phone: 201-756-2666 or 201-755-2781

Central Jersey/Masaya, Masaya Department, Region IV. A regional network. A paper, "Adventure in Hope," is available. Involved in several large shipments of aid. Hosted a visit by the mayor of Masaya. Founded: 2/1/86.

Montclair/Pearl Lagoon Sister City Project

Contact: Dick Franke
50 Oakwood
Upper Montclair , NJ 07043
Phone: 201-783-5896 or 201-744-4021

Montclair/Pearl Lagoon, Zelaya Sur, Special Zone II. Sister city is on the Atlantic Coast; English speaking, which makes correspondence easier, but harder to travel there. Founded: 1985. Official.

Morristown/Monimbó Sister Cities Project

Contact: Jim Burchell
39 Green Village Road, #304
Madison, NJ 07940
Phone: 201-765-9102

Morristown/Monimbó, Masaya Department, Region II. A new project, founded in August 1988. Historic parallel: Morristown was the military capital of the U.S. revolution, and Monimbó was the site of the first insurrection against Somoza in 1978.

Princeton/Granada Sister Cities Committee

Contact: James Laity
#3 Shirley Lane
Lawrenceville , NJ 08648
Phone: 609-896-2441

Princeton/Granada, Granada Department, Region IV. Delegations, including visit to Princeton by mayor of Masaya, Nicaragua, and mayor of Granada. Educational projects. Sells postcards with pictures from Granada. Children's art exchanges. Contacts with Princeton University. Founded: 2/87. Official (Princeton Borough Council, 3/88; Princeton Township, 5/88).

New Mexico

Southwest Organizing Project

Contact: Sofia Martinez
1114 7th Street N.W.
Albuquerque , NM 87102
Phone: 505-247-8832

Albuquerque/Estelí, Estelí Department, Region I. Adopted the "Rebeca Guillén" daycare center in Estelí; also works on environmental projects and community development. Emphasis on linking Nicaraguans with Chicanos in the U.S. Founded: 2/87.

New York

Brooklyn/San Juan del Río Coco Sister City Project

Contact: Susan Lyons & Donna Mehly
P.O. Box 356-A Times Plaza Station
Brooklyn , NY 11217
Phone: 718-282-0288 or 718-768-0953

Brooklyn/San Juan del Río Coco, Madriz Department, Region I. Sponsors an annual parade and picnic. Can share experience of organizing with a sister city in a war zone. Founded: 5/86.

Chelsea/El Jicaral Sister City Project
Contact: Mary Jean Chilcote
  & Fran Nesi
P.O. Box 1574, Old Chelsea Station
New York , NY 10113
Phone: 212-989-1592 or 212-255-9236
Chelsea/El Jicaral, León Department, Region II. Working on a water project. Has produced a Spanish ABC coloring book to send to Nicaragua. For copies, bulk rates for sale by other sister-city groups, contact Kathy Casey, 212-929-2362. Founded: 6/86.

**Lower East Side/Bluefields
Sister City Project**
Contact: Chris Idzik
P.O. Box 138
New York , NY 10009
Phone: 212-673-9174
Lower East Side, New York/Barrio Nueva York, Bluefields, Zelaya Sur, Special Zone II. Paired with Barrio Nueva York in Bluefields.Official — city council.

**North Manhattan/Colama
Sister City Project**
Contact: Dave Dubnau
790 Riverside Drive, #3E
New York , NY 10032
Phone: 212-281-1813
North Manhattan/Colama, Tipitapa, Managua Department, Region III. Based in a largely minority, working-class community in New York, about 75 percent Spanish-speaking. Colama is a barrio in the village of Tipitapa. Founded: 10/86.

Queens/Sébaco Sister City Project
Contact: Mark Landsman
108-46 63rd Avenue
Forest Hills , NY 11375
Phone: 718-897-0461
Queens/Sébaco, Estelí Department, Region I.

**Metro Act/Ciudad Hermana
Sister City Task Force**
Contact: Henrietta Levine
50 N. Plymouth Avenue
Rochester , NY 14614
Phone: 716-325-2560 or 716-473-3015
Rochester/El Sauce, León Department, Region II. Material aid: health care, school supplies, "Shoe Boxes for Peace." Political organizing; works cooperatively with other solidarity groups. Founded: 9/86.

**Upper Westside/Tipitapa
Sister City Project**
Contact: Carolyn Reed
370 Central Park West
New York , NY 10025
Phone: 212-678-6113
Upper Westside, Manhattan, New York City/ Tipitapa, Managua Department, Region III. Health and education projects. Founded: 9/86. Official—Community board endorsement, 3/87.

Utica/Barrio Camilo Ortega Project
Contact: Michael Bagge
  & Edie Weintraub
1314 Rutger Street
Utica , NY 13501
Phone: 315-732-2131 or 315-724-6528
Utica/Barrio Camilo Ortega, Managua, Managua Department, Region III. Projects: sending hospital supplies and working with a women's sewing cooperative. Founded: 1987. Official — mayor's proclamation.

North Carolina

Asheville Sister City Project
Contact: Imelda McKercher
36 Baird Street
Asheville , NC 28801
Phone: 919-967-2064

Chapel Hill Sister City Project
Contact: Diana McDuffee,
  Catherine McLeod & Jane Stein
222 Vance Street
Chapel Hill , NC 27516
Phone: 919-929-1614
Chapel Hill/San Jorge, Rivas Department, Region IV. Founded: 1/88.

Ohio

**Central American Solidarity
Association**
Contact: Ruth Gibson
647 Nome Avenue
Akron , OH 44320
Phone: 216-867-4542 or 216-864-9103
Akron/San Lorenzo, Boaco Department, Region V. Founded: 1988.

**Athens/Teustepe Sister
Community Association**
Contact: Frank Norton
P.O. Box 5683
Athens , OH 45701
Phone: 614-662-5075
Athens/Teustepe, Boaco Department, Region V. Medical aid, poultry project, child nutrition.

**Yellow Springs/Jícaro
Sister Village Project**
Contact: Steve Piatt & Hazel Tulecke
903 Xenia Avenue
Yellow Springs , OH 45387
Phone: 513-225-3197 or 513-767-1633
Yellow Springs/Jícaro, Nueva Segovia Department, Region I. Projects include a women's empowerment center in Jícaro, a program which "has presented both opportunities and challenges." Founded: 7/85. Official — mayor's proclamation.

**Sister City Project
of Youngstown, Ohio**
Contact: Jim Converse
Peace Council of Youngstown
2615 Market Street
Youngstown , OH 44507
Phone: 216-788-8848 or 216-782-2736
Youngstown/San Isidro, Matagalpa Department, Region VI. Affiliated with the Pittsburgh-San Isidro project. Coalition includes laid-off and unemployed steelworkers. Interested in farm projects. Founded: 1/87. Official — mayor's proclamation (5/88).

Oregon

Albany/Chichigalpa Sister City Project
Contact: James Power
P.O. Box 1025
Albany , OR 97321
Phone: 503-967-7595 or 503-926-3024
Albany/Chichigalpa, Chinandega Department, Region II.

**Portland-Corinto
Sister City Association**
Contact: Tim Calvert
& Margaret Thomas
3558 SE Hawthorne
Portland , OR 97214
Phone: 503-233-5181 or 503-295-7783
Portland/Corinto, Chinandega Department, Region II. A well-developed, active program, with delegations, construction brigades, material aid programs. Has video of Corinto. Portland is the home town of Benjamin Linder, the U.S. volunteer who was murdered by contras while working in Nicaragua. Founded: 9/84. Official (4/85).

Pennsylvania

**Pittsburgh/San Isidro
Sister City Project**
Contact: Jane Dirks & Jules Lobel
c/o Thomas Merton Center
5125 Penn Avenue
Pittsburgh , PA 15224
Phone: 412-361-3022 or 412-521-7109
Pittsburgh/San Isidro, Matagalpa Department, Region VI. Grassroots network in churches, schools, student and community groups. Works in collaboration with the Peace Council of Youngstown, Ohio. Founded: 6/86. Official.

Rhode Island

**Providence/Niquinohomo
Sister City Project**
Contact: Martha Bebinger
& Paula Donovan
69 Lenox Avenue
Providence , RI 02907
Phone: 401-861-5427 or 401-941-5697
Providence/Niquinohomo, Masaya Department, Region IV. Activities include constructing a health clinic and a school; photo exhibit; publication of a book of Nicaraguan poems. Founded: 11/84. Official — city council (4/85).

South Dakota

South Dakota/Yalí Sister City Projects
Contact: Thomas Lobe
414 E. Clark Street
Vermillion , SD 57069
Phone: 605-624-9241
Vermillion/Yalí, Jinotega Dept., Region VI.

Vermont

Bradford-Cardenas Friendship Project
Contact: Bud Haas & Holyoke Homer
Box 452
Bradford , VT 05033
Phone: 802-222-5701 or 802-222-5539
Bradford/Cardenas, Rivas Department, Region IV. Attempted unsuccessfully to obtain official endorsement. Founded: 1/87.

Ohio (cont.)
Yellow Springs
Youngstown

Oregon
Albany
Portland

Pennsylvania
Pittsburgh

Rhode Island
Providence

South Dakota
Entire state

Vermont
Bradford

Burlington-Puerto Cabezas
Sister City Program
Contact: Jo-Ann Golden & Roger Clapp
113 Church Street
Burlington , VT 05401
Phone: 802-864-0659 or 802-863-9572

Burlington/Puerto Cabezas, Zelaya Norte, Special Zone I. Made video of Puerto Cabezas, titled "Our Sister City." Experience shipping supplies to Nicaragua's Atlantic Coast. Knowledge about social, cultural and political situation there. Reforestation and family garden projects. Exhibition and photo book of the two cities by professional photographer Dan Higgins. Very active. Founded: 9/84. Official — city council resolution (9/84).

SouthWest Vermont Committee
on Nicaragua
Contact: Sophie Smith
P.O. Box 2810
Sandgate , VT 05250
Phone: 802-375-2287

Southwest Vermont/Escuela Somotillo, Chinandega Department, Region II. Main effort is to supply needs of elementary school, medical supplies, sewing materials. Founded: 3/86.

Washington

Bainbridge/Ometepe
Sister Islands Association
Contact: Kim Esterberg
P.O. Box 4484
Rollingbay , WA 98061
Phone: 206-842-8148

Bainbridge Island/Ometepe Island, Lake Nicaragua, Region IV. Has made videos documenting life in Bainbridge and life in Ometepe. Helped with a preschool. Participates in a 3-way exchange between Bainbridge, Ometepe, and the Gulf Island group in Canada. Founded: 11/27/86.

Jalapa/Port Townsend
Sister City Association
Contact: Doug Milholland
1829 Lincoln Street
Port Townsend , WA 98368
Phone: 206-385-6525

Port Townsend/ Jalapa, Nueva Segovia Department, Region I. Mayor of Port Townsend visited Jalapa, along with county commissioner and businesspeople. Projects include construction of children's playground with a handmade wooden carousel from Port Townsend. Electrical generator project. Founded: 12/83. Official — city council.

Seattle/Managua
Sister City Association
Contact: Roy D. Wilson
P.O. Box 24883
Seattle , WA 98124
Phone: 206-329-2974

Seattle/Managua, Managua Department, Region III. A large, well-established project. Special emphasis: bringing and sending delegations; cultural events; also building a multi-ethnic base. Regional coordinator, advisor to sister-city projects in northwestern U.S. Founded: 1/81. Official — city council (1984).

Spokane/Tipitapa
Friendship Association
Contact: Doug Segur & Renee Smith
E. 2608 4th Avenue
Spokane , WA 99202
Phone: 509-534-1668 or 509-326-0239

Spokane/Tipitapa, Managua Department, Region III. Hosted several delegations of Nicaraguans to Spokane.

CASA-Tacoma
Contact: Kaj Fjelstad
904 118th Street S
Tacoma, WA 98444

Tacoma/San Francisco Libre, Managua Department, Region III. Pacific Lutheran University-Sister School Project.

Thurston-Santo Tomás
Sister County Association
Contact: Marijke van Roojen &
    Peggy & Richard Smith
1958 Westridge Lane, NW
Olympia , WA 98502
Phone: 206-754-6765 or 206-754-8822

Thurston County/Santo Tomás, Chontales Department, Region V. Founded: 10/88.

West Virginia

Beckley/Mina El Limón
Sister City Project
Contact: Lee Adler
P.O. Box 1521
Beckley , WV 25802-1521
Phone: 304-252-2933

Beckley/Mina el Limón, León Department, Region II. Sponsors sister-program between West Virginia and Nicaraguan mining communities. Founded: 12/79.

Wisconsin

Wisconsin Coordinating Council on Nicaragua (WCCN)

Contact: Liz Chilsen, Executive Director
P.O. Box 1534
Madison , WI 53701
Phone: 608-257-7230

State of Wisconsin/Nicaragua (entire country). Coordinates cultural exchanges, delegations, educational and material aid activities to promote the official sister-state relationship that has existed between Wisconsin and Nicaragua since 1964. Sponsors the U.S.-Nicaragua Friendship Project, documenting the existence and activities of sister-city projects nationwide. Regional coordinator, advisor to sister-city groups in the midwestern U.S. Founded: 1984. Official — governor's proclamation, 1964.

Madison-Managua Sister City Project

Contact: Liz Chilsen
P.O. Box 1534
Madison , WI 53701
Phone: 608-257-7230

Madison/Managua, Managua Department, Region III. Programs include sister schools, Bikes Not Bombs campaign, exchanges between University of Wisconsin and the Nicaraguan National Autonomous University departments of limnology, math, medicine, and veterinary science. Official — city council.

Milwaukee/Ticuantepe Sister City Project

Contact: Todd Schlenker
1638 S. 33rd Street
Milwaukee , WI 53215
Phone: 414-671-4555

Milwaukee/Ticuantepe, Managua Department, Region III. Founded: 4/87. Official — city council (9/87).

Richland Center-Santa Teresa Sister City Project

Contact: Jane Furchgott
c/o Brewer Public Library
325 N. Central Avenue
Richland Center , WI 53581
Phone: 608-583-2431 or 608-583-2628

Richland Center/Santa Teresa, Carazo Department, Region IV. A small, conservative town in a rural, agricultural area. Emphasis has been on promoting pen-pal exchanges and showing slides of Santa Teresa. Donations of medical and school supplies. Founded: 3/87.

Río/Rapids Friendship Project

Contact: Carolyn Kenney
& Joyce Lobner
P.O. Box 1161
Wisconsin Rapids , WI 54494
Phone: 715-423-4991

Wisconsin Rapids/Rio Blanco, Matagalpa Dept, Region VI. Medical and school supplies; slide presentation in churches and schools. Founded: 7/87. Official — city council (4/88).

Wisconsin
Entire state
Madison
Milwaukee
Richland Center
Wisconsin Rapids

Sister Cities Listed by Nicaraguan Region, Department and City

Entire Country
State of Wisconsin

Region I

Department of Estelí
Condega: *Marin County, CA*
Estelí: *Albuquerque, NM*
La Trinidad: *Bucksport, ME*
San Juan de Limay: *Baltimore, MD*

Department of Jinotega
San Rafael del Norte: *San Rafael, CA*

Department of Madriz
San Juan del Río Coco: *Brooklyn, NY*
Telpaneca: *Fresno, CA*

Department of Neuva Segovia
Jalapa: *Boulder, CO; Port Townsend, WA*
Jícaro: *Yellow Springs, OH*
Ocotal: *Hartford, CT*

Region II

Department of Chinandega
Chichigalpa: *Albany, OR*
Corinto: *Port St. Lucie, FL; Portland, OR*
Escuela Somotillo: *Southwest Vermont*
Posoltega: *Bloomington, IN*

Department of León
Entire Department: *State of Minnesota*
El Jicaral: *Chelsea, NY*
El Sauce: *Rochester, NY*
La Paz Centro: *Amherst, MA*
León: *Berkeley, CA; New Haven, CT*
Malpaisillo: *Pittsfield, MA*
Mina el Limón: *Beckley, WV*
Nagarote: *Norwalk, CT*
Quezalguaque: *Brookline, MA*
Telica: *New Bedford, MA*

Region III

Department of Managua
Barrio Camilo Ortega, Managua:
   Utica, NY
Barrio William Diaz Romero, Managua:
   Al Frente de Lucha, Greeley, CO
Colama, Tipitapa: *N. Manhattan, NY*
Managua: *Madison, WI; Seattle, WA*
San Francisco Libre: *Tacoma, WA;*
   Newark, DE
Ticuantepe: *Milwaukee, WI*
Tipitapa: *Spokane, WA; Upper Westside,*
   Manhattan, New York, NY
Villa Carlos Fonseca: *Moscow, ID*

Region IV

Department of Carazo
San Marcos: *Concord, MA*
Santa Teresa: *Richland Center, WI*

Department of Granada
Granada: *Princeton, NJ*

Lake Nicaragua
Ometepe Island: *Bainbridge Island, WA*

Department of Masaya
Masaya: *Central Jersey, NJ*
Monimbó: *Morristown, NJ*
Nindirí: *Manhattan, KS*
Niquinohomo: *Providence, RI*
San Juan de Oriente: *Sacramento, CA*

Department of Rivas
Entire Department: *Bergen County, NJ*
Cárdenas: *Bradford, VT*
Quilalí: *Pomona Valley, CA*
Rivas: *Helena/Missoula, MT*
San Jorge: *Chapel Hill, NC*
San Juan del Sur: *Muir Beach, CA;*
   Newton, MA

Region V

Department of Boaco
Camoapa: *Arcata, CA*
San Lorenzo: *Akron, OH*
Teustepe: *Athens, OH*

Department of Chontales
Acoyapa: *Kalamazoo, MI*
Comalapa: *Worcester, MA*
Juigalpa: *Ann Arbor, MI*
Santo Domingo: *Tucson, AZ*
Santo Tomás: *Thurston County, WA*

Region VI

Department of Jinotega
Yalí: *Vermillion, SD*

Department of Matagalpa
Chaguatillo: *Athens, GA*
Esquipulas: *Milford, CT*
Matagalpa: *Gainesville, FL; Topeka, KS*
Río Blanco: *Wisconsin Rapids, WI*
San Isidro: *Pittsburgh, PA;*
  Youngstown, OH
San Nicolás: *Belfast, ME*

Special Zone I

Department of Zelaya Norte
Puerto Cabezas: *Burlington, VT*
Waspán: *Lexington, MA*

Special Zone II

Department of Zelaya Sur
Barrio Nueva York, Bluefields: *Lower
  East Side, New York, NY*
Bluefields: *Detroit, MI; Washington, DC*
Pearl Lagoon: *Montclair, NJ*

Special Zone III

Lake Nicaragua
Solentiname: *Martha's Vineyard, MA*

Department of Río San Juan
Entire Department: *State of Indiana, IN*

Europe's 209 Links With Nicaragua 10

On May 26-28, 1988, a European Conference on City-Linking with Nicaragua was held in Amsterdam, the Netherlands, organized by the Amsterdam City Council, NOVIB, Pax Christi, and the Dutch Nicaragua Committee in cooperation with the United Towns Organization of Paris and the Netherlands/ Nicaragua National City-Linking Council. The following list of official and non-official pairings was distributed at that conference.

For further information, contact:

Documentation-centre City-linking 'The Netherlands-Nicaragua'
Ronald van der Hijden
van Speykstraat 21   3572 XB   Utrecht   The Netherlands
telephone (o)30-718163

Achuapa: Bern (Switzerland); Cremona y Varesa (Italy)
Acoyapa: Münster (West Germany)

Bluefields: Florence (Italy); Lambeth (Spain); Orebru (Spain); Gerona (Spain)
Boaco: Perguia (Italy)

Chichigalpa: Hannover (West Germany); Wels (Austria)
Chinandega: Coventry (Great Britain); Eindhoven (The Netherlands); Leverkusen (West Germany); Molins de Rey (Spain); Motala (Sweden); North East Derbyshire (Great Britain)
Chontales: Cordoba (Spain); Cortona (Italy)
Cinco Pinos: Mollet de Valles (Spain)
Ciudad Darío: Lutterbach (France); Reading (Great Britain)

Ciudad Sandino: Charlottenburg (West Germany); Darmstadt (West Germany); Düsseldorf (West Germany)
Comoapa: Ciudad Rodrigez (Spain)
Condega: Augsburg (West Germany); Hildesheim (West Germany); Oostburg (The Netherlands); Schwegat (Austria); Venissieux (France)
Corinto: Aarlborg (Denmark); Arlberg (West Germany); Bremen (West Germany); Gotenburg (Sweden); Köln (West Germany); Le Havre (France); Liverpool (Great Britain); Puerto Genova (Italy); Rotterdam (The Netherlands)

Diriamba: Gävle (Sweden); Langenselbod (West Germany); Mainz (West Germany); Saarbrucken (West Germany); Villeneuve le Roi (France)
Diriomo: Soluthurn (Switzerland)

El Sauce: Offida (Italy)
El Viejo: Norwich (Great Britain)
Estelí: Anghiari (Italy); Bielefeldt (West Germany); Collegno (Italy); Delft (The Netherlands); Essen (West Germany); Evry (France); Graz (Austria); Malmö (Sweden); San Feliu de Llobregat (Spain); Sheffield (Great Britain); Stavanger (Norway); Turku (Finland); Vasteras (Sweden)

Granada: Badajoz (Spain); Breda (The Netherlands); Dos Hermanos (Spain); Torroella de Mongri (Spain)

Jalapa: Champigny (France); Disón (Belgium); Santa Coloma de Gramanet (Spain); Jyväskyla (Finland)
Jinotega: Cornella de Llobregat (Spain); San Michel sur Orbe (France); Sasuolo (Italy); Solingen (West Germany); Zoetermeer (The Netherlands)
Juigalpa: Communidad Autonoma de Santa Lucie (Spain); Den Haag (The Netherlands); Gandia (Spain); Köping (Sweden); Nottingham (Great Britain)

La Concha: Leeds (Great Britain)
La Libertad: Kiruna (Sweden)
La Paz Centro: Göttingen (West Germany); Grotagglie (Italy)
Las Cortezas: Halifax (Great Britain)
León: Ärhus (Denmark); Barcelona (Spain); Grugliasco (Italy); Hamburg (West Germany); Lund (Sweden); Luxemburg (Luxemburg); Neuville les Dieppe (France); Oxford (Great Britain); Salzburg (Austria); Tampere (Finland); Utrecht (Netherlands)

Managua: Amsterdam (The Netherlands); Camden (Great Britain); Hospitalet (Spain); Helsinki (Finland); Islington (Great Britain); Madrid (Spain); Stockholm (Sweden); Zürich (Switzerland)
Masaya: Alken (Belgium); Brugge (Belgium); Dietzenbach (West Germany); Leicester (Great Britain); Nijmegen (The Netherlands); Scandicci (Italy); Wiesbaden (West Germany)

Matagalpa: Borlange (Sweden); Clichy (France); Kalmar (West Germany); Karlsruhe (West Germany); Lancaster (Great Britain); Lewisham, London (Great Britain); Olten (Switzerland); Oulu (Fin); Sabadell (Spain); Tilburg (The Netherlands); Wuppertal (West Germany)
Matiguás: Saarlouis (West Germany)
Mina El Limón: Ansoain (Spain); Vaynor (Great Britain)

Nandaime: Barsinghausen (West Germany); Diemen (The Netherlands)
Nandasmo: Willebroek (Belgium)
Nueva Guinea: Hernani (Spain); Pitea (Sweden)
Nueva Segovia: Ciudad Segovia (Spain)

Ocotal: Alingsas (Sweden); Rubi (Spain); Santa Fé (Spain); Valencia (Spain)
Ometepe: Herne (West Germany)

Palacaguina: Arucies (Spain); Villa de Coslada (Spain)
Playas de Tapacalí: Mostoles (Spain)
Puerto Cabezas: Basel (Switz); Manchester (Great Britain); San Perez de Rivas (Spain); Viladecans (Spain); Villafranca del Penedes (Spain)
Puerto Morazán: Bristol (Great Britain); Oberhausen (West Germany)

Quilalí: Joensuu (Finland)

Rama: Aachen (West Germany); Maastricht (The Netherlands); Nieuwpoort (Belgium)
Region III (Río San Juan): Hesse (West Germany)
Río Blanco: Montauban (France)
Rivas: Haarlem (The Netherlands); Lille (France); Offenbach (West Germany); Talant (France)

San Carlos: Barcelona (Spain); Groningen (The Netherlands); Linz (Austria); Nürnberg (West Germany); Witten (West Germany)
San Dionisio: Amstetten (Austria)
San Francisco Libre: Fiano Romano (Italy)
San Isidro: Dortmund (West Germany)

San José de Bocay: Abanto y Zerbana (Spain)

San José de Cusmapa: Cavabeliz (Spain); Parla (Spain)

San Juan del Río Coco: Abadino (Spain); Fuenlabrado (Spain)

San Juan del Sur: Giessen (West Germany)

San Juan de Telpaeca: Ciempozuelos (Spain)

San Marcos: Biel (Switzerland)

San Miguelito: Waltrop (West Germany); Yverdon (Switzerland)

San Pierre de Corps: Chamberry (France)

San Rafael del Sur: Berlin-Kreuzberg (West Germany); Braunsweig (Federal Republic of Germany); Goslar (Federal Republic of Germany)

San Tomás: Mol (Belgium)

Santa Lucía: Bochum (West Germany)

Santa María: Ljunby (Sweden)

Santa Rosa del Peñon: Nacka (Sweden)

Sébaco: Harlow (Great Britain); Vaux en Vellin (France)

Solentiname: Mollis (Italy)

Somotillo: Frenchen (West Germany); Kaulinge (Sweden); Suolatie (Finland)

Somoto: Berlin-Wilmersdorf (West Germany); Fougères (France); Leganes (Spain); Luik (Belgium); San Remo (Italy); Várnamo (Sweden); Wilmerdon (Federal Republic of Germany)

Telica: Hallein (Austria); Liechtenstein (Liechtenstein)

Tipitapa: Campi Bisenzo (Italy); Duisburg (West Germany)

Tisma: Bradford (Great Britain); Frankfort (West Germany); Kreisbergstrasse (West Germany)

Totogalpa: San Fernando de Henares (Spain)

Trinidad: Delémont (Switz)

Villa Carlos Fonseca: Argan del Rey (Spain)

Villa Sandino: Zutphen (The Netherlands)

Waslala: Dorsten (West Germany)

Wiwilí: Freiburg (West Germany)

Yalaguina: Pinto (Spain)

U.S.-Nicaragua
Interest-Affiliated Groups

11

Academic Research

See Education; Information; Technical Aid and Exchange.

Agriculture

See also Construction; Environment; Technical Aid and Exchange.

Food First/Institute for Food and Development Policy

Contact: Frances Moore Lappé
145 Ninth Street
San Francisco, CA 94103
Phone: 415-864-8555

Information about food-related issues in the United States and throughout the Third World.

Guild House/HAP-NICA

802 Monroe
Ann Arbor, MI 48104
Phone: 313-761-7960

Raises funding to support Nicaragua's first scientific agricultural journal. Several environmental/ agricultural research projects, including a cooperative research center for oil palm on the Atlantic Coast, a honey cooperative, and A²MISTAD (see Construction). Publishes a newsletter.

North American Farm Alliance (NAFA)

P.O. Box 2502
Ames, IA 50010
Phone: 515-232-1008

Organizes tours of farmers hosted by Nicaragua's National Union of Farmers and Ranchers (UNAG), and a project to help displaced U.S. farmers obtain land in Nicaragua where they can live and farm.

Oxfam America

Contact: Silvia Sukop
115 Broadway
Boston, MA 02116
Phone: 617-482-1211

Provides emergency support to families displaced by war, promotes health and education in rural areas, and helps small farmers and farm communities with long-term developmental assistance. "Tools for Peace" program sends farm tools.

Ambulances

See Health; Veterans.

Appropriate Technology

See Technical Aid and Exchange.

Architecture

See Construction; Technical Aid and Exchange.

Arts and Culture

Arts for a New Nicaragua

439 Washington Street #4
Brookline, MA 02146
Phone: 617-738-9719

CASA Nicaragua - Chicago

Contact: Walter Urroz
P.O. Box 478435
Chicago, IL 60647
Phone: 312-728-5561

Cultural and information center, serving to facilitate exchanges between the U.S. and Nicaragua.

Academic Research

Agriculture

Ambulances

Appropriate Technology

Architecture

Arts and Culture

141

The Empowerment Project
Contact: Barbara Trent
13107 Venice Blvd.
Los Angeles, CA 90066
Phone: 213-390-9858
A media resource with videotape editing studio in Los Angeles. Producer of the award-winning "Destination Nicaragua."

Nicaraguan Cultural Alliance
Contact: Mary MacArthur
1627 New Hampshire Avenue, NW
Washington, DC 20009
Phone: 202-232-7510 or 202-686-0139
Promotes peace and understanding through cultural and artistic sharing and exchange. Sells postcards and attractive reprints of paintings by Nicaraguan artists. Publishes map of Nicaragua listing U.S.-Nicaragua sister cities.

Ventana
339 Lafayette Street
New York, NY 10012
Phone: 212-475-7159
North American artists, cultural workers and others who oppose U.S. intervention and destabilization efforts in Central America and the Caribbean. In Nicaragua, Ventana has sister-organization ties to the Sandinista Cultural Workers Association (ASTC).

Bicycles

See Technical Aid and Exchange.

Children

See also Education; Disabled; Health; Women.

Ecumenical Refugee Council
Contact: Sally Pettit
2510 N. Frederich Street
Milwaukee, WI 53211
Phone: 414-271-7719 or 414-332-5461
Has a "Godparent Project" which seeks sponsors to contribute $10 or $20 per month to "adopt" Nicaraguan orphans. Sends medical, food, other assistance.

Citizen Diplomacy

See Sister Cities.

Civil Disobedience

See Trade.

Conservation

See Environment.

Construction

See also Health.

A²MISTAD/Guild House
802 Monroe Street
Ann Arbor, MI 48104·
Phone: 313-761-7960
The "Ann Arbor-Managua Initiative for Soil Testing and Development (A²MISTAD)"; building a soil and water analysis laboratory for use by the Institute of Agricultural Sciences in Nicaragua. Fundraising activities include a "bowl-a-thon," door-to-door canvassing, and public presentations. A project of HAP-NICA.

Architects and Planners in Support of Nicaragua (APSNICA)
Contact: Steve Kerpin
P.O. Box 1151
Topanga, CA 90290
Phone: 213-455-1340
A volunteer organization which builds homes, schools and water systems in rural Nicaragua, and trains Nicaraguans in construction. Also provides technical assistance and material aid to the housing and planning ministries, placing architects planners and engineers in Nicaragua. Newsletter, "Framework."

Delegations

See Tours; Human Rights.

Development

See Human Rights, Religion, Technical, Trade.

Disabled

See also Health.

Denver Disabled Peace Project
Contact: Gary Handschumacher
829 REX
Louisville, CO 80027
Phone: 303-666-8214

Disabled International Support Effort (DISE)
2434 E. 23rd Street
Oakland, CA 94601
Phone: 415-436-0626
Sends material aid to the Organization of Disabled Revolutionaries in Nicaragua.

War Relief for Nicaraguans

Contact: Becky Pierce
P.O. Box 2040
Jamaica Plain, MA 02130
Phone: 617-282-3783 or 617-282-3783

Raises money to support victims of the contra war. Helps widows, orphans; provides physical rehabilitation, job training, and other assistance to disabled soldiers.

Disappeared

See Human Rights.

Education

See also Arts and Culture; Information; Libraries; Organizational Development; Nicaragua Network; Technical Aid and Exchange; Tours; Spanish Language Instruction.

American Friends Service Committee School Supplies Campaign

1501 Cherry Street
Philadelphia, PA 19102

The AFSC is an affiliate of the Quaker Church. The School Supplies Campaign supplies useful information and organizing packets for initiating a school supplies collection campaign.

Committee to Aid the UNAN

Contact: Irving Adler
RR1 Box 532
North Bennington, VT 05257
Phone: 802-442-2268

Sends supplies to aid the Universidad Nacional Autónoma de Nicaragua (UNAN), one of Nicaragua's national universities.

El Salvador

Committee in Solidarity with the People of El Salvador (CISPES)

Contact: Angela Sanbrano
P.O. Box 12056
Washington, DC 20005
Phone: 202-265-0890

National center of coordination, administration and information for the large Central American solidarity network, with over 450 local chapters and affiliates. Monthly newspaper, "the Alert!"

Going Home/SHARE Foundation

P.O. Box 24, Cardinal Station
Washington, DC 20064
Phone: 202-635-5552 or 202-635-5540

An interfaith campaign providing support to Salvadoran refugees returning from exile in Mesa Grande, Honduras. Volunteers accompany refugees and displaced persons from El Salvador as they return to their homes, witnessing and protecting the refugees from violations of their rights.

New El Salvador Today (NEST)

P.O. Box 411436
San Francisco, CA 94141-1436
Phone: 415-529-2114

Sister cities, developmental and self-sufficiency aid to war-torn Salvadoran communities, particularly in rural areas. Accompanies refugees returning to El Salvador. Currently there are five official U.S.-Salvadoran sister cities.

Embassy, Nicaraguan

Embassy of Nicaragua

1627 New Hampshire Avenue NW
Washington, DC 20006
Phone: 202-387-4371

Environment

See also Agriculture; Technical Aid and Exchange.

Environmental Project on Central America (EPOCA)

Earth Island Environmental Center
13 Columbus Avenue
San Francisco, CA 94111
Phone: 415-788-3666

Publishes several "Green Papers" dealing with environmental issues in Central America. Also organizes environmental restoration brigades and projects including sea turtle conservation campaign, environmental conferences, and "Peace through Parks," promoting creation of an international park on the Nicaraguan-Costa Rican border, both to demilitarize the region and to preserve endangered rainforests.

Minnesotans for the Environment of Central Americans (MECA)

Contact: Enrique Gentzsch
2926 West River Pkwy.
Minneapolis, MN 55406
Phone: 612-296-7823 or 612-722-1220

Works cooperatively with Project Minnesota/Leon. Focuses on concerns including waste water and solid/hazardous waste management.

Ethnic

See Organizational Development; Women.

Europe

Nicaragua Solidarity Campaign
20-21 Compton Tr.
London N1, EN
Phone: 01-226-6747

**Documentation-centre City-linking
'The Netherlands-Nicaragua'**
Ronald van der Hijden
van Speykstraat 21
3572 XB
Utrecht, The Netherlands
Phone: (o)30-718163

Farming, Food

See Agriculture.

Forests

See Environment.

Guatemala

See Human Rights.

Health

*See also Children; Disabled; Technical Aid
and Exchange; Veterans; Women.*

**Committee for Health Rights in
Central America (CHRCA)**
513 Valencia Street, #6
San Francisco, CA 94110
Phone: 415-431-7760
Medical aid; film and video available.

**National Central American Health
Rights Network (NCAHRN)**
Contact: Barbara Johnston
853 Broadway Avenue, #416
New York, NY 10003
Phone: 212-420-9635

*Shipments of medical supplies; placement of
health providers wishing to work in Central
America; organizer of annual North America-
Nicaragua Colloquium on Health; offers short
tours to Central America, speakers, slide shows,
film and educational materials. Quarterly
newsletter, "Links."*

**Nicaragua Hospital Emergency
Generator Fund**
P.O. Box 473
Santa Clara, CA 95052
Phone: 408-243-4359
*Sends diesel generators to solve the problem of
electrical blackouts at Nicaraguan hospitals.*

**Nicaragua Medical/Material
Aid Campaign**
577 Columbus Avenue
New York, NY 10024
Phone: 718-965-1057

Nicaragua Medical Aid
Contact: Paul Kranz & Wendi Moore
1400 Shattuck Avenue, Suite 7-125
Berkeley, CA 94709
Phone: 415-849-1644
*Helps other groups purchase medicine and medi-
cal equipment for delivery and distribution
through UNICEF at 10% of cost. Arranges
technical assistance by U.S. medical personnel;
facilitates emergency shipments of medicine or
equipment. Willing to inspect equipment to help
determine if it works.*

Vecino Project
Contact: Joanne Sunshower
10 Magnus Street
Somerville, MA 02238
Phone: 617-776-8186
*Built a health clinic in the city of Estelí. Places
health professionals for direct service in the Estelí
region.*

Honduras

See Information.

Human Rights

See also El Salvador; Information; Legal.

Americas Watch
36 West 44th Street
New York, NY 10036
*Researches and publicizes human rights condi-
tions in Latin America.*

Amnesty International
304 West 58th Street
New York, NY 10019
*Investigates and reports on human rights condi-
tions throughout the world. Organizes letter-writ-
ing campaigns on behalf of persons imprisoned,
tortured or otherwise subjected to political persecution.*

**Council for Human Rights
in Latin America**

511 E 12th Ave
Eugene, OR 97401-3608
Phone: 503-295-7783 or 503-484-5867

*Sponsors Fundación Centroamericana, run by
Central Americans, which promotes unity, communication and development on the grass-roots
level between all the nations in Central America.*

FINDING Campaign

1020 S. Wabash, #401
Chicago, IL 60605-2215

*International campaign to free individuals "disap-
peared" in Guatemala.*

Washington Office on Latin America

110 Maryland Avenue NE
Washington, DC 20002
Phone: 202-544-8045

*A non-governmental human rights organization
supported by religious organizations, private
foundations and individual donors.*

Witness for Peace

P.O. Box 29497
Washington, DC 20017
Phone: 202-269-6316

*A faith-based organization; sends short-term and
long-term delegations to document contra atrocities in Nicaraguan war zones. Newsletter, lobbying, slide shows.*

Information

*See also Arts and Culture; Education;
Libraries; Nicaragua Network; Religion.*

Agencia Nueva Nicaragua (ANN)

1260 National Press Building
Washington, DC 20045
Phone: 202-662-7630

*Independent, non-profit international news ser-
vice focusing on Nicaragua and Central America. Publishes a weekly bulletin.*

Central American Historical Institute

Intercultural Center
Georgetown University
Washington, DC 20057
Phone: 202-625-8246

*An independent research group. Publishes
"Envío," monthly packets of in-depth reports on
various aspects of Nicaraguan society. Affiliated
with the Instituto Histórico Centroamericano at
the Jesuit-run Central American University,
Managua, Nicaragua.*

Central America Resource Center

P.O. Box 2327
Austin, TX 78768
Phone: 512-476-9841

*A non-profit information clearinghouse; dis-
tributes books and other publications, including a
biweekly compilation of news articles selected
from major U.S. and Mexican newspapers; and
the Directory of Central America Organizations,
listing over 1100 groups across the U.S. Sells
customized mailing lists.*

Contra Watch/Global Options

P.O. Box 40601
San Francisco, CA 94140
Phone: 415-550-1703

*Resource center and clearinghouse for informa-
tion about Nicaraguan contras and their supporters. Monthly newsletter, "Contra Watch."*

DataCenter

464 19th Street
Oakland, CA 94612
Phone: 415-835-4692

*Information on corporations, labor, industries,
neoconservatives, Central America. Research
services for community and activist groups.*

**Fairness and Accuracy in Reporting
(FAIR)**

666 Broadway, Suite 400
New York, NY 10012
Phone: 212-475-4640

*Monitors the accuracy and bias of the U.S. news
media in reporting peace-related issues; pressures
the media to include peace viewpoints. Newsletter, "Extra!"*

Honduras Information Center

Contact: Roxanna Pastor
One Summer Street
Somerville, MA 02143
Phone: 617-625-7220

*Educates about the situation in Honduras and its
relationship to events in the rest of Central
America, publicizes human rights violations in
Honduras, and reports on U.S. use of Honduras
as a base for intervention in the region.*

**Latin American Studies Association
Task Force on Nicaragua**

Contact: Prof. Harvey Williams
Sociology Department
University of the Pacific
Stockton, CA 95211
Phone: 209-946-2101

*Conducts annual two-week field seminars to
introduce Latin Americanists to research sources
in Nicaragua.*

Human Rights (cont.)

Information

North American Congress on Latin America (NACLA)
Contact: Martha Doggett
& Marc Edelman
151 West 19th Street
New York, NY 10011
Phone: 212-989-8890 or 212-989-8892

A non-profit research institute. Publishes NACLA Report on the Americas, providing detailed analysis of U.S.-Latin American issues and political, social and economic questions.

PeaceNet/Institute for Global Communications
Contact: Joanne Scott
3228 Sacramento Street
San Francisco, CA 94115
Phone: 415-923-0900

The world's first computer network for peace. Enables users throughout the U.S. and in 70 other countries to communicate with each other through electronic mail, conferences, databases, and a user directory. Includes the Central America Resource Network (CARNet).

The Voz Summary
P.O. Box 8151
Kansas City, MO 64112
Phone: 816-361-1101

A bi-weekly summary of news originating from Nicaragua, based on daily broadcasts of the Nicaraguan government's short-wave radio, La Voz de Nicaragua.

Journalism

See Information.

Legal

Center for Constitutional Rights
666 Broadway, 7th Floor
New York, NY 10012
Phone: 212-614-6464

Christic Institute
1324 North Capitol Street, NW
Washington, DC 20002
Phone: 202-797-8106

Currently waging a lawsuit on behalf of two U.S. journalists who survived a contra terrorist bombing in 1984. The lawsuit indicts key players in the Iran/Contra scandal, linking them to cocaine smuggling and other crimes. Publishes video, audio tapes, written documentation of the lawsuit, and a newsletter.

Movement Support Network
666 Broadway, 7th Floor
New York, NY 10012
Phone: 212-477-5652
Hotline: 212-614-6422

An anti-repression project of the National Lawyers Guild and the Center for Constitutional Rights. Provides legal aid to groups experiencing harassment. If an incident occurs, call their hotline. Publishes a "Harassment Update." Also sponsors visa denial project on behalf of Nicaraguans denied U.S. travel visas.

National Lawyers Guild/ Central America Task Force
Contact: Cathy Potler
853 Broadway, #1705
New York, NY 10003
Phone: 212-254-5700

Promotes educational, legal, and solidarity activities challenging U.S. intervention in Central America. Has filed lawsuits, conducted War Crimes Tribunals, sent delegations to the region.

Libraries

See also Arts and Culture; Information.

Nagarote Library Link
Contact: Barbara Hudgins
25 Chestnut Street, 1-H
Norwalk, CT 06854
Phone: 203-866-6040

Provides Spanish-language books, audiovisual materials and equipment, card catalogs to a Nicaraguan public library. Interested in sending U.S. librarians to volunteer in Nicaragua. Seeking student volunteers and donations of subscriptions to Spanish-language periodicals.

Living in Nicaragua

See also Information.

Committee of U.S. Citizens Living in Nicaragua (CUSCLIN)/ Through Our Eyes Publications
Distribution Committee
P.O. Box 4403-159
Austin, TX 78765

Distributes "Nicaragua Through Our Eyes," newsletter of the Committee of U.S. Citizens Living in Nicaragua (CUSCLIN).

Material Aid

See Agriculture; Arts and Culture; Construction; Disabled; Education; Health; Shipping; Technical Aid and Exchange.

Information (cont.)

Journalism

Legal

Libraries

Living in Nicaragua

Material aid

Media

See Arts and Culture; Information.

Medical

See Health; Technical Aid and Exchange.

Municipal Foreign Policies

See Sister Cities.

Networking

See Information; Organizational Development; Nicaragua Network; Sister Cities.

Nicaragua Network

Nicaragua Network National Headquarters

2025 "I" Street, N.W. #212
Washington, DC 20006
Phone: 202-223-2328
News hotline: 202-223-NICA

Organizes delegations; harvest, construction and environmental brigades; speaking tours; political lobbying both nationwide and regionally. Sponsors the "Let Nicaragua Live!" campaign, which provides aid to war refugees.

Regional Contacts:

Atlanta Committee on Central America (ACLA)

Contact: Robin Singer
P.O. Box 4184
Atlanta, GA 30302
Phone: 409-377-1079
Southeast coordinator: GA, FL, and AL.

Central America Resource Center/ Nicaragua Solidarity Committee

Contact: Gary Prevost
Newman Center
1701 University Avenue, S.E.
Minneapolis, MN 55414
Phone: 612-379-8799 or 612-378-1460

Books, audiovisual materials; publishes Directory of Central America Classroom Resources K-12, a catalog for teachers. Upper Midwest coordinator for Nicaragua Network, covering the states of MN, SD, ND, IA.

El Centro de la Raza

Contact: Debra Ross
2524 16th Avenue South
Seattle, WA 98144
Phone: 206-329-2974
Regional coordinator: WA, OR, ID, MO.

Latin America Assistance

Contact: Emily Jones
P.O. Box 7219
San Antonio, TX 78207
Phone: 512-492-5239
Texas regional coordinator.

New England Central America Network (NECAN)

Contact: Julie Dow
1151 Massachusetts Avenue
Cambridge, MA 02138
Phone: 617-491-4205
Regional coordinator: CT, MA, RI, VT, ME, NH.

Nicaragua Information Center

Contact: Rick Lewis
P.O. Box 1004
Berkeley, CA 94701
Phone: 415-549-1387

Has a 300-book resource library, speakers bureau. Publishes "Nicaraguan Perspectives," the only nationally-distributed magazine about Nicaragua in the U.S. Regional coordinator for Nicaragua Network for CA, NV, AZ, UT, HI.

Nicaragua Solidarity Committee of Greater New York

Contact: Julie Spriggs
339 Lafayette Street
New York, NY 10012
Phone: 212-674-9499
New York regional coordinator for Nicaragua Network.

Nicaraguan Embassy

See Embassy, Nicaraguan.

Organizational Development

See also Information; Nicaragua Network; Sister Cities.

Central American Solidarity Alliance

Contact: Julie Boss
1151 Massachusetts Avenue
Cambridge, MA 02138
Phone: 617-776-8293 or 617-491-6972
Produces the "Let Nicaragua Live" Calendar which serves as a fundraiser for solidarity groups.

Interreligious Foundation for Community Organization, Inc. (IFCO)
402 W. 145th Street
New York, NY 10031
Phone: 212-926-5757

Organizes intensive "Central America Information Week" educational campaigns in selected states and congressional districts. Targets middle Americans, with simultaneous indepth outreach to Black and Hispanic communities, drawing linkages between Nicaragua and ethnic groups' struggles for justice in the U.S.

Peace Development Fund
Contact: Meg Gage
P.O. Box 270
Amherst, MA 01004
Phone: 413-256-8306

Provides financial grants to groups working for peace. Also offers training and advice on fundraising and other aspects of organizational development.

Orphans

See Disabled; Children.

Partners of the Americas

See Sister Cities.

Refugees

See El Salvador; Human Rights; Nicaragua Network.

Religion

See also Education; El Salvador; Human Rights; Information; Organizational Development.

CEPAD Newsletter
Contact: Bob Buescher
32867 SE Hwy 211
Eagle Creek, OR 97022
Phone: 503-637-6411

English-language newsletter of Nicaragua's Evangelical Committee for Aid to Development (CEPAD).

Interreligious Task Force on Central America
475 Riverside Drive, Room 563
New York, NY 10115
Phone: 212-870-3383

Provides educational, theological, liturgical and programmatic resources focusing on the theme of partnership between people of faith in North and Central America.

Religious Task Force on Central America
1747 Connecticut Avenue, NW
Washington, DC 20009
Phone: 202-387-7652

Publishes "Central America Report," a bimonthly journal.

Southern New England & New Hampshire Conference of United Methodist Church
Contact: Eric Swanfeldt
34 Maple Avenue Ext.
Uncasville, CT 06382
Phone: 203-848-3856 or 203-848-7468

Has a "covenant relationship" with the Iglesia de Cristo de Nicaragua.

Research

See Information; Technical Aid and Exchange.

Resource Centers

See Education; Information.

Science

See Technical Aid and Exchange.

Shipping

Quixote Center-Quest for Peace
Contact: John Kellenberg
P.O. Box 5206
Hyattsville, MD 20782
Phone: 301-699-0042 or 212-832-1913

Major coordinator of material aid shipments to Nicaragua. Can advise on how to ship goods.

Sister Churches

See Religion.

Sister Cities

See also El Salvador; Europe; Embassy, Nicaraguan.

Boston CASA
Contact: Kathy Brown
CASA/1151 Massachusetts Avenue
Cambridge, MA 02138
Phone: 617-492-8699

Provides advice and support for groups in eastern Massachusetts wishing to initiate and develop sister-city projects with Nicaragua or El Salvador.

Center for Innovative Diplomacy

Contact: Michael Schuman
17931 Skypark Circle, Suite F
Irvine, CA 92714
Phone: 714-250-1296

Dedicated to reducing the risks of nuclear and conventional war by encouraging direct citizen and city involvement in foreign affairs. Publishes a quarterly magazine, the "Bulletin of Municipal Foreign Policy."

National Association of the Partners of the Americas

2001 "S" Street NW
Washington, DC 20009

Oversees "partner state" programs between the United States and Latin America. Founded in the 1960s under Kennedy's "Alliance for Progress." Calls itself "nonpolitical" but receives significant money from the U.S. government, as well as major U.S. corporations. Collaborates with U.S. government in Latin America through agencies such as the Agency for International Development (U.S. AID).

Northern California Ecumenical Council (NCEC)

Contact: Janine Chagoya
942 Market Street, Room 706
San Francisco, CA 94102
Phone: 415-433-6057

Frequent tours to sister cities in Nicaragua. Has developed relationships with daycare centers, health facilities, churches, and schools. Assists groups on the west coast wishing to develop sister-city projects with Nicaragua.

Sister Cities International

1625 "I" Street, NW, Suite 424-26
Washington, DC 20006
Phone: 202-293-5504

Umbrella network for over 1,000 U.S. sister-city affiliations worldwide. "Nonpolitical"; partly funded by U.S. government. Has not worked with many U.S.-Nicaragua sister cities since the Sandinista revolution. SCI's member cities pay dues on a sliding scale based on the size of the U.S. city.

U.S.-Nicaragua Friendship Project

Contact: Liz Chilsen, WCCN
P.O. Box 1534
Madison, WI 53701
Phone: 608-257-7230

Promotes cooperation and information-sharing among U.S.-Nicaragua sister cities.

Wisconsin-Nicaragua Partners

1321 Temkin Avenue, #12
Madison, WI 53703
Phone: 608-231-2591 or 608-231-2124

The Wisconsin affiliate of Partners of the Americas, a U.S. government-sponsored sister-state program. NOTE: See "National Association of Partners of the Americas."

Spanish Language Instruction

Casa Nicaragüense de Español

2330 W. Third Street, Suite 4
Los Angeles, CA 90057
Phone: 213-386-8077

Two- to eight-week programs of Spanish language training, political education, family living, and community activities in Managua; weekend trips outside of Managua.

Nuevo Instituto de CentroAmérica (NICA)

Contact: Beverly Treumann
P.O. Box 1409
Cambridge, MA 02238
Phone: 617-497-7142

Intensive Spanish-language instruction in Estelí. Participants live in the homes of Nicaraguan families and share in community life in Estelí; in addition, they meet with government officials, members of community organizations, opposition representatives, and others.

Sports

See also Technical Aid and Exchange.

Baseball Diplomacy Inc.

12335 Santa Monica Blvd.
Los Angeles, CA 90025

"Bats Not Bombs." Organizes sports delegations between the U.S. and Nicaragua. "We want to compete on ball fields, not battlefields."

Technical Aid and Exchange

See also Education; Health; Construction.

Bikes Not Bombs

Contact: Ken Hughes
P.O. Box 56538
Washington, DC 20011
Phone: 301-589-1810 or 301-589-1810

Sends bicycles and bicycle spare parts to ease Nicaragua's transportation problems and to promote environmentally sound transportation policy. Maintains bike shops in Nicaragua for assembly, repair and training Nicaraguans in bicycle repair.

NicaTech
P.O. Box 95815
Seattle, WA 98145-2815
Phone: 206-722-7018 or 206-634-0870
Water-quality testing, hydroelectric plant, machine shop, communication links for refugee communities, especially in the El Cuá-Bocay region of northern Nicaragua.

Nicaragua Appropriate Technology Project (NICAT)
3112 Alderwood Avenue
Bellingham, WA 98225
Phone: 206-671-8303
Housing, potable water systems, sanitation, and other humanitarian projects in close cooperation with Nicaraguan development agencies.

Puente de Paz (Bridge for Peace)
c/o Arkansas Peace Center
Contact: Bob Bland
1039 Overcrest Street
Fayetteville, AR 72703
Phone: 501-442-7423 or 501-565-3581
Develops potable water systems in Nicaraguan war zones.

Science for People/Science for Nicaragua Committee
Contact: Michael Harris
897 Main Street
Cambridge, MA 02139
Phone: 617-547-0370

TECNICA
Contact: Suzanne Lyons
3254 Adeline
Berkeley, CA 94703
Phone: 415-655-3838; tele
Technical training, assistance in cooperation with Nicaraguan ministries. "Job placement" for volunteers with technical skills.

Tours

See also Education; Human Rights; Sister Cities; Spanish Language Instruction; Technical Aid and Exchange.

Center for Global Education
Contact: Sara Nelson-Pallmeyer
Augsburg College
731 21st Avenue South
Minneapolis, MN 55454
Phone: 612-330-1159
Offers a variety of "experiential education programs" that examine the problems of social change, in order to build international awareness, inform debate on foreign policy, and contribute to a more just and peaceful world.

Marazul Tours
250 W. 57 Street, Suite 1311
New York, NY 10107
Phone: 212-582-9570 or 800-223-5334
Political-cultural tours to Nicaragua, with bilingual guides.

Tropical Tours
2330 West Third Street, Suite 4
Los Angeles, CA 90057
Phone: 800-854-5858 or 213-389-4123
Organizes group tours, specializing in socio-political aspects of Nicaragua including aspects of Nicaraguan society such as health, agriculture, education, culture, religion, women's issues and the labor movement.

Tur-Nica
929 Douglass Street
San Francisco, CA 92114
Phone: 415-647-6220
Travel agency organizing educational tours of Nicaragua.

Trade

Coffee for Peace
P.O. Box 2435
Fort Bragg, CA 95437
Phone: 800-422-3380 or 707-964-8640
Distributes and sells Nicaraguan coffee processed in Canada, thus legally bypassing the U.S. embargo on trade with Nicaragua.

Friends of the Third World/ Cooperative Trading
611 West Wayne Street
Fort Wayne, IN 46802-2125
Phone: 219-422-6821
Imports Nicaraguan coffee processed in Holland and Canada.

Pueblo to People
1616 Montrose #1027
Houston, TX 77006
Phone: 713-523-1197
A nonprofit organization that sells crafts and agricultural products produced in Central America and the Philippines to support grassroots organizations of the poor.

Trade For Peace, Inc.
P.O. Box 3190
Madison, WI 53704-0190
Phone: 608-255-6274

A nonviolent, civil disobedience project that imports postage stamps and various crafts to protest the U.S. embargo on trade with Nicaragua. Detailed knowledge of the embargo's legal scope and exemptions from the embargo.

Transportation

See Shipping; Technical Aid and Exchange; Tours.

Veterans

Bill Motto VFW Post 5888
P.O. Box 664
Santa Cruz, CA 95061

Organized Concord Naval Action to block shipping of U.S. weapons from the Concord Naval Base in California to Central America. Also organized "Veterans Fast for Peace Action Team" and a Ben Linder memorial construction brigade, which rebuilt a health post destroyed by contras.

Veterans Fast for Life/
Veterans Peace Action Team
P.O. Box 586
Santa Cruz, CA 95061
Phone: 408-426-7822

Organizes study tours of conflict zones in Nicaragua to show solidarity and to demonstrate opposition to the contra war.

Veterans of the
Abraham Lincoln Brigade (VALB)
799 Broadway, Room 227
New York, NY 10003
Phone: 212-674-5552

Veterans of the fight against fascism in the Spanish Civil War prior to World War II. Organizes "Ambulances for Nicaragua." Members include Bill Gandall, a veteran of the U.S. military campaign against Sandino in the 1920s.

Vietnam Veterans Against the War
P.O. Box 408594
Chicago, IL 60640
Phone: 312-327-5756

Fighting against the "next Vietnam." Publishes a national newsletter, "The Veteran."

Video

See Arts and Culture.

War Relief

See Disabled; Nicaragua Network; Veterans.

Water

See Construction; Environment; Technical Aid and Exchange.

Women

See also Children; Health.

MADRE Women's Peace Network
121 West 27 Street, Room 301
New York, NY 10001-6207
Phone: 212-627-0444

Women's health and child care projects in Nicaragua and El Salvador. A very active program of twinning day centers in the U.S. with centers in Nicaragua, with over 30 U.S. centers paired.

Somos Hermanas
3543 18th Street
San Francisco, CA 94110
Phone: 415-621-3870

A multiracial national network of lesbian and non-lesbian women opposing U.S. intervention in Central America.

Where to Find Groups in the Directory of Interest-Affiliated Organizations

Agencia Nueva Nicaragua: *Information*

American Friends Service Committee School Supplies Campaign: *Education*

Americas Watch: *Human Rights*

A²MISTAD/Guild House: *Construction*

Amnesty International: *Human Rights*

Architects and Planners in Support of Nicaragua (APSNICA): *Construction*

Arts for a New Nicaragua: *Arts and Culture*

Atlanta Committee on Central America (ACLA): *Nicaragua Network*

Baseball Diplomacy Inc.: *Sports*

Bikes Not Bombs: *Technical Aid and Exchange*

Bill Motto VFW Post 5888: *Veterans*

Boston CASA: *Sister Cities*

CASA Nicaragua-Chicago: *Arts and Culture*

Casa Nicaragüense de Español: *Spanish Language Instruction*

Center for Constitutional Rights: *Legal*

Center for Global Education: *Tours*

Center for Innovative Diplomacy: *Sister Cities*

Central America Resource Center: *Information*

Central America Resource Center/Nicaragua Solidarity Committee: *Nicaragua Network*

Central American Historical Institute: *Information*

Central American Solidarity Alliance: *Organizational Development*

CEPAD Newsletter: *Religion*

Christic Institute: *Legal*

Coffee for Peace: *Trade*

Committee for Health Rights in Central America (CHRCA): *Health*

Committee in Solidarity with the People of El Salvador (CISPES): *El Salvador*

Committee of U.S. Citizens Living in Nicaragua (CUSCLIN): *Living in Nicaragua*

Committee to Aid the UNAN: *Education*

Contra Watch/Global Options: *Information*

Council for Human Rights in Latin America: *Human Rights*

DataCenter: *Information*

Denver Disabled Peace Project: *Disabled*

Disabled International Support Effort (DISE): *Disabled*

Documentation-centre City-linking 'The Netherlands-Nicaragua': *Europe*

Ecumenical Refugee Council: *Children*

El Centro de la Raza: *Nicaragua Network*

Embassy of Nicaragua: *Embassy, Nicaraguan*

The Empowerment Project: *Arts and Culture*

Environmental Project on Central America (EPOCA): *Environment*

Fairness and Accuracy in Reporting (FAIR): *Information*

FINDING Campaign: *Human Rights*

Food First/Institute for Food and Development Policy: *Agriculture*

Friends of the Third World/Cooperative Trading: *Trade*

Going Home/SHARE Foundation: *El Salvador*

Guild House/HAP-NICA: *Agriculture*

Honduras Information Center: *Information*

Interreligious Foundation for Community Organization, Inc.: *Organizational Development*

Interreligious Task Force on Central America: *Religion*

Latin American Studies Association Task Force on Nicaragua: *Information*

Latin America Assistance: *Nicaragua Network*

MADRE Women's Peace Network: *Women*
Marazul Tours: *Tours*
Minnesotans for the Environment of Central Americans (MECA): *Environment*
Movement Support Network: *Legal*

Nagarote Library Link: *Libraries*
National Association of the Partners of the Americas: *Sister Cities*
National Central American Health Rights Network (NCAHRN): *Health*
National Lawyers Guild/Central America Task Force: *Legal*
New El Salvador Today (NEST): *El Salvador*
New England Central America Network (NECAN): *Nicaragua Network*
Nicaragua Appropriate Technology Project (NICAT): *Technical Aid and Exchange*
Nicaragua Hospital Emergency Generator Fund: *Health*
Nicaragua Information Center: *Nicaragua Network*
Nicaragua Medical Aid: *Health*
Nicaragua Medical/Material Aid Campaign: *Health*
Nicaragua Network National Headquarters: *Nicaragua Network*
Nicaragua Solidarity Campaign: *Europe*
Nicaragua Solidarity Committee of Greater New York: *Nicaragua Network*
Nicaraguan Cultural Alliance: *Arts and Culture*
NicaTech: *Technical Aid and Exchange*
North American Congress on Latin America (NACLA): *Information*
North American Farm Alliance: *Agriculture*
Northern California Ecumenical Council: *Sister Cities*
Nuevo Instituto de CentroAmérica (NICA): *Spanish Language Instruction*

Oxfam America: *Agriculture*

Peace Development Fund: *Organizational Development*
PeaceNet/Institute for Global Communications: *Information*
Pueblo to People: *Trade*
Puente de Paz (Bridge for Peace): *Technical Aid and Exchange*
Quixote Center-Quest for Peace: *Shipping*

Religious Task Force on Central America: *Religion*

Science for People/Science for Nicaragua Committee: *Technical Aid and Exchange*
Sister Cities International: *Sister Cities*
Somos Hermanas: *Women*
Southern New England and New Hampshire Conference of United Methodist Church: *Religion*

TECNICA: *Technical Aid and Exchange*
Through Our Eyes Publications-CUSCLIN: *Living in Nicaragua*
Trade For Peace, Inc.: *Trade*
Tropical Tours: *Tours*
Tur-Nica: *Tours*

U.S.-Nicaragua Friendship Project: *Sister Cities*

Vecino Project: *Health*
Ventana: *Arts and Culture*
Veterans Fast for Life/Veterans Peace Action Team: *Veterans*
Veterans of the Abraham Lincoln Brigade: *Veterans*
Vietnam Veterans Against the War: *Veterans*
The Voz Summary: *Information*

War Relief for Nicaraguans: *Disabled*
Washington Office on Latin America: *Human Rights*
Wisconsin-Nicaragua Partners: *Sister Cities*
Witness for Peace: *Human Rights*

Appendix: Sample Resolutions by Local Governments

An ordinance creating a Sister City relationship between the City of Corinto, Nicaragua, and the City of Portland, Oregon; approving the Articles of Incorporation for the non-profit corporation, the Portland-Corinto Sister City Association, Inc.; and declaring an emergency.

The City of Portland ordains:

Section 1.
The Council Finds:

1. That the Sister Program created by President Eisenhower has increased international understanding between cities of the world.
2. That the City of Portland, through its two sister city relationships with Sapporo, Japan, and Guadalajara, Mexico, has benefited from increased understanding and cultural ties with these two cities and their countries.
3. That a significant number of Portland residents have visited Nicaragua and, specifically, the Pacific seaport city of Corinto, Nicaragua; and as a result of these visits, a number of new relationships have been developed between individuals, churches, labor organizations, businesses, schools, health clinics and other organizations in the two cities.
4. That a substantial number of Portland citizens have expressed an interest in maintaining continuous, ongoing contact with the city of Corinto, Nicaragua.
5. That the Mayor and City Council of Corinto, Nicaragua, have expressed their desire to form a Sister City relationship with the City of Portland.
6. That the Portland-Corinto Sister City Association is currently supported by funds raised in the Portland community and, therefore, does not require and has no intention of requesting city funds for operation of the Portland-Corinto Sister City Program.
7. That in order to facilitate functioning, financing and other matters relating to the program, it is desirable to form a non-profit corporation to be managed by a Board of Directors.
8. That attached to this ordinance is a form of Articles of Incorporation for the Portland-Corinto Sister City Association, Inc., which includes the initial directors of the corporation.

Now, Therefore, the Council Directs:

a. The creation of a Sister City relationship between the City of Corinto, Nicaragua, and the City of Portland, Oregon.
b. Approval of the Articles of Incorporation for the non-profit corporation, The Portland-Corinto Sister City Association, Inc.

Section 2.
The Council declares that an emergency exists because it is necessary for the non-profit corporation to become incorporated and functioning at the earliest possible time: therefore, this Ordinance shall be in force and effect from and after its passage by the Council.

Passed by the Council,
Commissioner Mike Lindberg
David E. Judd:bas
March 29, 1985

An official resolution should state your case clearly. It should develop your argument and include important relevant issues. It should conclude with a request for action.

The "findings" section states the *evidence and arguments* in favor of the proposed action.

Reference to a broad historical precedent legitimizes the request; a local precedent adds further justification.

Demonstrate pressing *local interest.*

Show that *research and preparatory work* have been done.

City officials are more comfortable if they can prove *little or no cost to taxpayers.*

This is a finer detail than most resolutions require; here it indicates that a stable organizational structure is planned.

Describe the *action to be taken* upon passage of the resolution.

Some resolutions, like this one passed by the Wisconsin State Legislature, present the findings in a series of "whereas" clauses, and spell out the actions to be taken with statements that begin, "be it resolved."

The State of Wisconsin 1987 Senate Joint Resolution 39.
Enrolled Joint Resolution Relating to Memorializing Congress to End Aid to Contra Forces in Nicaragua.

Whereas, the state of Wisconsin and its citizens have maintained, since 1965, a special sister-state relationship with the government and people of Nicaragua; and

Whereas, the friendship between the peoples of Wisconsin and Nicaragua has been nurtured by humanitarian aid and educational and cultural exchanges; and

Whereas, on August 7, 1987, the presidents of El Salvador, Honduras, Guatemala, Nicaragua and Costa Rica adopted a peace plan, and President Oscar Arias of Costa Rica has received the Nobel Peace Prize for his efforts in spearheading the development and adoption of that peace plan; and

Whereas, the Arias Plan demonstrates the commitment of Central Americans to determine policy for their region, recognizing the potentially harmful influence of the superpowers, including the Soviet Union; and

Whereas, the United States government, with bipartisan congressional support, has been sending aid to the insurgent contra forces seeking to overthrow the elected government of Nicaragua; and

Whereas, military aid to the contras has undermined the relationship and friendship between the peoples of Nicaragua and the United States and has heightened tensions between the two nations; and

Whereas, elimination of aid to the contra forces does not constitute an endorsement of the present government in Nicaragua or its policies; now, therefore, be it

Resolved, by the Senate, the Assembly concurring, that the legislature of the state of Wisconsin, on behalf of the residents of this state, hereby requests the Congress of the United States to end funding for additional military aid to the contras in Nicaragua and, instead, to support appropriations for humanitarian aid to improve the health, education and standard of living for the people of our sister state; and, be it further

Resolved, that duly attested copies of this joint resolution be transmitted by the senate chief clerk to the President of the United States and to each of the members of the U.S. congressional delegation from this state.

Representative Thomas A. Loftus,
Speaker of the Assembly

Senator Fred Risser,
President of the Senate

October 29, 1987

Findings and ballot initiative wording from Ann Arbor, Michigan.
Approved by voter referendum in the April, 1986 election.

This resolution follows essentially the same format as the Portland, Oregon resolution, except that it was approved by voters through a municipal ballot referendum rather than through city council action.

Findings:

1. The vast expenditures for war in Central America divert resources from solving the causes of strife in Central America, and diminish the federal funds available for the vital needs of our city and our nation, needs such as public safety, housing, health care, education, transportation, economic development, and the creation of jobs.
2. The U.S. government is currently providing hundreds of millions of dollars in military aid each year to the governments of El Salvador, Guatemala, and Honduras where systematic human rights abuses by government-sponsored and government-tolerated groups continue.
3. Our tax dollars are enabling the contras to wage war against the people of Nicaragua.
4. The massive U.S. government arms build-up and continual military maneuvers in Honduras increase tensions in an already explosive region and make full-scale U.S. military intervention more likely.
5. The U.S. government is materially supporting continuing aerial bombing of civilians in rural El Salvador.
6. U.S. government pressure is undermining Costa Rica's long-standing position of neutrality in the region and is militarizing the only Central American country without a standing army.
7. Many of the actions of the U.S. government in the region are in violation of international law.
8. We the people of the City of Ann Arbor, as citizens and taxpayers, share in the ultimate responsibility for these actions.

An Ordinance Establishing Initiatives for Peace in Central America:

Shall the city adopt an ordinance requiring 1) the City Clerk to convey to the federal government a statement by the people of Ann Arbor expressing the desire that our tax dollars be spent on peaceful not military purposes in Central America, supporting the right of self-determination; and 2) the City to establish a Central America Sister City Task Force to facilitate educational, cultural, and peaceful exchanges?

The City of Ann Arbor ordains:

Section 1.
The City Clerk shall convey the following statement to our representatives in Congress and to the President:

I.   The people of the city of Ann Arbor desire that our foreign aid dollars to Central America be used for life, not death; for reconstruction, not destruction; for economic prosperity, not economic destabilization.
II. The people of the city of Ann Arbor support the right of self-determination and the peaceful settlement of conflicts in the region.
III. The people of the city of Ann Arbor respect the role of international law in the settling of international disputes and request that the United States government return to its former acceptance of the jurisdiction of the International Court of Justice at the Hague.
IV. The people of the City of Ann Arbor oppose the involvement of the United States government in the conflicts in Central America by means of continued military aid to the governments of El Salvador, Guatemala, and Honduras.
V.   The people of the City of Ann Arbor oppose the use of our tax dollars for the purpose of overthrowing or destabilizing the government of Nicaragua, and for the aerial bombing in El Salvador.

VI. The people of Ann Arbor ask that federal funds now being used to promote destruction in Central America be redirected to the promotion of services vital to the welfare of our citizens, needs such as housing, health care, educaton, transportation, public safety, economic development, and the creation of jobs, as well as towards the similar needs of the people of Central America.

Section 2.

That Chapter 8 of the Code of the City of Ann Arbor is amended by adding a new section 1:235 which shall read as follows:

1:235. In order to foster communication and peaceful relations with the people of Central America, there is hereby created a seven member Central America Sister City Task Force, to be appointed on nomination of Mayor with approval of Council within 30 days of the effective date of this section, which shall:

A. Establish a sister city relationship with a city or cities within the countries of Costa Rica, El Salvador, Guatemala, Honduras, and Nicaragua.
B. Encourage community groups such as churches, educational institutions, businesses, unions, and civic organizations to raise private funds, materials, and volunteers to facilitate educational and cultural exchanges between the people of the selected sister cities and the people of Ann Arbor.
C. Report to the Mayor and Council and to the people of Ann Arbor on its work, actions, and further recommendations within six months and again within one year after the passage of this ordinance, after which the Task Force shall cease to exist.

Suggested Reading

Central America

Barry, Tom and Deb Preusch, *The Central America Fact Book*. New York: Grove Press, 1986. More facts than you can shake a big stick at.

Barry, Tom, Deb Preusch, and Beth Wood, *Dollars and Dictators: A Guide to Central America*. New York: Grove Press, 1983.

Galeano, Eduardo, *Open Veins of Latin America, Five Centuries of the Pillage of a Continent*. New York: Monthly Review Press, 1973.

Hamilton, Nora, Jeffrey Frieden, Linda Fuller, and Manuel Pastor, Jr., *Crisis in Central America: Regional Dynamics and U.S. Policy in the 1980s*. Boulder: Westview Press/PACCA, 1988.

LaFeber, Walter, *Inevitable Revolutions: the United States in Central America*. New York: Norton, 1983.

Pearce, Jenny, *Under the Eagle: U.S. Intervention in Central America and the Caribbean*. Boston: South End Press, 1982.

History

Bermann, Karl, *Under the Big Stick: Nicaragua and the United States Since 1848*. Boston: South End Press, 1986. Highly readable, informative.

Booth, John A., *The End and the Beginning: The Nicaraguan Revolution*. Boulder, Colorado: Westview Press, 1982.

Center for Research and Documentation of the Atlantic Coast, *Trabil Nani: Historical Background and Current Situation on the Atlantic Coast of Nicaragua*. New York: The Riverside Church Disarmament Project, 1985. Analyzes relations between the Nicaraguan government and the indigenous people of the Atlantic Coast, including Miskito Indians.

Elman, Richard M., *Cocktails at Somoza's: A Reporter's Sketchbook of Events in Revolutionary Nicaragua*. Cambridge, Massachusetts: Apple-wood Books, 1981.

Macaulay, Neill, *The Sandino Affair*. New York: Quadrangle Books, 1967.

De Nogales, Rafael, *The Looting of Nicaragua*. New York: Robert M. McBride & Co., 1928.

Rosengarten, Frederic, *Freebooters Must Die! The Life and Death of William Walker, the Most Notorious Filibuster of the Nineteenth Century*. Wayne, Pennsylvania: Haverford House, 1976. William Walker was a U.S. mercenary who invaded Nicaragua in the 1850s and attempted to declare himself president of the country.

Walker, Thomas H., *Nicaragua, the Land of Sandino*. Boulder, Colorado: Westview Press, 1981.

Wall, James T., *Manifest Destiny Denied: America's First Intervention in Nicaragua*. University Press of America, 1981.

Human Rights

Brody, Reed, *Contra Terror in Nicaragua*. Boston: South End Press, 1985.

Cabestrero, Teófilo (translated by Robert R. Barr), *Blood of the Innocent: Victims of the Contras' War in Nicaragua*. Maryknoll, New York: Orbis Books; London, England; Catholic Institute for International Relations, 1985.

Dutcher, Mary, *Nicaragua: Violations of the Laws of War by Both Sides, February-December, 1985: An Investigative Report*. Washington, DC: The Washington Office on Latin America, 1986.

Nicaragua (general)

Collins, Joseph, *Food and Farming in the New Nicaragua*. San Francisco: Institute for Food and Development Policy, 1983.

_____, and Francis Moore Lappé (photographs by Peter Barnes), *Now We Can Speak: A Journey Through the New Nicaragua*. San Francisco: Institute for Food and Development Policy, 1982.

Davis, Peter, *Where is Nicaragua?* New York: Simon and Schuster, 1987.

Hirshon, Sheryl and Judy Butler, *And Also Teach Them to Read*. Connecticut: Lawrence Hill and Co., 1983. Focuses on the Nicaraguan literacy campaign of 1980,

159

which successfully reduced the country's illiteracy rate from 54% to 12%.

Meisalas, Susan, photographer, *Nicaragua*. New York: Pantheon Books, 1984.

Miller, Valerie, *Between Struggle and Hope: the Nicaraguan Literacy Crusade*. Boulder: Westview Press, 1985.

Randall, Margaret, *Sandino's Daughters*. Vancouver: New Star Books, 1981.

Rosset, Peter and John Vandermeer, eds., The *Nicaragua Reader: Documents of a Revolution Under Fire*. New York: Grove Press, 1983.

_____, Nicaragua, *Unfinished Revolution: The New Nicaragua Reader*. New York: Grove Press, 1986.

Ruchwarger, Gary, *People in Power: Forging a Grassroots Democracy in Nicaragua*. South Hadley, MA: Bergin & Garvey, Inc., 1987.

Somoza Debayle, Anastasio, *Nicaragua Betrayed*. Boston: Western Islands, 1980. The dictator's statement after fleeing the country. Approximately the same length as *Mein Kampf*; not nearly as honest.

Walker, Thomas W., ed., *Nicaragua In Revolution*. New York: Praeger, 1982.

_____, *Reagan vs. the Sandinistas: the Undeclared War on Nicaragua*. Boulder: Westview Press, 1987.

Nicaraguan Revolution

Black, George, *Triumph of the People: The Sandinista Revolution in Nicaragua*. London: Zed Press, 1981.)

Cabezas, Omar, *Fire from the Mountain: The Making of a Sandinista*. New York: Crown, 1985.

Deighton, Jane, *et. al. Sweet Ramparts: Women in Revolutionary Nicaragua*. London: War on Want, Nicaragua Solidarity Campaign, 1983.

María Vilas, Carlos (translated by Judy Butler), *The Sandinista Revolution: National Liberation and Social Transformation in Central America*. Berkeley, CA: Monthly Review Press, 1986.

Selser, Gregorio, *Sandino*. Monthly Review Press, New York, 1981.

Spalding, Rose J., ed., *The Political Economy of Revolutionary Nicaragua*. Winchester, Mass.: Allen and Union, 1987.

Weber, Henri (translated by Patrick Camiller), *Nicaragua: The Sandinist Revolution*. New York: Schocken Books, 1981.

Organizing and Fundraising

Ayvazian, Andrea, Randall Kehler, Ben Senturia, *Thinking Strategically: A Primer on Long-Range Strategic Planning for Grassroots Peace and Justice Organizations*. Amherst, Massachusetts: Exchange Project, 1988. How to avoid burnout and give your project stability for the long haul. An important book. (Also see the Exchange Project's organizational listing under "Interest-Affiliated Groups.")

Brody, Ralph, Ph.D., *Fundraising Events: Strategies and Programs for Success*. New York: Human Sciences Press, 1988.

Flanagan, Joan, *The Grassroots Fundraising Book: How to Raise Money in Your Community*. Chicago: The Swallow Press, Inc., 1977.

_____, *The Successful Volunteer Organization*. Chicago: Contemporary Books, Inc., 1981. If you've only got time to read one book about organizing and fundraising, this one covers the bases. Well-written, knowledgeable and to the point.

Kahn, Si, *Organizing: A Guide for Grassroots Leaders*. New York: McGraw-Hill, 1982.

Klein, Kim, *Fundraising for Social Change*. Washington, DC: CRG Press, 1985.

National Network of Grantmakers (Jill R. Shellow, ed.), *Grant Seekers Guide: Funding Sourcebook*. Washington, DC: Moyer Bell Ltd.)

Seltzer, Michael, *Securing Your Organization's Future: A Complete Guide to Fundraising Strategies*. New York: The Foundation Center, 1987.

Periodicals

Barricada Internacional. A weekly, English-language version of the Sandinista newspaper Barricada. $30/year. Send subscription to: Barricada Canada, P.O. Box 398, Station E, Toronto M6H 4E3, CANADA.

Bulletin of Municipal Foreign Policy. A quarterly publication of the Center for Innovative Diplomacy, 17931 Skypark Circle, Suite F, Irvine, CA 92714. Reports regularly on U.S.-Nicaragua sister city projects, as well as other city-based initiatives including South Africa divestment, nuclear-free zoning, sister cities with the Soviet Union. Correspondents in 120 U.S. cities. $15/year.

Nicaragua (general)

Nicaraguan Revolution

Organizing and Fundraising

Periodicals

Central America Information Bulletin. A weekly publication of the Agencia Nueva Nicaragua (ANN), an independent Nicaraguan news organization. $25/year. Send subscription to: Agencia Nueva Nicaragua, Washington Bureau, 1260 National Press Building, Washington, DC 20045.

Envío. A monthly in-depth analysis of current events and issues in Nicaragua edited by an international team of analysts at the Central American Historical Institute, Intercultural Center, Georgetown University, Washington, DC 20057. At $25/year, it is the best resource for regular updating on Nicaragua.

NACLA Report on the Americas. Published bi-monthly by the North American Congress on Latin America, an independent non-profit organization founded in 1966 focusing on the political economy of Latin America. Subscriptions: $20/year. Write to: NACLA, 151 W. 19th Street, 9th Floor, New York, NY 10011.

Nicaragua Through Our Eyes. The official publication of the Committee of U.S. Citizens Living in Nicaragua. Describes daily life, the political situation and solidarity projects in Nicaragua with personal testimony. $10/year. Send to Through Our Eyes Publications, Distribution Committee, P.O. Box 4403-159, Austin, TX 78765.

Nicaraguan Perspectives. A publication of the Nicaraguan Information Center, P.O. Box 94701 1004, Berkeley, CA 94701.

Update. Monthly packets of three or more reports published by the Central American Historical Institute, Georgetown University, Washington, DC 20057; phone 202-687-5676. $27/year to individuals; $50/year to institutions and overseas.

Poetry

Cardenal, Ernesto, *Apocalypse and Other Poems.* New York: New Directions, 1977. We're big fans of Ernesto Cardenal, and this volume is one of his best.

_____, *Love.* Crossroad, 1981. Prose meditations

_____, *Psalms.* Crossroad, 1981. Reconstruction of David's psalms, hymns of praise and community laments.

_____, *Zero Hour and other Documentary Poems.* New York: New Directions, 1980.

Darío, Ruben (Lysander Kemp, translator), *Selected Poems.* Austin: University of Texas, 1965. Known internationally as the father of the modernist movement in Spanish-language poetry, Darío is a major reason for Nicaragua's reputation as a "nation of poets."

_____, *Poetic and Prose Selections.* Boston: Heath, 1931.

_____ (edited by George Umphrey and Carlos Garcia Prada), *Selections from the Prose and Poetry of Ruben Darío.* New York: MacMillan, 1928.

Johnson, Kent, trans., *A Nation of Poets: Writings from the Poetry Workshops of Nicaragua.* Los Angeles, CA: West End Press, 1985.

White, Steven F., ed., *Poets of Nicaragua, A Bilingual Anthology, 1918-1979.* Greensboro, North Carolina: Unicorn Press, 1982. Nicaraguan poetry after Ruben Darío but before the revolution.

Religion

Berryman, Phillip, *The Religious Roots of Rebellion: Christians in Central American Revolutions.* Maryknoll, New York: Orbis Books, 1984.

Cabestrero, Teófilo (translated by Robert R. Barr), *Ministers of God, Ministers of the People: Testimonies of Faith from Nicaragua.* Maryknoll, New York: Orbis Books; London: Zed Press, 1983.

Cardenal, Ernesto, *The Gospel of Solentiname,* 4 vols. Maryknoll, New York: Orbis Books, 1976. Transcripts of scriptural dialogues between peasants living on the island of Solentiname, Nicaragua. Ernesto Cardenal is a Catholic priest and world-renowned poet, currently active within the Nicaraguan government. Highly recommended.

Lernoux, Penny, *Cry of the People: United States Involvement in the Rise of Fascism, Torture, and the Persecution of the Catholic Church in Latin America.* New York: Penguin, 1980.

Randall, Margaret, *Christians in the Nicaraguan Revolution.* Vancouver, Washington: New Star Books, 1983.

U.S. Citizens Living and Working in Nicaragua

Everett, Melissa, *Bearing Witness, Building Bridges: Interviews with North Americans Living and Working in Nicaragua.* Philadelphia: New Society Publishers, 1986.

McGinnis, James, *Solidarity With the People of Nicaragua*. New York: Orbis Books, 1985.

Ridenour, Ron, *Yankee Sandinistas: Interviews with North Americans Living and Working in the New Nicaragua*. Willimantic, Connecticut: Curbstone Press; New York: distributed by The Talman Co., 1986.

U.S. Government Publications

Rudolph, James D., *Nicaragua, A Country Study*. Washington, DC: Headquarters, Department of the Army: For sale by the Supt. of Docs., U.S. G.P.O., 1983.

U.S. Department of State, *The Challenge to Democracy in Central America*. Washington, DC: U.S. Department of State, 1986.

U.S. Department of State, *Nicaraguan Biographies: A Resource Book*. Washington, DC: U.S. Department of State, 1988.

U.S. Intervention in Nicaragua

Burns, E. Bradford, *At War in Nicaragua: The Reagan Doctrine and the Politics of Nostalgia*. New York: Harper & Row, 1987.

Chomsky, Noam, *Turning the Tide: U.S. Intervention in Central America and the Struggle for Peace*. Boston: South End Press, 1985.

Cockburn, Leslie *Out of Control: The Story of the Reagan Administration's Secret War in Nicaragua, the Illegal Arms Pipeline, and the Contra Drug Connection*. New York: Atlantic Monthly Press, 1987. Engaging, gripping reading.

Dickey, Christopher, *With the Contras: A Reporter in the Wilds of Nicaragua*. New York: Simon and Schuster, 1985.

Diederich, Bernard, *Somoza and the Legacy of U.S. Involvement in Central America*. New York: Dutton, 1981.

Diskin, Martin, ed., *Trouble in Our Backyard: Central America and the United States in the Eighties*. New York: Pantheon Books, 1983.

Eich, Dieter and Carlos Rincon, eds., *The Contras: Interviews with Anti-Sandinistas*. San Francisco: Synthesis Publications, 1985.

Kornbluh, Peter, *Nicaragua: The Price of Intervention*. Washington, DC: Institute for Policy Studies, 1985.

_____ and Michael T. Klare, *Low Intensity Warfare: Counterinsurgency, Proinsurgency and Antiterrorism in the Eighties*. New York: Pantheon, 1988.

Miles, Sara, "The Real War: Low-Intensity Conflict in Central America," *NACLA Report on the Americas*, Volume XX, No. 2, April/May 1986, pp. 17-48. A seminal work analyzing the army's operating doctrine in Central America under the Reagan administration which, according to the army itself, is "the most likely form of conflict the U.S. Army will be involved in for the remainder of this century." The army defines "low intensity conflict" as "total war at the grassroots level." Pretty intense.

The National Security Archive, *The Chronology: The Documented Day-by-Day Account of the Secret Military Assistance to Iran and the Contras*. New York: Warner Books, 1987. This book does what the Tower Commission report should have done: gives the who, what, when and where. Each day unfolds in a brief entry.

Omang, Joanne and Aryeh Neier, *The CIA's Nicaragua Manual: Psychological Operations in Guerrilla Warfare*. New York: Vintage Books, 1985. This is the CIA's contra training manual, containing recommendations for political assassination, that created a scandal when news of its existence reached the U.S. news media.

Sanchez, James, *Index to The Tower Commission Report*. Jefferson, NC: McFarland, 1987.

The Tower Commission Report: The Full Text of the President's Special Review Board. New York: Bantam Books, 1987.

U.S. Citizens Living and Working in Nicaragua

U.S. Government Publications

U.S. Intervention in Nicaragua

References

New Pilgrims in the Americas

1. Dawn Jax Belleau, "Nicaragua: The Wisconsin Connection" (series of articles), *Sheboygan Press*, January 26-31, 1987. The cited quotation appeared in a story titled "Our Enemy, Our Friend," January 26, p. 1.
2. Jeff Jones, ed., *Brigadista: Harvest and War in Nicaragua; Eyewitness Accounts of North American Volunteers Working in Nicaragua* (New York: Praeger Publishers, 1986), p. 13.
3. *Mexico Daily News*, November 9, 1986.
4. *Milwaukee Daily Journal*, November 23, 1986.
5. William D. Davidson and Joseph V. Montville, "Foreign Policy According to Freud," *Foreign Policy*, Vol. 45, Winter 1981-82, pp. 145-57. Quoted in Gale Warner and Michael Shuman, *Citizen Diplomats: Pathfinders in Soviet-American Relations* (New York: Continuum Books, 1987), pp. 5-6.

Chapters one and two owe a substantial debt to Michael Schuman at the Center for Innovative Diplomacy in Irvine, California. Direct quotations from his works are credited in the text. Additional inspiration has been taken from the following publications:

Michael H. Shuman, *Building Municipal Foreign Policies: An Action Handbook for Citizens and Local Elected Officials* (Irvine, California: Center for Innovative Diplomacy, 1987).
_____, "Dateline Main Street: Local Foreign Policy," Foreign Policy, Vol. 65, Winter 1986-87.
Gale Warner and Michael Shuman, *Citizen Diplomats: Pathfinders in Soviet-American Relations* (New York: Continuum Books, 1987).

Do-It-Yourself Foreign Policy

1. Warner and Shuman, pp. 4-5
2. *Id.*, 14.
3. Shuman, *Building Municipal Foreign Policies*, pp. 10, 15.
4. *Id.*, p. 10; and Warner and Shuman, pp. 20-21.
5. Alvin Toffler, *The Third Wave* (New York: William Morrow and Company, 1980), pp. 405-6, 408.

6. John Naisbitt, *Megatrends* (London: Futura, 1984), p. 160., quoted in Shuman, *Building Municipal Foreign Policies*, p. 7.
7. George Gallup, Jr., *Forecast 2000: George Gallup, Jr., Predicts the Future of America* (New York: William Morrow and Company, Inc., 1984), pp. 135-6, 138.
8. Janice E. Perlman, "Grassrooting the System," in *U.S. Capitalism in Crisis*, (Union for Radical Political Economics, 1978), p. 306.
9. Sheldon Wolin, *Democracy* magazine, Fall, 1982. Quoted in Harry C. Boyte, *Community is Possible: Repairing America's Roots* (New York: Harper & Row, 1984), p. 213.
10. Jerome Levinson and Juan de Onís, *The Alliance that Lost Its Way: A Critical Report on the Alliance for Progress* (New York: Twentieth Century Fund, 1970), p. 44.
11. *Id.*, pp. 44, 51-2, 55.
12. *Id.*, pp. 34-5.
13. Arthur Schlesinger, "The Alliance for Progress: A Retrospective," in *Latin America: The Search for a New International Role* (New York: John Wiley & Sons, 1975), p. 64.
14. *Id.*, pp. 64, 73.
15. "Twisted Sisters: Foreign Policy for Fun and Profit," *New Republic*, June 22, 1987, p. 16.
16. *Partners*, quarterly newsletter of the National Association of Partners of the Americas, Inc. (Washington, DC), Vol. 19, No. 2, June 1987, p. 2.
17. Wisconsin Governor John W. Reynolds, Executive Office Release 64-349, June 27, 1964.
18. *Newsweek*, March 31, 1986.
19. Harry C. Boyte, *Community is Possible: Repairing America's Roots* (New York: Harper & Row, 1984), p. 27.
20. Center for Innovative Diplomacy, *The CID Report*, Volume 3, Number 1, Winter 1986-87, p. 6.
21. Larry Agran, October 1987 speech at a Riverside Church Disarmament Program National Teach-In, New York City, printed as "Commentary: Irvine Mayor Calls for a City-Based Foreign Policy," *Bulletin of Municipal Foreign Policy*, Vol. 2, No. 1, Winter 1987-88, p. 5.

22. Los Angeles Mayor Tom Bradley, "Municipal Responsibility in International Affairs," keynote address to the Congress of the National League of Cities, Seattle, Washington, December 10, 1985. Quoted in Shuman, *Building Municipal Foreign Policies*, pp. 4-5.

23. Shuman, "Dateline Main Street: Local Foreign Policy," *Foreign Policy*, Vol. 65, Winter 1986-87, pp. 170-1.

How to Begin

1. Harold L. Nix, *The Community and Its Involvement in the Study Planning Action Process* (Atlanta, Georgia: U.S. Department of Health, Education and Welfare), pp. 25-27.

2. *Id.*

3. Arthur J. Vidich and Joseph Bensman, *Small Town in Mass Society: Class, Power and Religion in a Rural Community*, pp. 29-33.

4. Nix, pp. 7-8.

5. Saul Alinsky, *Reveille for Radicals* (New York: Vintage Books, 1969), p. 65.

6. Nix, pp. 11-14.

7. Telephone interview with Roy Wilson, December 15, 1987.

8. Liz Koch, "Marchers Bridge Nicaragua/U.S. Gap," *The Phoenix*, July 29, 1986, p. 1.

9. "Nicaragua and the U.S. Media — A History of Lies," *Extra! the Newsletter of FAIR (Fairness & Accuracy in Reporting)*, Vol. 1, No. 4, October/November 1987, p. 1.

10. Timothy Crouse, *The Boys on the Bus* (New York: Random House, 1973), pp. 19-20.

11. Judy Butler, interview with George Vukelich, January 1987.

12. Sue Lyons of the Brooklyn/San Juan del Río Coco Sister City Project wrote a considerable part of the how-to section on working with news media.

13. Joan Flanagan, *The Successful Volunteer Organization* (Chicago: Contemporary Books, Inc., 1981), pp. 170-171, 192.

Coming Face to Face

1. The beginning of this chapter is an edited version of "Esterberg's Quest Turns Up Nicaraguan Sister Island" by Theresa Morrow, *Bainbridge Review*, January 21, 1987.

2. Portland, Oregon Mayor Brent Shirley, letter to President Ronald Reagan, March 12, 1986.

3. Harry C. Boyte, *Community is Possible: Repairing America's Roots* (New York: Harper & Row, 1984), p. 153.

4. Some of the information which appears in this chapter was taken from a "Steve's Travel Tips to Nicaragua," written by Steve Watrous of Milwaukee.

5. Zachary Sklar, "Bringing the War Home in Nicaragua," *The Nation*, February 9, 1985, p. 138.

6. "People to People" (editorial), *Gainesville Sun*, January 18, 1987.

7. Paul Hollander, *Political Hospitality and Tourism: Cuba and Nicaragua* (The Cuban American National Foundation, 1986), pp. 9, 19, 21-22.

8. Alister Mathieson and Geoffrey Wall, *Tourism: Economic, Physical and Social Impacts* (London and New York: Longman, 1982), pp. 135-6, 171, 173.

Friends in Need

1. Peter Davis, *Where is Nicaragua?* (New York: Simon & Schuster, 1987), pp. 234-5.

2. Gary Gunderson and Tom Peterson, "What We Think: American Views on Development and U.S.-Third World Relations," *Needs*, June 1987, p. 6. Quoted in *Food First Action Alert: "U.S. Foreign Aid: Help That Hurts,"* by Kevin Danaher (San Francisco, CA: Institute for Food and Development Policy, 1988), p. 1.

3. Nick Eberstadt, "The Perversion of Foreign Aid," *Commentary*, June 1985, p. 19.

4. *Id.*

5. Andrew E. Rice and Gordon Donald, Jr., "A Constituency for Foreign Assistance," in *U.S. Foreign Assistance: Investment or Folly?*, ed. by Gerry Feinstein and John Wilhelm (New York: Praeger, 1984), p. 358. The statistics cited come from Gallup polls sponsored by the Chicago Council on Foreign Relations in 1982.

6. Harry Reasoner, "The Reasoner Report," American Information Radio, February 19, 1974. Quoted in the Wisconsin-Nicaragua Partners newsletter, Vol. 1, No. 2, Spring 1974, p. 5.

7. Eberstadt, *id.*, pp. 19, 33.

8. James Bovard, "The Continuing Failure of U.S. Foreign Aid," USA Today, September 1986, p. 15.

9. Rice and Donald, *id.*, p. 360.

10. Carl Bakal, *Charity, U.S.A.* (New York: Times Books, 1979), pp. 266-7.

11. *Id.*

12. Bovard, p. 11.

13. Bakal, *id.*, pp. 25, 254.

14. Bovard, p. 11.

15. "Managua, Nicaragua," words by Albert Gamse, music by Irving Fields. Copyright 1946 by Regent Music Corp.. Current copyright, The Richmond Organization.

16. John Gerassi, *The Great Fear in Latin America* (London: Collier-Macmillan Ltd., 1963), pp. 174-5.
17. *Time* magazine, November 15, 1948.
18. Philip Caputo, *A Rumor of War* (New York: Ballantine Books, 1977), p. xiv.
19. Eberstadt, *id.*, p. 24.
20. *New York Times*, April 14, 1986.
21. F. Johnette Frick, "Surveying Nicaragua Behind the Headlines," *Narragansett Times*, August 13, 1987.
22. William Warren, "The Long Ride from Niquinohomo to Providence," *George Street Journal* (Brown University), November 26, 1986.

Helping Hands

1. Melanie Bartmess, "Students Discover Jalapa, Nicaragua," *Port Townsend Leader*, March 27, 1985.
2. Letter from Grant School teachers to Senator Dan Evans, June 4, 1985.
3. Richard J. Walton, "Niquinohomo: A Report from Providence's Sister City in Nicaragua," *The NewPaper*, Sept. 25-Oct. 2, 1985.
4. Bill Warren, "The Clinic Project, Brick by Brick," *Hermanas/Sisters* (newsletter of the Providence-Niquinohomo Sister-City Project), Winter 1987.
5. Steven Kinzer, "Nicaraguan Clinic American-Made," *New York Times*, September 2, 1986.
6. Douglas Hadden, "City to City Project Brings Practical Help to Nicaragua," *The Observer*, August 13, 1987, p. 1.
7. Warren, *id.*
8. Kinzer, *id.*

9. Central American Historical Institute, "Interview with Nicaragua's Minister of External Cooperation," *Update*, August 25, 1987, p. 2. Excerpted and translated from an interview that appeared in three parts in *Barricada*, Nicaragua, on July 27, 28 and 29, 1987.
10. Laura Berger, "A Week in a Nicaraguan Health Center," *Wisconsin Coordinating Council on Nicaragua (WCCN) Update*, June-August 1987, p. 7.
11. "An Invitation to U.S. Farmers," *Barricada Internacional*, May 29, 1986.

For Ann Arbor, Nicaragua Becomes a Reality

1. "The Talk of the Town," *The New Yorker*, August 17, 1987.
2. *Id.*
3. Allison Downing, "A Meeting of Two Homes," quoted in *Trucking to Nicaragua: A Sister City Adventure*, unpublished manuscript by Kurt Berggren, pp. 17-18.
4. Dave Vayo, "De Ciudad a Ciudad/From City to City," song dedicated to the people of Juigalpa, Nicaragua and Ann Arbor, USA. Quoted in Berggren, p. 24.
5. Downing, *id.*, quoted in Berggren, pp. 18-19.
6. Tom Rogers, special report in the *Ann Arbor News*, November 24, 1986.
7. *Id.*
8. *Id.*
9. *Id.*
10. Berggren, p. 52.
11. Tom Rieke, "The Road to Nicaragua," *Car and Driver*, March 1988, p. 125.
12. Berggren, p. 98.
13. *Id.*, pp. 99-100.

Index

About the Authors

Sheldon Rampton

Sheldon Rampton has been a missionary, a typesetter and a journalist. He grew up in Las Vegas, Nevada and attended Princeton University, graduating *magna cum laude.* In addition to working for newspapers in Las Vegas and Wisconsin, he has published articles in Europe, the United States and Latin America. Since 1985, he has served as editor for the Wisconsin Coordinating Council on Nicaragua's *Sister State Update,* and is a former member of the WCCN board of directors. He lives in Portage, Wisconsin, where he is the adoptive father of four cats, Smoky Bear, Tiger, Blondie, and Michael, Jr.

Liz Chilsen

(photo by Ellen Curry)

Liz Chilsen has worked as a photographer for ten years. While a photographic archivist at the State Historical Society of Wisconsin, she studied the role of visual imagery in U.S. movements for social change. She first visited Nicaragua in 1984 with a delegation of North American artists. A former member of the WCCN board of directors, she became the organization's executive director in 1987. Chilsen has traveled extensively in Nicaragua, documenting the impact of the war on daily life, Wisconsin-Nicaragua sister-state projects, and the U.S.-Nicaragua sister-city movement. Her photographs have appeared in numerous publications and exhibitions.